Real Hollywood Stories

BOCO MEDIA, LLC
Published by BoCo Media, LLC, Boulder, CO,
and Tatra Press, LLC, Suffern, NY

First Published in the United States of America

1 3 5 7 9 10 8 6 4 2

Cover Design: Dan Ragland
Book Design: Dan Ragland
Distributed by National Book Network (NBN), Lanham, MD 20706
(800) 462-6420; (717) 794-3800 www.nbnbooks.com

ISBN 10: 0-9776142-5-5
ISBN 13: 978-0-9776142-5-7
The Library of Congress has catalogued this edition as follows:
Raab, Scott
Real Hollywood Stories, by Scott Raab
Library of Congress Control Number: 2008921458

Acknowledgment is hereby made to *Esquire* magazine, a unit of Hearst Communications,
for granting publication rights to portions of certain chapters contained herein.

Publisher Contacts:

Boco Media, LLC	Tatra Press, LLC
979 Utica Circle	292 Spook Rock Rd.
Boulder, CO 80304	Suffern, NY 10901
www.bocomedia.com	www.tatrapress.com
(303) 818-0963	(845) 357-4843

For Lisa and Judah

REAL
Hollywood STORIES

Inside the minds of 20 celebrities, with one A-list writer

Scott Raab

BoCo Media, LLC
BOULDER, CO

TATRA PRESS, LLC
SUFFERN, NY

Contents

Going Hollywood: Foreword

When I wrote my first Hollywood profile – Mickey Rourke at the bottom of the barrel, in 1994 – I was already in my 40s and only a year or so removed from peddling columns to my local alternative weekly for $40 a pop. But even as I tried to establish myself as a well-paid glossy-magazine hack, I never set out to become a practitioner of 'celebrity journalism' – I was a serious writer, thank you very much, complete with a Master of Fine Arts degree from the Iowa Writers' Workshop and a half-assed, half-done novel – much less a specialist in profiling such crackpots, curs, and hooligans (I'm looking at you, Miss Ann Coulter) as fill this book.

I pitched Mickey to my editor not knowing that Mick's publicist was a lying shitheel, or that the movie Mick was shooting with Tupac Shakur would go direct to video, or that Rourke and I would hate each other. I just wanted to know more about him and his career swan-dive: I thought he'd be a good story. And when I got the green light, I dived in – I holed up with as many of his films as I could get my hands on, read everything about him I could find, spent most of a month trying to spend as much time with him as his lunacy would allow, and talked to anyone who knew him who would return my calls.

When I was done reporting, I believed that I knew more about Mickey Rourke's story than anybody else alive who hadn't slept with him. And then I wrote it. Yeah, it's 'just' a celebrity profile, but it's still the same as any good story – you dig into it as deep as possible, and then you write the hell out of it as quick as you can.

For the celebrity profiler, every job's a blind date, and the sweaty fat girl is always you. When the chemistry's right – with Robert Downey Jr., or Bill Murray – it's heaven, and it's magical for the story. And when the chemistry sucks – Hi, Nic! Cheers, Ewan! – it's utter misery, and also very good for the story.

It's the story I crave – and the story is about real human connection, good and ill. Always. It's not my job to plug the star's latest project, to fix his or her place in the firmament of American culture, or to fill space with "duh" quotes from family, friends, and co-workers. My job is to learn everything I can about my subject's life and work, and then to forge an actual human link, however brief or twisted – and finally, to write the hell out of it as quick as I can.

I love my job. If many of the people I write about are difficult, cranky, and possibly insane – and a lot of them are, or once were – I suppose that says plenty about me, too. But like 'em or not, these people fascinate me – even Ryan Seacrest – and I wanted to get to know them better, and enjoy a few laughs doing so.

That's the thing about a blind date: If you show up on time, wearing your best shirt and biggest smile, you could have a great time. Hell, they may even forget that you have a tape recorder running.

– Scott Raab, December, 2007

Real Hollywood Stories:
Introduction

I called Scott Raab last week after I finished reading a story about Sean Penn he'd just completed for one of *Esquire's* fall issues. I called him and told him that there is no writer I enjoy reading more than Scott Raab. Just the day before, I'd asked one of my editors (or maybe it was an entire group of editors) what we would do without Scott Raab. Literally. I said: "What the f*** would we do without Scott Raab?"

Every time I read something new by Scott Raab I realize all over again that there is no one like Scott Raab. Scott is one of those occasional men who have no precedent and no antecedent. You can't say that he is like anyone else or that anyone is like him. What do I mean by that?

One of the great assets of Scott's writing is that it can give offense. It is aggressive. It is opinionated – no, not opinionated; it is certain. Writing is not easy for Scott (though his stories rarely show the pain) and as a result, Scott's stories often express anger at the difficulties inherent in their creation. He rails against the indignities and stupidities of the world, yes, but mostly he's pissed at the impossibility of his art. His profile of Ryan Seacrest (Chapter 4) is an excellent example. Though ubiquitous in the popular culture, Mr. Seacrest was not – how you say – interesting. Which can present a problem for a writer endeavoring to be not only interesting but entertaining. Mr. Seacrest, though quite possibly Satan's spawn, bore the brunt.

I think in some ways, Scott blames his subjects for being willing to be written about by him. If they had refused him access, after all, he wouldn't have to go through this. As a result, they have to earn their way into his good graces. He is tough on them because they must prove to him that they are worthy of the pain they will inevitably cause him. In the new Sean Penn story I just read (Chapter 3), here is Scott's initial description of Penn:

"I crane my neck to see that the auteur is in the house, looking like a Little Rascal gone to seed. No shave, red eyed, hank of hair askew, hands jammed in the pockets of his jeans.... His face is lined much deeper than when I first met him, but that was back in '97, fifty thousand cigarettes and a sea of booze ago, before he copped Best Actor, saved the city of New Orleans and turned traitor to the homeland, any single one of which exploits would have put a dent in Superman."

Damn. Concise *and* angry. Caustic,

sarcastic, honest and, in the end, kind of loving. And the rhythm. The rhythm of Scott's sentences is unpredictable. Unlike lesser writers, he doesn't let the reader be lulled by easy patterns. He wants his words and phrases and sentences to be noticed, and to achieve that effect, he makes us a little uncomfortable, sticking an adjective where we expect a verb, surprising us with cadence. These aren't riffs; they're planned.

About 17 years ago, I was introduced to Scott Raab by a semi-renowned writer of fiction who had advised Scott to send me some of his work. I was new to a job and desperate for things to do, so when I received "Me, Tommy Boitano" in the mail, I read it. It was a short story. About a shoe salesman whose one claim to fame was that he had fucked Elizabeth Taylor. From the moment I read it, I knew there was something different about this guy. What that difference was, exactly, was hard to pinpoint. But in the years since I encountered "Tommy" it's become clear to me that Scott's best work is fueled by a combination of rage and affection.

Read his Paul Newman profile. Scott clearly feels something like love for Mr. Newman (Chapter 8) – love and admiration. But like many men, Scott doesn't express that love and admiration directly. He has to make Newman (who maybe can act a little, and, who maybe has helped the planet by donating more than $100 million to charitable causes) earn it.

Newman has to prove to Scott, throughout the profile, that he's more than some pretty-boy actor dilettante fuckwad like all the other pretty-boy actor fuckwads (and Scott would use that term affectionately) that populate Hollywood. Newman stands up to Scott's battering and the result is that the reader finds a new depth of respect for the man for being able to do so. Of course, certain of Newman's relatives – mostly his brother – were less than charmed by Scott's method of expressing his admiration, and let us know about it.

The other thing that "Tommy Boitano" was, that most every story Scott has written for magazines since was, is funny. Comic might be a better term, except that a comic outlook presupposes some inherent optimism. So, let's say funny. They're funny because Scott sees the joy in language and the absurdity apparent in every aspect of life.

I remember in one of Scott's sports pieces, he wrote about Don Zimmer – one of the last great characters in baseball, a sport Scott loves more than life itself. I remember Scott getting a glimpse of 68-year-old Zimmer waddling to the showers and noting, as Scott put it "the dowsing rod of his manhood" and then recording Yankee manager Joe Torre's reaction to having seen the same thing: "I'm sorry I saw [THAT]." Who else would dare record that for public consumption? I'll tell you who: No one.

– David Granger, editor in chief, Esquire, *fall 2007*

Chapter One

Bill Murray

Mensch

There are worse spots to wait for Bill
Murray than the Vince Lombardi Rest Area on the New Jersey Turnpike.
Sure, the place smells like piss and feels like a peep-show booth, but it's
got the Jersey-rest-stop Grand Slam: A TCBY, A Nathan's Famous, a Burger
King, and a Cinnabon. Although only the Burger King and Cinnabon are
open at 9:00 A.M., which is now.

I'm hanging on a bench fronting the parking lot, thinking about
Murray. I've got some history with this guy, and it goes beyond being old
enough to know firsthand what a startling joy he was to watch on
Saturday Night Live – the glorious seventies *SNL*, when 11:30 P.M. on
Saturdays meant taking communion, except with a bong – or seeing
Stripes on June 12, 1981, one of the two best boy-girl dates of my life, or
believing *Lost in Translation* is a perfect movie and that Murray's work in
it ranks with the very finest performances ever put on film.

With Murray, the history is personal. And I wouldn't raise this sort of
thing here if what I actually know didn't say something important and
revealing about this particular guy:

He's an utter douche bag.

Oh, wait... that was Mickey Rourke. It gets confusing, writing dozens of celebrity profiles over so many years.

What I meant to say about Bill Murray is, he's a mensch. We met when *Esquire* put him on the cover as Santa Claus in 1998. We weren't profiling him, so he had nothing to gain by pandering to the writer, but he invited me to a dinner party Disney was throwing for the premiere of *Rushmore*. And he told me to ask my wife to join us.

That was special. In my experience, no celebrity treats any journalist with such consideration, and for good reason: We're like talk-show hosts but without the depth, gravitas, or clout. You hit your mark, pitch your product, and get the hell outta there.

Later, after Murray had won Best Supporting Actor awards for *Rushmore* from the National Society of Film Critics, the Los Angeles Film Critics Association, and the New York Film Critics Circle – he also was nominated for a Golden Globe – he got stiffed by the Academy: no Oscar nomination. Murray called to invite us to a party at his home; his wife, Jenny, had bought a fancy dress, and since they weren't going to Los Angeles for the ceremony, they were throwing an Oscar bash of their own

Cutting Room Floor: Murray

THE PITCH: Going from *Saturday Night Live* to *Caddyshack* is one thing. Becoming one of Hollywood's finest, oddest actors is something else entirely.

SCENE: An *Esquire* photo shoot for the December, 1998, cover. Writers rarely go to these things, but Murray and I had already met to work out the story – a fictitious lunch where Santa and Bill talk Christmas – and I was there so Murray had someone to talk to while the photographer put him through hours of trying on Santa hats and fake beards.

BACKSTORY: Murray posed for the cover of *Esquire* as a last-minute favor in '98 – a couple of other cover subjects had fallen through. But it was also before *Rushmore* opened, and years away from *Lost In Translation*, so Bill's film career was not exactly at its apex. By December, 2004, his next time on the cover, he was as hot as any actor in America. And every bit as regular a guy as he had been years before.

so that she could wear it.

That party – on March 21, 1999 – was the other best boy-girl date of my life. My wife was pretty pregnant, so we bought her a nice dress-up outfit, and I borrowed a suit from *Esquire*'s fashion folks and bought myself a hat, and we drove up to Murray House – and if *Shakespeare in Love* hadn't whipped *Saving Private Ryan* for Best Picture, we would've copped the Oscar pool, which as I recall, was a four-figure payout. There were at least a hundred guests, but the only celebrity I saw there, besides Bill Murray, was Tim Meadows – and it was a grand time. I don't remember Jenny's dress, but the host wore a white tux and did hilarious faux-presenter shtick, riffing karaoke-style in front of a massive, muted TV during the awards broadcast.

So that's the truth about Murray: The cat's way cool. Beyond ordinary cool, which any yutz with large enough fame and money can pretend to be. He's pure Chicago jagoff cool, a big soul who deals with people, "important" or not, on the square and loves to share the good times – an Everymaniac.

CONFLICT: Because he was in the middle of filming *Broken Flowers*, my only shot at spending enough time with Murray to get a decent interview done was on Yom Kippur. I'm not a particularly observant Jew, but YK is the Big One – our most solemn, heavy-duty holiday. Heck, when I was a kid, Sandy Koufax refused to pitch in a World Series game scheduled on the Day of Atonement; was I really going to work that day?

Yep.

WISH I'D WRITTEN: The first time I met him, Murray was reminiscing about Christmas when he was a kid. He started describing a book he loved, *Why The Chimes Rang*, retelling the story in great detail: poor boy, small town, cathedral bells haven't rung in years, and on Christmas the citizens place lavish gifts on the altar in hope of hearing those bells. Nothing works, until the boy leaves his single little silver coin on the altar. And by the time Murray's finished telling it, he's blinking back his tears.

By the way, that's the truth about Mickey Rourke, too: douche bag.

Murray's waving from the front passenger seat of a silver Ford Expedition as it pulls up at the rest area. Gibby the Teamster – that's how Bill introduces him – is driving. Gibby and Bill are both working on a Jim Jarmusch movie that just began shooting. Gibby looks nice – casual shirt, a touch of premature gray around the temples, no visible weaponry – and as for Bill, he looks tired, tousled, stubbly. He's got on an orange gimme T-shirt from some executive jet service, a pair of old shorts, and scuffed sneakers.

Murray always has looked like who and what he truly is, a working-class Irish stiff, the fifth kid of a nine-child clan squeezed into a small house just north of Chicago proper, soft of heart yet gimlet-eyed. And though he has aged sleekly into his mid-fifties, smooth and handsome enough to play a dapper man without smarm, he still has the ancient acne pock going for him and the crooked caddy's grin that tells you he knows just how far over par you'll shoot – and how much you'll tip – before you even tee it up.

The morning's plan calls for Bill to ride with me; we'll follow Gibby's spoor to the shoot, in a parking lot at Newark Airport – hence the Vince Lombardi, which is both on Murray's way down from his home near New York City and not far from where I live. But before we leave, I ask if maybe we ought to bring along some Cinnabons.

"Heck, *yeah*," Murray says. "Everyone loves Cinnabons."

We load 'em up – three boxes, each holding half a dozen, maybe sixty pounds of frosted manhole covers – and set out for Newark. Gibby's got the lead foot, and the highway's heavy with trucks all the way to the airport. Murray and I talk about the Cubs, who haven't yet collapsed. Murray, whose attachment to pro sports, particularly the Chicago teams, borders on pathology, had flown back and forth to see the Cubs at Wrigley on the weekend before the Jarmusch movie shoot started, and he insisted that his trailer be crowned with a satellite dish so he can watch baseball when he isn't acting.

It's a decent enough trailer – parked in the short-term lot of Terminal B – but on the small side, nothing fancy.

"The one I had in Rome had a fireplace," Murray chuckles.

"A fireplace?"

"A fireplace." Murray sounds sardonic; I'm unsure if he's joshing about the fireplace. He spent five months in Italy this past winter making *The Life Aquatic with Steve Zissou*, due out this Christmas, his third film with director Wes Anderson. Apparently, fireplace or no, it wasn't fun, at least for Mr. Bill. All the action takes place on a boat – Murray's character is a Jacques Cousteau type seeking to avenge his partner's death by shark – but Murray won't discuss the awful details.

"It's like talkin' about war stories," he says. "I can't even think about it. My impression of Italy before doing this job was that it's one of the greatest, most beautiful places in the world. After this job, if you say 'Italy' to me, it's like a whole lotta cockroaches in one room – you don't know what to deal with first. It was by far the hardest job I've ever had, and I always work hard. I work the same hard on all of 'em. But this one – I've been kidding about it, saying they almost broke me, and they may have and I just don't know it yet."

Well, I say, I'm sure it's gonna turn out to be a good –

"God *damn* it," Murray snarls, "the movie better be the greatest movie ever made. If it's not, I'm gonna kill Anderson. He's a dead man. If it's not the greatest movie ever made, or in the top ten, he may as well just move to China and change his name to Chin, and he better get himself a small room in a small town – and even then, I'll hunt him down."

Murray grabs a box of Cinnabons and hauls them over to the makeup trailer along with a couple of CDs – Prince, the Stones – and comes back to flip on the Ryder Cup. Golf for Murray is not a passion so much as a religion; his 1999 book, *Cindarella Story* – surely the best-written showbiz memoir since John Houseman's *Unfinished Business* and arguably the best golf tome since Tom Watson's *Putz!* – is subtitled *My Life in Golf.* Interviewing Murray while the Ryder Cup's on is like farting in shul. He''s wolfing a Cinnabon one-handed, no mean feat, working the clicker with his other hand, and running down the set caterer's breakfast options for my benefit.

"Gibby was havin' some oatmeal. Want some oatmeal? They make a nice breakfast burrito. You could have a vegetarian one, or you can get it with bacon and hot sauce in it – the garbage-can one." He turns to Steve, his wee-but-wiry boy assistant: "I'll take a small one." To me: "You gonna have one?"

All right. Gimme the garbage can

Murray pushes a box of Cinnabons across the table. "Here," he says. "But pace yourself."

I can't eat these, too, man. I got fat.

Murray nods and grins. "And it feels good to get there. You have the largesse to eat enough and move so little that you actually gain weight. 'Hey, I've made my bones, and I can afford to go on out and have a nice veal.' That's the line I use to myself whenever it gets really shitty on a movie: 'Jesus Christ, I could be eatin' veal in a nice restaurant. What the hell am I doin' here?'

"To me that is indulgence: I'm gonna have myself some veal, which assumes you're gonna have a little pasta on the side and some red wine, too. You've earned that – and the sensation of the veal going into your belly and the feeling you've earned it become a compound-comfort thing. And then you get heavier. *Get in the hole! Uhhhh!* He skunked that fucking putt."

On the TV, the U.S. is getting smoked by the Europeans, but Steve has brought the burritos...and the burritos are spectacular.

"Isn't it *great?*" Murray says, chewing. "This is movie life. This is one of the good things."

Murray's movie life spans roughly three dozen films over three decades, and its arc is peculiar as hell. On the heels of his four seasons on *Saturday Night Live*, he stole *Caddyshack* in 1980; by '84, with *Ghostbusters*, he was huge, the box-office king of broad comedy. During that same stretch, though, Murray also did *Where the Buffalo Roam* and *The Razor's Edge* – neither movie was a success, but you could see even then that this guy was an actor alive, open every moment, fun to watch – and, in an uncredited, underwritten role in *Tootsie* in '82, he held serve and then some onscreen with Dustin Hoffman.

"I got *noticed* in *Tootsie*," Murray says now. "I mean, I was some sort of movie star then, on a junior level – I had done *Caddyshack* and *Stripes* – but not of an adult nature yet. Those movies had done well, but they weren't the same thing. I remember meetin' Jimmy Stewart at the Cannes festival, he had no fuckin' idea who I was. Of course, I'm not sure he knew who his *wife* was. But I figured, Well, *shit*, I'll walk up to him and say hello--'I'm so-and-so, I'm an actor, and I like your stuff.' And sometimes when you say you're an actor, they at least fake it – 'Oh, sure sure.' He couldn't even swing that."

But after *Ghostbusters* hit the jackpot, in that ancient age when grossing more than $100 million meant something special, Murray more or less walked away from his career. For four years.

"I didn't have a plan. Once you've been on top in terms of box office and stuff like that, when you've really been up there – I sort of decided *not* to stay up there. I didn't want to stay up there. My life"– Murray's first kid was born in '82, his second in '85; he now has six children, all boys – "required more of my time. To be a bachelor and in the movies is the greatest, because you've got nothin' else to do.

"It's like Tiger Woods: As long as he didn't have a girlfriend, he was unquestionably the greatest golfer in the world. And people, myself included, said, 'Well, wait'll he finds a girl. He'll find that his time's gonna be different. His life *is* gonna get more complicated.' And it did for him, and it does for everyone."

Murray's comeback took another four years. There was delight along the way – *Scrooged, Quick Change* (which he co-directed), *What About Bob?* and *Mad Dog and Glory*, with Murray playing a gangster and Robert De Niro as a timid cop – but it wasn't until *Groundhog Day* that Murray became a major star again.

"That was sort of the turning point. That was the first time the New York press went, 'Hey, wait a minute – this is a real movie here, not just that broad thing.' It also was – they're proud of the *Saturday Night Live* people. New York claimed them as their own in a way, and people were glad for me. We'd lost Johnny and Gilda; they were truly beloved New Yorkers while they were here, significant, influential people. They made a lot of friends, and they touched a lot of people.

"I remember that there was a caricature of me in *The New Yorker,* comin' outta the ground. And it was so cute and it was so great. That felt good. It wasn't an Academy Award, but it was somethin' I liked a lot. It was more significant."

After *Groundhog Day*, a new generation of directors wanted to work with Murray: Tim Burton on *Ed Wood*, the Farrelly brothers on *Kingpin*, Wes Anderson, Sofia Coppola, Jim Jarmusch.

"Because I didn't embarrass myself in my earlier run," he says, "I was desirable. I never made any movies were people went, 'Ohhhh, you can't,' because there are people who make choices that're so bad that you can never look 'em in the eye again."

He laughs. "I've done some that didn't make it all the way across the Atlantic, but there were none that were really the death knell, and people appreciate that. Wes, Sofia, this guy Jarmusch – these are people who've got real cinema *stuff*. They're not dabblers. And it's not like you're working with some bully or some blowhard. And I think I'd learned enough about makin' movies that I really felt like I was – not a journeyman, but a master. Well, master sounds a little vain. I'm a guy that – I can do it. I feel like I can do it. I really feel that I can do pretty much anything."

It's time for Murray to get to work – "Fifteen

minutes, brother," shouts wee-but-wiry Steve through the trailer's open door, which means it's time for the beastly Waterpik to blast Bill Murray's gums free of Cinnabon and burrito.

"This thing was my concession to aging," he says, mouthing the nozzle and starting it up. "You ever done this? It feels *good*!"

It pulses, loud as a jackhammer. Murray's standing in profile at a small sink and mirror in the middle of the trailer, working the thing around his mouth, bending to the mirror to keep his torso out of the range of any blowback or leakage. It's like watching a Buster Keaton short.

Amazing you can do that without soaking your shirt, I say when he's finished.

"These are the gifts," he says. "That's the first time I ever did it with cold water. I wouldn't do that again. But I'm telling you, it feels great. You gotta be able to figure out how to get the drool out of your mouth – and you put a little bit of hydrogen peroxide on it, and it kills all the germs in your mouth and also makes your teeth whiter. It's an old Rosemary Clooney trick. My mother told me that.

He burps. Cinnabon?

"Absolutely. I gotta go to work now. I know we've gotten a *lot* done, but I'm basically locked in a bus for the rest of the day."

But before he goes, he slips me a photo. From the Oscar party – a close-up of my wife's fingers laced over her swollen belly.

"Isn't that nice?" he asks. "The missus remembered and gave it to me to give you. She said, 'Ohhhhh, I've got a good picture,' and I'm thinkin', How good a picture could this be? Well, it really is a good picture."

Oh, yeah. It's beautiful. My wife's gonna cry when she sees this.

"Of course she will," Murray says. "Maybe you'd better save it – you know, pull it out to show her when you really need it."

A week later, Murray's still in the trailer, but the

Teamsters have hauled it up to a different location, in Sloatsburg, a small New York town just across the New Jersey border. Murray's not only tired – his shooting days are running from 11:00 A.M. to 2:00 A.M. or later – he's now hocking phlegm, too. TheraFlu helps some. Chicken soup. Tea. Blueberry muffins. He offers whiskey, but he's not having any. And he's got cigars, an assortment of Cubans. He's not smoking, but he insists, and who am I to say no to a Cohiba?

Outside the trailer, a swarm of townsfolk and children – on bikes, on foot, on scooters – gathers. Every time he leaves for makeup or to shoot another scene, Murray autographs their hats, papers, arms, whatever.

"The thing that's really breathtaking and most pleasing," he says, "is just the number of times people say, 'You've given me so many laughs over the years.' They say, 'I hope you don't mind me sayin' so.' I say, 'That's the nicest thing I could ever hear.' That makes me feel good, like I did somethin worthwhile with my life. At least there's something on that side of the ledger, you know?"

But there are some things Bill Murray won't do for his public. *Inside the Actors Studio*, with James Lipton, for instance.

"I met that guy a while ago and he said, 'You're never gonna do the show, are you?' I guess I've been invited before, but I always had a problem with it being called *Inside the Actors Studio*. When I was at *Second City*" – the legendary Chicago improv troupe where Murray, Belushi, and other golden-age *SNL*-ers honed their chops – "we always had a bit of an attitude about the Actors Studio. *The Actors Studio* – yeah, they had a couple of good actors. So? Do we all have to get down and worship 'em? It always bothered me. And when he called the show *Inside the Actors Studio* – well, what're you talkin' to Meg Ryan for, or any number of these people they've got now who couldn't find the Actors Studio with a phone book? It's so hard *not* to take yourself seriously just day to day. The idea of going up there and being trumpeted and fellated for so long..."

He trails off, shaking his head. By any current standard of celebrity, Murray is a real oddball, practically a hermit. He doesn't shill for his movies or bare his soul for the press. No publicist. No agent. No shit.

"I've never had a publicist," he says, "and I don't have an agent – and it's great. It's *great*. I wish I'd done it a long time ago."

So how do people get scripts to you?

Murray shrugs. "I really don't know," he says.

"Jeez, you seem so Zen about it. Do you worry?

"About what?"

Well, you've got a big family to feed, a great career...

"I seem *sad* about it?"

Not sad – Zen. Zen.

He laughs. "I thought you said sad."

You wanna work, you gotta get scripts, right?

"*Ehhhh,*" he says, and shrugs again. "If they want me, they'll find me."

One other thing Murray won't do: He won't say what he whispered to Scarlett Johansson at the end of *Lost in Translation.*

"I guess the answer is, there's somethin' that makes it impossible to tell," he says. "But I'll tell ya a good story about it. I'm gettin' on the ferry at Martha's Vineyard, and some guy yells out from across the way, 'Bill, what'd ya say to her?' Everyone hears him ask, and I pause for a second with my mouth open and start to speak. And as I start to speak, the foghorn sounds, about a twenty-five-second blast, and I just"--Murray starts moving his lips silently--"I acted it out like I was saying something really sincere, and the crowd laughed so hard. it was great. I couldn't have bought that moment."

It's late – 10:00 P.M. – but it's the middle of Murray's work-

day. He puts on a suit, his costume for a scene in which Sharon Stone will try to seduce him. The Cubs are on the dish playing the Mets; it's tied in the eighth inning when Steve pops in whith a ten-minute warning.

"I gotta work," Murray says. "Take another cigar. Stay and watch the end of the game."

You don't mind?

"Fuck, no. But I should ask this guy Soapy to come in and watch it, too, if you don't mind. He's a good guy."

What about Gibby?

"Well, Gibby's gone home for the weekend."

Bill, one last question: Were you really pissed off at the Oscars last year?

"Pissed off?"

Yeah – that you didn't win Best Actor. You looked mad.

"I was actually joking. My first movie I got nominated for a Canadian Oscar – for *Meatballs*. For *MEATBALLS*. And who am I up against? George C. Scott. So he wins the award and I stand up and go: 'That's it – let's get the hell outta here.'

"So, I'm tellin' this story to someone I'm sittin' next to, and when Sean Penn wins, I think they're goin' to a commercial. I say, 'That's it – I'm outta here,' and I start to get up, and Billy Crystal sees me and he's like, 'Whoa, Bill, sit down.' He thinks it's *serious*. I was just screwin' around, and he thought it was real – because I'm such an effective actor, I guess."

Okay, fine. But I know how pissed off I was that you didn't win: plenty. You earned it.

"You know what? I had it the best of anybody. The best was to get to go all the way to it, have all that fun, and walk away – not to have to be on TV the next morning doing an interview about how you won the Oscar. We had a *great* time. And the thing is, *the movie is the prize*. In time, nobody remembers who won the damn Oscar; they just remember the movie if it was good. If you had said to me, 'You could be in *Mystic River* and win the Oscar or you could be in your movie and not win'– not a fuckin' chance. No contest. I loved the whole experience. It's a great, great movie."

Murray hails Soapy from the bottom of the trailer steps.

"Excuse me, young fella," he says. "Can you go in there and watch the game for me? Just keep an eye on it."

"*Heh-heh-heh,*" says Soapy. "No problem."

Soapy's not a young fella. He's a white-haired, big-knuckled union man, and he's got a thickset, cross-eyed colleague in tow. They take the couch without a struggle.

"Hey," Soapy says. "How you doin'?"

Super, Soapy. You?

"*Heh-heh-heh*. I have to watch TV. You have to keep your eyes open to do that."

I fire up another Saint Luis Rey – *oooh,* baby. Velvet. A velvet torpedo. This is movie life. This is one of the good things.

So's Bill Murray.

Chapter Two

Larry David

Kvetchmeister

To look at Larry David – bespectacled, bald, and basset-eared, a long-limbed fifty-four-year-old fellow draped in untucked cotton and baggy corduroy, sipping lukewarm decaf – you would never glean his anguish. To hear him whistle as he works, tilted back in his office chair, whistling and humming, laughing at his own image on the TV screen, you would not sense his suffering. Even knowing his show – HBO's *Curb Your Enthusiasm*, a half-hour Sunday-night faux vérité schmuckfest starring David as himself, the ex-New York City stand-up who cocreated *Seinfeld* and has stewed wealthily ever after out here in Los Angeles, drenched in self-loathing – still you would imagine, to watch him in the editing room, that he is a happy man.

You would be wrong. He is a touchy man, Larry David. A touchy, touchy man. If you doubt this, pay him a compliment. Call him – as I do when he takes a break – a comic genius.

"Are you out of your mind?"

I didn't make it up, I say. Comic genius: That's the tag.

"What tag?" he shouts. "Where's the tag? There's no tag!"

Ah, but there is. Tom Shales – America's least unknown TV critic – wrote that you were a comic genius, flat-out. And he's not the only one.

"Genius tag – what is that? That's ridiculous. What the hell does it even mean?"

His arms are crossed. His legs are crossed, too. His endless brow furrows above narrowed eyes. One hand snakes up to knead the base of his neck. I spot a small bottle of hot sauce on his desk – Cholula – and attempt a soothing transition.

Cholula, I say. Good stuff.

"I don't think I've ever had it in my life," he says.

Sorry if I've made you uncomfortable, I say.

"Oh, no. No. This is just a natural state. It's a natural state. This is not a sign of discomfort for me."

He purses his lips, balloons his cheeks with air, and blows it all out, nice and slow.

"Genius," he moans. "That'll be the end of me, by the way, if people ever read anything like that."

His anger and despair are half joking, but no more than half. One of *Curb Your Enthusiasm's* pleasures is watching a man without a boss or a job, a man with a name, half a billion dollars, and a loving wife, piss vinegar and blow up over a parking space. It is somehow reassuring to know that even in what passes for his real life, all his money and acclaim can't protect David from his own vanity, shame, and gloom, or force him to enjoy being ... Larry David. He knows this much: The end of him is coming, yes, as it comes to every man. Meanwhile, things fall apart. In the roaring of God's silence, in the face of certain doom, Larry David is a noiseless, ceaseless echo: one Jew kvetching.

"He's happy," Laurie David, his wife, insists. "He just doesn't want anyone to know. Everybody calls him grouchy, but he's not – not really. He's the most loyal, sweet person you'll ever meet. This guy can't go past an empty restaurant without feeling guilty – like he should be eating in there, helping them out. He's such a softy."

But comedy is melancholy work, a tough job for a softy. Something bad must happen for comedy to click; mockery must be made. Someone had to be the first to crawl from the cave and inch along the glacier's rim, only to slip and slide back down, cracking his skull. And somebody else had to watch, busting a gut.

Stand-up is even worse: You crack open your own head, pause for the laugh, do it again – but bleed funnier this time. You're the heir of every jester who displeased his king and wound up bent upon the chopping block. The last sound he ever heard was the tinkle of his bells; his exit line was, "Prithee, I killed in Saxony." You're that someone now – the loser paid to say what no one else will say. You'll die up there one night.

In 1970, Larry David graduated from the University of Maryland, went back to his native New York City, found a two-room apartment with two roommates, made the rounds of employment agencies, drove cabs, sold bras, worked as a paralegal, and got fired from or quit every job he ever held. Then he went to a comedy club one night and thought, I can do that.

He was right. He was cerebral and skewed, distant and deadpan. He was brilliant. He just couldn't take the dying.

He'd open by thanking God that he had not been born a wealthy Spanish landowner, "because I could never be sure about whether to address the help using the *tu* form or the *usted* form. If I use *usted*, I don't want them to think I'm being condescending. But if I use *tu*, I don't want them to feel so familiar that they think they can just help themselves to anything in the refrigerator."

Then he'd move on to his death-camp stuff.

"You know," he'd muse, "if he'd given me a compliment, Josef Mengele and I could have been friends: 'Larry, your hair looks very good today.' 'Really? Thank you, Dr. Mengele!'"

And: "You know what I really admired about Hitler? He didn't take any shit from magicians."

Fellow comics adored him. Most clubgoers, drooling for their ration of Dice Clay dick jokes, loathed him. Loudly.

"I was in fear every night of going onstage in front of these audiences," David recalls. "I knew I had to go on, but I really didn't want to. It was bad. There were some bad nights. If I was bumped--'So-and-so came in and you can't go on' – that was fine. That was great news."

Sometimes David would bump himself, just stalk offstage in the middle of his set. Sometimes fights would break out between hecklers and fans in the crowd while David stood watching.

Laurie David met him then, years before they married. She was Letterman's talent coordinator. He was ... Larry David.

"He was a mess," she says now. "No future, no dough, no potential. When we first started seeing each other, I literally sat down with a girlfriend, and on a paper placemat I wrote 'Pro' and 'Con.' The 'Con' list had fifteen, twenty things on it. He had this disgusting apartment. He had a

Cutting Room Floor: David

THE PITCH: He made Seinfeld *Seinfeld*, and a billion bucks to boot. But what sort of sick, twisted mind does it take to make America laugh at incest, bestiality, and sponge cake?

SCENE: Straight out of any episode of *Curb Your Enthusiasm*: It's the morning after the premiere show of *Curb's* second season, and the phone rings in the editing room. "I got better?" Larry David snarls into the mouthpiece after listening for two seconds. "What does that mean, 'I got better?' No, it didn't get better. How did you even get through? 'I got better.'" Down slams the phone. "There's no compliment that can ever be delivered in a way that makes you feel good," scowls David. "The guy on the phone told me, 'I saw the show; you were better.' Oh, I personally got better? Oh, thank you – thanks for the call. Who are these idiots that say that?"

BACKSTORY: I was in no hurry to fly, especially out of Newark, after 9/11, but the chance to profile David, who generally shuns publicity, was too rich to pass up. So on 9/22, I flew to Los Angeles, and spent the next two days trying to guilt Larry into doing something with me beyond sitting and talking in the editing and looping rooms.

No dice. But that didn't mean Larry was unmoved by the drums of war. "I bought the gas masks, small ones for the kids, little gas masks. Then I got the antibiotics. I got flashlights and first-aid kits. So today

cup and a spoon. He was this comedian who'd walk off stages if everybody wasn't paying attention. He refused to travel, refused to go anywhere. He never did anything to try to be successful, not for one second. He just pursued his craft. The 'Pro' list had one thing on it: He's funny."

In 1988, NBC gave one of David's stand-up buddies – the less overtly twisted and far more ambitious Jerome Seinfeld – a shot at a sitcom pilot, and Jerry asked Larry to come out to L. A. to help create a show. It worked out pretty good. David wrote sixty-odd scripts, and for the first seven seasons of Seinfeld's nine-year run, he poured his soul's bitter sap over every

I'm listening to the radio and an expert, he's talking about this thing of people going out and buying – he's just making a list of the things that I did. The gas masks, they're going to be useless; the antibiotics, more harm than good; so I just threw out all that money."

CONFLICT: Larry David vs. Larry David: "I used to have dreams where there would be a battle going on in my living room, people ducking under chairs, killing each other. It was a war. I'd walk into the room – this was in my house – and I'd go, What the hell is going on here? And it's two sides fighting each other with guns in the middle of my living room – and I would duck down behind the couch. And all of a sudden one of the soldiers came up to me and pointed a gun and said, 'Do a set' – pointing a gun to my head.

"I'd go, 'Do a set? But there's a battle going on. I can't go do a set.' There was a little stage area at the end of the living room where I could actually go up in the middle of all this fighting and perform, so I would duck under the bullets and go up on the stage and take the microphone."

WISH I'D WRITTEN: The onscreen verbal warfare between David and Richard Lewis on *CYE* is the byproduct of a 40-year-old friendship between the two, but the friction is no mere contrivance. "I love this opportunity on camera to literally infuriate him," Lewis told me. "I sometimes think of things the night before that might provoke him, and why not? He does so many takes, I started calling him 'Citizen David.'"

episode. He became a rich man. He became a Los Angeleno. He became a comic genius. Yet he was still ... Larry David. He was still the same guy who had moved to L. A., briefly, ten years before, to write and perform on *Fridays*, ABC's lousy copy of *Saturday Night Live*, and, earning real money for the first time in his life, bought himself a convertible. Cruising Santa Monica Boulevard one day, top down, he was at a red light when some yutz waiting for a bus recognized him.

"Your show stinks!" the guy hollered.

David pulled the convertible over and put the top back up. "It was never down again," he says now. "Never."

Sixteen years later, newly armed with his *Seinfeld* Emmys and his syndication gelt, the comic genius bought himself a Porsche. He didn't crave a Porsche – "a 911," he says, "whatever it was" – but Seinfeld, who has collected two of every three Porsches ever built, had been hocking him about how great they are and taunting him about the old-fart Lexus David was driving.

"Then I heard they had the Tiptronic," David says, "which is an automatic. Okay, now I can get it, because you don't have to shift. I didn't want to shift. There are other things to do in the car – radio dials, food every now and then, you want to take a note or two. Why would anybody want to shift?"

David drove his new Porsche for a week before returning it to the dealer at a loss of twelve grand.

"I was so self-conscious driving it that I couldn't pull up anywhere I was going. Even a restaurant – I would park blocks away. I was too embarrassed."

When I ask Seinfeld about this, he snickers. "Yeah, Larry thought that people actually gave a shit that he was driving a Porsche. He thought people noticed. In L. A."

David, who now drives the gas-electric-hybrid Toyota Prius on his show and in what passes for his real life, shrugs at the memory.

"I couldn't adapt," he says. "I was uncomfortable."

"Why would I do anything?" David

asks as we walk back to the editing room from lunch. "I never do anything." Come on – anything you want.

"If I never do anything," he says, "it would be very odd for me to do something, don't you think?"

I thought we discussed going to Disneyland on the phone.

"I wouldn't even go there with the kids," he says. "I hate it. With a passion."

The Davids have two young daughters, which is no small miracle when you consider how hard it was to drag David to the altar. "He asked me to marry him," says Laurie David, "and it took three years to get him to do it. He went through a period where he had cold feet. Literally. His feet were ice-cold all the time. He was always ordering special slippers to get his feet warm. We'd go into a jewelry store, and I'd look at a ring and look over, and he wouldn't even be in the store. He'd be out on the street. His neck got bright-red with hives every time he went into a jewelry store.

It was a total nightmare. He was so panicked. He was afraid that he wouldn't be funny anymore if he was happy. One day I just gave him a martini, and we got on a plane and went to one of those drive-in places in Las Vegas. Nobody cared that we didn't have a wedding. Our families were just glad it was done. They couldn't take it anymore."

Three years? I've got two days here. Two days to uphold the celebrity-profile convention – dating back to when stone-eyed Homer accompanied ox-pronged Achilles to a Thracian brothel – requiring the subject and the writer to do something quirky and pseudo-revealing together. Since the invention of kneepads, this activity has nearly always been mediated in advance by the star's publicist, but David employs no publicist, rejects any definition of star that includes him, and isn't exactly eager to do anything with me.

Look, I tell him, Sean Penn does very little press, and he took me out on his boat.

"That's one place you would never get me to go. I can't stand boats. I would never get on a boat. God, do I hate them."

Drew Carey and I went bowling.

"Uh-huh."

Hey, Albert Brooks went with me to the Universal Studios theme park. We went on two rides.

"He did that? I can't believe it."

He did. So, Disneyland?

"Why? The lines –"

If there are lines, we'll leave.

"Right. Maybe tomorrow."

He meant to say never but didn't want to hurt my feelings. He's such a softy.

Safely back in the editing room, David sits and begins

to rotate his shiny egg of a head while kneading the base of his neck. His face is an old man's grimace. When he's finished, he resumes whistling – snatches of some vaguely familiar, opera bouffe air I can't quite place.

"Always a big whistler," Seinfeld confirms later. "Master of the obscure musical reference. I'd say, 'Wait, I know that; it's the Ronzoni jingle, isn't it?' It was like working with a calliope."

Curb's narrative structure is invariably *Seinfeld*ian – the pebble of a mishap dropped into a pond ripples and builds to a tsuris tsunami – but the streamers tied to David's gnarled maypole of an id now flap free of any network standards and practices. It always was a delight to see what David managed to slide past the censors at NBC when *Seinfeld* reigned: onanism, cunnilingus, and shrunken phalli; the death by poisoned envelope of George Costanza's fiancée; fleecing a child with severe immune deficiencies out of victory at Trivial Pursuit. *Curb Your Enthusiasm*, though, makes all that seem like *Touched by an Angel*.

In the final scene of the episode he's working on this afternoon, David climbs out the window of a theater ladies' room after getting hugged there by a prepubescent lass who has rushed out of his arms and into the crowded lobby, screaming, "Mommy, Mommy, that bald man's in the bathroom and there's something hard in his pants!"

The viewer knows that the hard thing in David's pants is a water bottle he's attempting to hide, but the folks in the lobby do not; David's leaving through the window because he hears them coming to lynch him.

"It's a funny show, isn't it?" he asks as the credits roll. "It might be my favorite."

It's not easy, picking a favorite. Two prior episodes have explored at length the power of the word *cunt* – once as a typo in a newspaper obituary David wrote to honor his wife's aunt. Last season, at a meeting of incest survivors, David devised a fictional incident of his childhood abuse at the wandering hands of an imaginary uncle. Here, pedophilia. Next season – bestiality?

"Yeah, I'll probably tackle it," David says, smiling. "I actually have an idea for it. If you can't take the high dive, what's the point? I don't feel that's risky at all – because I know it's making me laugh. I know if we can execute it the way I see it, it'll work. I mean, to me, there's not even a chance that it won't work."

Whatever works: That is the kamikaze's credo and the comic's. If he crashes and dies, it won't be for lack of stomach. And if watching *Curb* leaves you loathing Larry David half as much as he loathes himself, well, that's fine. Just as long as it makes him laugh.

Even on his worst nights doing stand-up, he never doubted his chops; that soft, David never was. But *Seinfeld* taught him that commercial success could be more crushing than stand-up-comedy failure, brutal to sustain, a treadmill to creative oblivion. David assumed the *Seinfeld* pilot would never make it, and when NBC liked it enough to ask for four more episodes, he began unraveling. "I had no confidence," he says. "I wasn't interested in having anything to do with television. That only came about because of my relationship with Jerry. I was living in New York, doing stand-up at night, fucking around, getting by. I had a car, I was playing golf, I had no responsibilities.

"Four shows – all right, it wasn't that traumatic. Maybe somehow I could write four shows. Somehow. So we do the four shows, and I'm thinking, Okay, that's the end of this crap. And then we're picked up for thirteen. Thirteen shows. Oh, my God – that's impossible. I can't do it. I'm welling up with fear and anxiety. I feel myself starting to cry.

"Then it gets picked up for another twenty-two. All of a sudden I've got this huge undertaking that I am emotionally ill-equipped to handle. It was so big. It was like, Yeah, cancel the show. Take me out of my misery – because I don't think I can do this."

Even as he mounted the summit of the sitcom world, David remained ... Larry David. Each season, he prayed that NBC or Jerry would pull the show's plug. Each year, he frayed a little more under the pressure to keep topping himself. In 1996, he quit the highest-rated sitcom on television – quit writing, quit producing, and quit watching it. And – being Larry David – not with any sense of triumph or success.

"People would say, You deserve it. I'd go, What do you even mean – I deserve it? What do I deserve? I don't deserve anything."

As for his *Seinfeld* money, it's a running joke on *Curb*. When David confronts a network exec about swiping shrimp from his take-out order, the guy hollers, "You know what, Larry? Take your $475 million and buy yourself some fucking shrimp." And when David's manager loses his Lakers courtside seats after David trips and injures Shaquille O'Neal, David asks what he can do to make up for it and his manager screams, "Buy the team!"

If Larry David isn't happy, it's not the money's fault.

"I like having it; I'm not gonna deny that. I never made more than $7,000 a year until I was thirty-two. I had my share of so-called character-building years. It's great to have it. But I wasn't happy when some of those numbers were published. People look at me and go, Oh, you must be so happy. Nobody knows what's going on inside a person's head. You don't know anything, no matter who they are."

When I see him still rubbing his neck and grimacing at the office the next morning, I ask him about it. "I have a condition. I'm not in pain – I just can't turn too well. I haven't had any range of motion in my neck for fifteen years now. It's the muscles. There was a time when I was in pain, but I'm not anymore."

So let's go get a massage. My treat.

"I don't like to indulge myself like that. Somebody working on my body for an hour – I feel like I'm wasting my time."

All right, here's the plan: We jump in the Prius and drive to the Museum of Tolerance. It's five minutes from here.

"You're not serious. The Museum of Tolerance?"

Come on. Five minutes.

"What's in the Museum of Tolerance anyway?"

I'm not sure. It's some kind of Holocaust memorial.

"Oh, God. You want me to go to the museum and mock the Holocaust. You want to end my career."

He's not even half joking now; maybe he's not joking at all. He has seen careers wither, fade, and die. Another running joke on this year's *Curb* is David's fruitless, season-long effort to pitch a new sitcom, based on the rigor mortis suffered by Jason Alexander and Julia Louis-Dreyfus – played straight by Alexander and Louis-Dreyfus – cast forever in the shadows of their *Seinfeld* characters. And David has had his own near-death experience: *Sour Grapes*, the movie he wrote and directed after Seinfeld. It was not good, and it did not do well.

"I survived it," David says.

The kamikaze has it good. The comic has to die and live to die again: His life is shtick; shtick is his life. The point where David's *Curb* persona ends and the man himself begins isn't easy to discern, not even in the mirror. "The person on the show actually has more character than I do," he says with dour cheer. "He's not as bright, but inside, he has more character. I'd rather be the person on the show."

Whatever cries and whispers lurk in Larry David's depths are flung up on the screen in *Curb* – or lodged tightly in his neck. You needn't love yourself to be a narcissist; you can be just as transfixed by self-loathing. But to milk your misery for laughs and money, that is some kind of genius.

Screw happy: If your deepest fear is of not being funny, then happiness is a threat, not a goal. David's boyhood chum Richard Lewis, the Yid in black beside whose self-lacerating comedic stylings David's are but a hymnal whisper, once persuaded David to see a psychotherapist, many years ago, back in New York.

"I recommended mine," says Lewis, who often pops up on *Curb* whining in disharmony with David. "We'd go to group with the doctor, and afterward we had aftergroup. Larry went to these aftergroups, and one night he just stood up and said, 'I've had it. I don't want to hear you people. You're not helping me, I can't help you – this is insane.'

"He just stormed out of this person's house. The whole group ran after him, ten neurotic people chasing a guy fleeing from therapy. He wound up in a phone booth. I said, 'Larry, come on – you should go back.' He said, 'I'm not coming out.' We ultimately all left, and I don't think he's been in therapy since.

"Larry gets to his neuroses not from a Method school — he's the Olivier of neurosis. I don't think in real life he suffers that much internally. I hope not. His obsessiveness is to make good art and be a good father and husband. I think. I say that about people, and then you read the next day that someone was dressed up like Peter Pan on top of a bicycle."

Not to worry. David's Tao of Eternal Discomfort trumps any notion of personal transformation. "I realized I could speak to this person every day for two hours for the rest of my life," David says of therapy, "and I'll be exactly the same. All you're doing is exacerbating everything by exploring yourself so deeply. It's too much. You can learn too much about yourself. I think there's a limit."

David is happy doing *Curb* – ten episodes a season, shot on the fly, documentary-style, with a few pages of outline and no censors – perhaps too happy. Being Larry David, he yearns to return to what he failed at best: stand-up comedy.

"I think I finally could get an audience who would be on my side. I've never done it under those conditions. I'd like to see what that would be like. Once you're up there and you've got the right audience, there's nothing like it. It's not something that you forget. I'm gonna go back."

Maybe. But Richard Lewis has nudzhed David to tour with him for years without success.

"It would be fun touring," Lewis says, "doing some gigs with him, and I think it would be great for people to see him live. Now he would be able to handle that heckler."

Seinfeld is less sanguine. "Now that he's got a little celebrity, maybe it would be different. But not that different. Stand-up is a very unforgiving medium. And a Richard Lewis – Larry David double bill would be some sort of neurosis-protein-shake spectacular."

Laurie David is altogether dubious about her husband – with or without Lewis – getting back up there again.

"I don't see this happening so fast – because to get your act together, you have to hit the clubs. You have to travel. And we all know he's not traveling. He's not going anywhere."

He's certainly not going anywhere with me. No Disneyland. No massage. No Museum of Tolerance. When he mentions that he has a dental appointment, I beg to come along. No dice.

He points at my tape recorder.

"I feel sorry for you," he says. "Having to go through all those tapes – it's not gonna be good. Whaddya got? Nothing. You got nothing here. I'm bad at these things. I keep seeing what I'm saying in print and I freeze up. I warned you."

Warned me? You invited me to come. I flew out here during wartime for this. Out of *Newark*, for pity's sake.

"Was anyone else on the plane?"

Yeah – Norm Mineta and the Sri Lanka Hotfoot Ballet Troupe.

"You know, normally I love a good pall, but this is beyond pall. Anything where the society as a whole would be depressed would probably have buoyed my spirit a little bit – but not this. This is a bit much. Those are nice sneakers, by the way."

You don't think the laces are a trifle long?

"They're making laces long these days. Have you noticed that? So, Albert Brooks – did you go into editing with him, too?"

No. Look, don't worry about this story. I'll make you look good.

"I don't care. If you called me up and said you're not gonna write it, I'd say that's great. I would encourage you not to."

But you might not like the part where I leave my wife and son back at ground zero and you won't go anywhere with me. How it was too much of a favor to ask of the big-shot comic genius to go to Disneyland.

"That's very funny," he says. "That's fine. Just keep away from the genius thing. That's embarrassing. I don't want people reading about that. They'd have to lock you up if that's what you thought about yourself. You wouldn't be able to walk around in society."

God forbid. Why, that would make you ... Larry David.

Chapter Three

Sean Penn

Patriot

The screening room on the Sony lot in Culver City is much larger than the crowd, maybe a couple dozen industry types, gabbing behind me, waiting for the movie to unreel. I'm down in front, hissing into my cell, getting one last update from the wife back in New Jersey on game four of the Cavs-Pistons series. Sean Penn has yet to show.

The Cavs, God love 'em, get the W despite my wife's lousy play-by-play, just as the yakking in the room goes hush. I crane my neck to see that the auteur is in the house, looking like a Little Rascal gone to seed. No shave, red eyed, hank of hair askew, hands jammed in the pockets of his jeans, Penn's standing at his center seat a few rows back, staring at the still-blank screen while we all stare at him.

"I think it speaks for itself," he croaks, squinting, pitched forward like a pirate on the plank. "I hope you like it."

Uh-oh. Old-school celebrity-journalism rules are few and simple: If you tape, bring lots of batteries. Before you leave your hotel, floss and pee – in that order. Above all, beware the screening. You can't avoid it if your star has a movie coming out, but watching it before you hook up is lose-lose: If it sucks, you must pretend you loved it anyhow; if you adored it – in fifteen years, this has occurred exactly never – the star won't believe you mean it. In 1998, I sat through a screening of *The Muse* before I met with Albert Brooks, and I had to spend the rest of our two-day date basically telling a fat girl her ass was awesome. And now the man-beast it took eight men to hold back in *Mystic River* – Penn had to be fed oxygen between takes, and Clint Eastwood, the director, had to keep piling on extras to restrain Penn; viewed in slow motion or real time, nobody in the scene is "acting" – looks skittish enough to pinch a jagged brick into his briefs.

Worse, Penn doesn't act in the new film; he directed it. And while you can slice the greatest-living-actor hoo-ha eight ways to Sunday – however you cut it, Sean Penn, forty-seven, has been part of that pie for years – the three movies he has directed are small, dark, and difficult. *The Indian Runner*, based on a Springsteen song from *Nebraska*, is a Cain-and-Abel variant; *The Crossing Guard* is about a guy seeking to murder the drunk driver who killed his daughter; and *The Pledge* is the story of a retired cop's fruitless quest to nail a serial killer preying on little blond girls. All three are worthy films – the latter two are anchored by top-notch work from Penn's pal Jack Nicholson, the soundtracks glisten, and the meandering subservience of plot to character brings back the sweet seventies of Ashby, Altman, and Cassavetes. Their palette of emotion, though, runs from broody and dismal to grimly redemptive exhaustion. Put it this way: At Cannes, *The Indian Runner* got a long standing ovation. "Now I know," Penn said to the audience, "what it feels like to be Jerry Lewis."

And tonight: *Into the Wild*, from the 1996 nonfiction bildungsroman best-seller about Christopher McCandless, a rich kid with itchy feet and high ideals whose hunger for freedom, truth, goodness, purity, nature, and self-knowledge led him on a two-year journey that ended in Alaska, where he made his home in an abandoned bus for four months and starved to death. It's a lovely, sad, and inspiring book. You can see right away why a moviemaker would want to turn it into a movie, and just as fast you can think up good reasons not to – starting with the fact that it's a lovely, sad, inspiring book about a rich kid who slowly starves to death, alone in an abandoned bus.

Yet the movie – I shit you not – is better, a fearless, full-hearted beauty. Penn wrote it big, shot it epic – spacious skies, fruited plains and amber waves of grain, and, in all her fearsome majesty, Alaska – got Eddie Vedder to cough up an open-road opera, and gave Vince Vaughn a few precious minutes to hot-wire the whole operation, in return for which Vince gave Sean something missing from his prior movies: fun.

But what lifts *Into the Wild* to greatness is the no-name who plays the dead kid – Emile Hirsch. It's a game physical performance – he's visibly skeletal by movie's end – but that ain't half its depth. On the page, McCandless is framed by irony and the author's judgments; on the screen – Hirsch is there almost every second – he's an immense spirit, overflowing with joy. And Penn never judges or distances himself; he celebrates.

Early on, here is Hirsch hunkered on the sun-dazzled roadside, munching an apple, goofing.

"You're really good," he tells the fruit, his voice throaty with lust and rising in beatific wonder. "You're like a hundred, a *thousand* times better than any apple I've ever had. You're a super apple. You're so tasty. You're so organic. So natural. You're the apple of my eye."

Then, with the camera already tight on him, he crooks his starry-eyed mug right into the lens, grinning madly. And as Eddie Vedder's jet-engine roar torques into a "gonna rise up" lyric, well, good gosh, you'd have to be a golem not to feel goosebumps and some kind of love. Which means you'll likely sniffle come the end.

And what beyond that you'd ever ask of any movie, screening or not, I surely don't know.

After the lights come up, Penn still looks tight as

a fist. The man needs a drink, maybe two or three. His face is lined much deeper than when I first met him, but that was back in '97, fifty thousand cigarettes and a sea of booze ago, before he copped Best Actor, saved the city of New Orleans, and turned traitor to the homeland, any single one of which exploits would have put a dent in Superman.

Alcohol awaits at a Beverly Hills hotel where one of *Into the Wild's* producers is staying, and Penn leads the way in a burbling new blue-and-gray Shelby GT500. He's at the hotel entrance by the time my rented Grand Prix limps in, standing next to some gent in a dark suit who turns as I follow them inside, offers a rumpled smile and a paw to shake, and says, "I'm Jack."

You look sort of familiar, is what I want to say, but truth is, I'm struck dumb. Bend me over and call me Mabel, is what I'm thinking – it's John Joseph Nicholson, right here, of all places, smack-dab in the middle of a Sean Penn profile. What the fuck.

"I just flew in from New Jersey," is what I finally do manage to say when we join the group in the bar's small seating area.

"Why would anyone ever want to leave New Jersey?" asks Jack.

"You're a Neptune boy," I say.

"Close enough," Jack says.

Manasquan High School, class of '54, is what I want to tell him, but the line between celebrity hack and ass-kissing dork is already plenty blurry, as any soi-disant journalist will tell you. So there's Jack, seventy years old and still looking like the cock of the walk, and Sean, thick veined and muscular and bolting mojitos, and Sean's missus – Robin Wright Penn, an actress of consummate skill, also the sole owner of shiksadom's most exquisite face, not counting my own wife's – and Bill Pohlad, producer, a long, lean, friendly Minnesotan, son of the billionaire Twins owner, plus two guys I don't recognize.

Penn, it turns out, was pissed off because the projector's bulb at the screening was too hot, so the film didn't look as crisp as it should've.

"It made me feel edgy," he says. "I don't want anybody to see it when it's not the way it oughta be."

It really is a gorgeous movie, I tell him, which doesn't count as kissing ass because it's absolutely true.

"Yeah," says Penn. "That's why. I knew it would play and all that, but it made me crazy.

"That kid looks like Leonardo," Nicholson says, meaning Hirsch and DiCaprio, and he's right. "You better keep him working, or they'll eat him alive."

When Penn mentions that Hirsch lost forty pounds over the course of *Into the Wild's* eight-month shooting schedule, Nicholson chuckles.

"I just played a guy dying of cancer," he says. "And I didn't lose an ounce."

Nicholson's drinking coffee – "brown vomit," he calls it – at midnight. When he wants to smoke, he lights up. This may be a nation of laws, not men, yet every place makes exceptions, and in Los Angeles, it's Jack. But ten years of living close to San Francisco have changed the Penns: When they need a fix, they step outside.

"Sean's brilliant," says Nicholson. "He knows how to tell a story. He knows how to help actors deal with pressure. He understands it's all on you, all of it, every goddamn day."

Jack turns to Pohlad, launching a monologue that starts in Moscow, at a film festival – Russian whores get a cameo – winds into a disquisition about why governorship is fine for a movie star ("Every state should have one") but not the presidency, which somehow melds into an opaque anecdote about mending fences with screenwriter Robert Towne after a twenty-odd-year feud, leading to the possibility of making a sequel to *The Last Detail*, which segues into Brando's last will and testament as Marlon's ultimate act of revenge upon his executor, Hollywood titan Mike Medavoy, and ends at last with the thought that moviegoers are no longer able to connect emotionally with a good old-fashioned film.

"It's like a dead nerve," he says. "A whole generation – maybe two generations now – all they know are special effects. Not just all they know. That's all they want."

By the time the Penns return, Jack's talking about trying hypnosis for the cigarettes, which brings to mind Harry Dean Stanton, who's eighty-one, still smoking proudly, and it's Tuesday night – Harry's band is playing at a café not far from here. Or was – it's way too late.

"You know what Harry says about smoking?" Robin asks Jack. "'I'm gonna go out the way I wanna go out' – and you should go out the way you want to go out."

"You're his favorite wife," Jack tells her. "He keeps saying Sean is just his beard. Harry loves you."

Penn laughs. "I can't blame him for that," he says.

"Are you trying to get laid?" says his wife.

Penn's eyebrows waggle. I don't think he's acting.

"I gotta go," says Nicholson. "I've got the second half of the basket-ball game TiVoed."

I know how it turns out, I say.

"Don't fuckin' tell me," he growls, getting up to leave. "I don't wanna know."

I just . . .

"*No!*" he yells, hurrying away. "Don't say another fuckin' word."

Penn doesn't need another drink, but he wants one. Not a mojito – some beastly, malodorous shellac, the color of spit snuff. Pohlad's eyes look like pinwheels; he's still lost in Nicholsonia, somewhere between Moscow and Mulholland Drive.

"That's Jack," Penn tells him. "He speaks in some Joycean dialect. Ya gotta go slow. Never mind the lyrics. Just listen to the melody."

I hook back up with Penn late the next morning in Santa Monica, at a postproduction place where he's

color-timing *Into the Wild* – going over it frame by frame with his editor and cinematographer, making sure that each shot matches the next, fixing any flaws before he sends his baby out into the world. It's grueling labor for a middle-aged man who may well be hungover and fresh-laid, requiring much spring water and a soup-'n'-sashimi lunch. He's wearing Hollywood business haggard – dark blue suit, dark blue open-necked dress shirt, mussed hair, stubble, shades. To smoke, he heads out to a patio deck by the rooftop parking lot, four stories above the street and

Cutting Room Floor: Penn

THE PITCH: The guy who's been whining for ten years that he doesn't want to be an actor anymore (because he'd rather write and direct) finally proves why.

SCENE: At the Peninsula Hotel in Beverly Hills, in the bar, sitting around a long, low table with Penn and his wife and their personal assistant and a film producer and a film editor and another guy and, yeah, Jack Nicholson. As it ran in the story, the scene doesn't address the reporting circumstances. I didn't have my tape recorder with me and I wasn't taking notes. I've worked like that a few times over the years, and I've developed a mnemonic device: I build a house in my head – my own real-life house, actually – and I store phrases and details inside each room. Afterward, I make notes as soon and as fast as I can.

BACKSTORY: When I first profiled him in 1997, Penn had plenty of time to relax. We spent a long day on his boat, hung out one night an L.A. bar he co-owned, and met for lunch and a long interview the day after that. This time out, he was working 12-to-18 hour days on *Into The Wild*, sweating over every post-production detail with absolutely no time to kick back and talk.

For much of two days, I stood by as he sat for hour after hour at a lab in Santa Monica, color-timing the film – don't ask – and whenever he'd take a smoke break, we'd huddle out on the deck for another interview snippet. To be fair – and trust me, Sean Penn is both a across from a dental office with a penguin atop its sign.

"That used to be a diner," Penn says. "The Penguin Diner. We hung out there when I was in high school. I guess they kept the penguin."

You like northern California?

"Love it."

Miss anything about L.A.?

"No. We come down and visit my mother. But it's a much better situation, particularly with the kids – much better."

---

swell guy and a good man – he was clear from the get-go that this was how we'd have to do things this time around. No problem: Part of my job is to take whatever I can get – always.

CONFLICT: I wasn't sure that he would be all right with me using the stuff from the Peninsula. It wasn't off-the-record, but I asked him about using it anyway – in general – and he said, "Go ahead. I trust you." I maybe betrayed that trust by using the banter about his wife and Harry Dean Stanton. Light-hearted as it was – and even taking into account that Mrs. Penn is a celebrity in her own right, and a heck of a thespian, too – I read it now and cringe. And I'll bet Robin and Sean cringed, too. Sorry.

WISH I'D WRITTEN: This goes back to that '97 profile. Penn was ready to quit acting then, and I spoke about that with his friend and director, Tim Robbins, who gave me the best explanation I've ever heard about how hard a job acting can be for some actors:

"There's very few jobs I know of where you work twelve to fifteen hours a day, six days a week, where you have to be emotionally tied up if you take your work seriously. There are people who work overtime, and work as hard as we do, but that's in a disconnected way emotionally. If you're playing your emotions and you're accepting them honestly and getting into the character, it's exhausting. It's a tough profession. I think that there's an image of it as being this really glamorous, easy-to-do thing – we're overpaid and we're spoiled. I'm sorry, but it couldn't be farther from the truth."

Sean and Robin's son and daughter – Hopper and Dylan – are teenagers now. Penn's father, Leo, an actor and director who was blacklisted on both coasts back in the 1950s, died in 1998. His little brother, Christopher – one heck of an actor himself: fiery, funny, and scary as hell, often all at once – died early in 2006, barely forty years old. When I say how much I liked his brother's work, Penn grunts.

"Lived right over there," he says. "See that clock tower? Right below that."

He's silent until I mention my own favorite Chris Penn role – Chez Tempio in *The Funeral*.

"One of the great performances in film history as far as I'm concerned," he says. "The size of his talent, the size of the things he was able to convey – there's not a young actor out there who can do that. In the world of younger leading boys, he was a younger leading man.

"He got to do some great things, and he did 'em great. Forty's not the age to go. It's a lot different from a parent goin'. He was a beautiful boy, and it's a stinker."

And that's that. Penn doesn't trade in sound bites or open his heart for show. He's ready to go back inside, to work.

Movie magic's afoot at another postproduction nest of dweebs nearby – "the *Star Trek* convention," Penn calls it as he jerks the Shelby into another parking garage. Counting Penn and Jay Cassidy, his editor, nine folks are staring at the onscreen face of an actress who shall remain nameless here, because what they're doing is using a laser pointer to mark which of her zits need to be removed from one of her close-ups.

"It's reality," Penn says. "But it's not appealing reality."

"More blemishes," says the guy holding the pointer, circling her blebs.

"There's one there," says someone else.

"And there – yeah."

"And that one, on her forehead."

"Yeah – the pimple."

"What about this small one?"

"No," says Penn. "Leave that."

During his next cigarette, he talks about choosing Hirsch to carry a movie that sends him roaring down white-water rapids, back-floating naked as a jaybird down an Alaskan river, slogging uphill through waist-high snow, and dropping close to a third of his body weight.

"I'd seen him in *Lords of Dogtown*, and I thought he was electric in that, very physical. The way I wrote that rapids scene – the idea is that he's so in that zone, that immortal zone, that he's just gonna make it. I didn't want Emile to know how to do it, yet I was gonna throw him into that rapid in a kayak.

"He took a look at it, and he was intimidated by it – and it was intimidating. So I said, 'If I do it, will you do it?' I didn't know that I could make it, but I knew that I'd be okay if I didn't. Well, I didn't – about three quarters down, I went down. It was good because he got to see that a) you could do it, and b) you could survive if you didn't. He made it four times in a row. He just has this natural-born balance. Extraordinary. He never didn't make it."

Then Penn laughs – a surfer/stoner hoo-hoo-hoo, just like Spicoli back at Ridgemont High.

"Well, he didn't one time at the end. But it was fantastic."

Emile Hirsch is on the phone from Berlin, where he's
doing *Speed Racer*.

Are you playing Speed?

"I am." He sounds delighted.

I sing him the first line: Go, Speed Racer.

Hirsch finishes the chorus. Unlike his balance, his voice is not extraordinary.

How much weight did Penn make you lose?

"I went from 156 to 115. There was a lot of motivation and running and determination and suffering. Mostly suffering."

Self-doubt?

"The first day. I had to go over this hill and down into snow up to my belly button, and I had to carry this thirty-pound backpack. And I'm tryin' to scrape my way back up this hill, which is really steep, to get back and do the take again. The prop guy throws down this rope, and I hear Sean go, 'What're you doin'?' The prop guy says, 'I was gonna help him up the hill,' and I hear Sean go, 'Nope – no way.' And I'm at the bottom of this hill, digging in the snow.

"I'm just like, *Ohhh, fuuuck* – this is gonna be hard. I remember gritting my teeth, fighting through my Texas-sized anxiety attack, and just working my way up the hill. And I ended up doin' it twelve times."

Sadistic son of a bitch.

"I never doubted Sean. I completely trusted him in every way as a director. He knows – he just knows. He saw in me that I was ready to die making this movie. And I think he liked that. This wasn't, Oh, the take's over, let me go kick my feet up in my trailer while I get a massage. This was, I have a couple minutes after finishing the take, let me lie on my cot and shiver. But love every single second of it."

Floating naked downstream – you loved that, too?

"It was freezing. I remember getting in and being wracked with the cold and getting out and doing it over and over. And I remember in the trailer afterward, where you're supposed to warm yourself up, I was trying to describe what it was like to a production assistant, but I was slurring my words. Hypothermia was setting in. I freaked out and put this big warm bag on my head – a hot pad, like a water pad. And Sean came in and said, 'That was one of the *gnarliest* things I've ever seen an actor do' – and he slammed the door.

"I was just like, *Hell*, yeah. That was worth every chilled moment."

You must have suffered some major shrinkage.

"It was so cold, you got bigger afterward. *That's* the kind of cold it was. It was so cold, it was *huge*."

Like Hirsch says, Penn knows; Penn always has
known. At fourteen, working on *Little House on the Prairie* as an extra on a hot day, he decided he should stay in character – and in his prairie outfit – through lunch. When shooting resumed, he promptly passed out.

"Sunstroke," he explains.

You're big on commitment.

"Yeah. I like that part of it, whether it's on the acting side or the directing side, where whatever you do is driven by the love of the feeling when you merge with the thing. You're not gonna hold back. You leave doubt behind. It's that freedom from one's own bullshit. It rises ya up."

Penn's en route from a meeting with another director – he's acting next week, playing a border-patrol agent – to more postproduction work on *Into the Wild*, from 6:00 P.M. tonight to 6:00 A.M. tomorrow. He's wearing work boots, gray work pants, a dark sweatshirt beneath a plain blue zippered jacket, and gold-rimmed glasses – "cheaters," he calls them – looking, all in all, like hammered poo.

You're no kid anymore – how do you keep your energy up?

"Rage."

Rage?

"Rage."

Good – I've got some role-playing I'd like to do. I'm Sean Hannity.

Do you want the U.S. to win the war?

"That's the wrong question. 'Winning the war' — I think we're past that point in human evolution where there's such a thing as winning wars. You know what that's like asking? You're on the third date and you're uncomfortable, so you look at the other person in silence and say, 'What're you thinking?' That's what that question is."

I can't tell whether he's just groggy or going Joycean on me.

So, Sean . . . what're you thinking?

"I gotta get on this Spanish like a motherfucker — the Spanish I have to speak in this movie next week."

Ten years ago, Penn was through with acting. He wanted only to direct. Ten years ago, he was done with politics, too; he had just finished working on Tom Hayden's failed campaign for L.A. mayor. And ten years ago, he told me about trying to interview Charles Bukowski. Penn and the old master were longtime friends.

"I'd already talked to him about all of the things I was interested in, but buildin' the spontaneity again was hard. So we tried to break up where we were. We went to the track. We were at the track all day, and somewhere it just went silent. So we went to dinner, and we're sittin' there, and it was very quiet.

"He wanted to help me out. He knew I needed more stuff, and he was tryin' to think what to talk about. I couldn't figure out anything. We got out in the parkin' lot — all we could hear was my shoes, my new shoes hittin' the gravel. He stopped. And he said, 'I'll tell ya one thing: I wouldn't wear loud shoes.'"

Now I mention Bukowski, tell Penn that he told me a story ten years ago, but before I can even begin to retell it, he says — in Bukowski's ravaged timbre — "I wouldn't wear loud shoes."

His work boots don't squeak, but Penn himself has become the footwear equivalent of a brass band playing Sousa on July 4. He has forked over tens of thousands of dollars to place himself on the public record in *The Washington Post* and *The New York Times* about the Iraq war; he has written tens of thousands of words for the *San Francisco Chronicle* about his trips to Baghdad and Tehran; he went to New Orleans in the wake of Katrina, found a boat and a rifle, and literally rescued dozens of flood victims; and for his trouble, he has been more vilified than any Tinseltowner since Hanoi Jane. If patriotism is the last refuge of those star-spangled scoundrels who report while you decide, their turncoat of choice is none other than.

So, Hannity aside, what's that like?

"Here's what: If you have any Irish blood" – Penn's mother, actress Eileen Ryan, is half Irish, half Italian – "then your first sip of whiskey as a child is gonna kick your ass. When they first come out swingin', it's that first sip of whiskey. But by the time you're done with that glass? Gimme more. Gimme more. I'm drunk with it."

He shakes his head and laughs again, that surfer laugh.

"The exemption they make for actors – because you occupy the position they only dreamed about as a child, you can't be an American, too. You don't get both, because that's just too much. Oh, God – you caught me being me? *Fuck* you."

Penn kept acting for the payday, and because working with directors like Terry Malick and Eastwood helped restore his sense of purpose and fun. What drives Penn's political commitment is love – of father, kids, and country. Leo Penn received the Distinguished Flying Cross in World War II, and in his ad in the *Times*, Sean, recalling the flag draping his dad's coffin, wrote:

> *Our forefathers entrusted that flag and what it should stand for, whether in times of bliss or terror, to our fathers and mothers. And they have entrusted it to us. The responsibility "for which it stands" is ours. That flag is my father and I want him back.*

"How would you like this legacy as a father?" Penn says now. "You're Sean Hannity or Bill O'Reilly, and you're on camera in the archives saying this: 'XY equals Z. XY equals Z. XY equals fucking Z.' Cut to one year later – 'XY equals Z, my ass. Show those loops to their children when they grow up. And between X, Y, and Z are 3,465 dead Americans and 600,000 dead civilians in Iraq.

"There's baggage attached to coming out publicly on stuff, but there's baggage – in my view, more damaging baggage – to goin' and jerkin' off on Jay Leno's show, philosophizing about *Uncle Buck* or whatever you're hawkin'."

Whoa – you just dissed John Candy, and I resent that. Very much.

"I like John Candy. The reason I picked *Uncle Buck* is because I already let that slip about ten years ago as an offhanded thing, and I heard from the actors in it, so nobody new is gonna get mad."

Who's your favorite president?

"Of all time?"

All time.

"I'm a Thomas Jefferson guy."

Been to his memorial?

"I went with my daughter."

Underrated – the memorial, not Jefferson.

"When I was a kid, I stenciled on the back of my bedroom door – it was my message to my parents – his quote: 'Our children are born free, and their freedom is a gift of nature and not of those who gave them birth.'"

How old were you?

"Eleven or twelve – somethin' like that."

Any of that coming back to bite you in the ass now?

"Yeah," he says, laughing. "But I still agree with it."

Penn once was even more famous and reviled than he is today, for different reasons. Married to Madonna, tossed in jail for assault – that sort of stuff. He doesn't talk about those things. I don't blame him. Under perfect circumstances, it takes a good long time and plenty of work to become some semblance of a grown man anyway, and part of it is learning to keep your mouth shut – but what the hell, Sean Penn: Do you ever look back at yourself and ask, Who the *fuck* was that?

"I regret the future," he says. "I find the future potentially regrettable, starting with this death thing."

Sure, sure – but you, the you back then, was that a you you recognize today?

"Yeah. In that sense, I don't know that I've changed that much, really. I am suspect of cathartic moments in people's lives. I think you learn more about how to wreak havoc without witnesses than avoid committing the crime."

Well, something's changed: You made a splendid movie, pal. Confident. Free. You found a vision you haven't had before as a director.

"Hey! It takes practice."

Now you have to worry about what Jack Nicholson said – about the dead nerve. The audience that won't connect. Or can't.

"They'll get back there. Chocolate cake is not a need; it's a luxury. Dreaming is a need – a survival need. And it can pass up epochs – generations can die off – but it's in the DNA of mankind. It cycles back to the

49

point where people say, 'No, no, no, no – I'm not gonna. I'm not gonna not dream, and I'm not gonna *not* feel.' Even if you get a numb generation, that's not the death of it. It has an Easter.

"I'm committed to the idea – and I always have been – that the audience doesn't always know when they're being lied to. And the lies do have damage that they leave behind. But there's always hope that they know when they're bein' told the truth. D'you believe good can triumph over evil? I say, you might as well – but I'm not without that worry."

By the time I get to the postproduction place that night, LeBron has dropped forty-eight on the Pistons, it's almost 1:00 A.M., and Penn is sitting out back, smoking, happy, and relaxed. Tonight, they've wrapped up early.

"All right," he says. "Let's go to Fifth and Arizona."

There is vodka at Fifth and Arizona. Vodka and tonic with ice in a sweating glass at a bar packed with white kids who paid a ten-dollar cover to dance badly to a remix of Edwin Starr's "War."

"Induction, then destruction," Starr roars. "Who wants to die?"

Earlier that day, talking about mortality, Penn had said, "I don't have a desire to live forever," and he talked about his first visit to the bus where Chris McCandless died.

"It was overwhelming in a lot of ways, but what killed me is, his boots are still sittin' there – in the bus. Sittin' right next to each other where he left 'em."

But when I asked Penn what made young McCandless and *Into the Wild* so important to him – he spent ten years just chasing the film rights – he said only, "If you read the book and see the movie, the answer's there as far as I can tell."

Far as I can tell – Penn's no self-interpreter – this guy unwinding glass by sweating glass is the most dangerous type of man: He's an idealist. He actually believes – in art, in patriotism, in action above words and truth beyond irony. No wonder the poor bastard needs a drink.

Chapter Four

Ryan Seacrest

Fiend

Ryan Seacrest, history's greatest monster, has a full plate this morning. The KIIS-FM phone lines are lit, his cohost, Ellen K, has the latest on the 911 tape of Yanni's allegedly battered girlfriend, today's call-in theme – dishonesty – hasn't reached liftoff yet, and Monique on line 2 says that her hubby, Carl, thinks Ryan's gay.

"Is Carl gay?" Seacrest snaps. "Is Carl gay?"

Monique, who has phoned in from somewhere in the sprawling tar pit of lost souls known as Los Angeles to own up to once denting a parked car without leaving a note, says her man Carl is not gay.

"Welllll," says Ryan, "how can Carl be so sure?"

Ellen K – I'm fairly sure that her K does not stand for Kafka or Kant; Kewpie is a possibility – leans toward her microphone. "I wish I had a gay ATM for every time someone asked me that question," she says. "I would be so rich."

"Thanks for the call," says Seacrest. "And tell Carl to stop hatin'. And if he thinks I am – c'mon, Carl, show me your moves. See if I'm turned on."

Oh, he's an enigma all right, big-grinning Ryan Seacrest, a mystery wrapped in a shroud of boyish bonhomie so thick, you'd need a pitchfork to pierce it. His green eyes glazed with pale gold, his patch of dirt-brown bedhead mussed just so, his chipmunk cheeks and square jaw dotted by winsome stubble – put him in khaki shorts and a blue bandanna and you've got the world's richest Eagle Scout. Yet, at thirty-one, he seems so goddamn old. Choppers as big and white as dentures, wrinkling neck, rutted brow, the faint smell of sour coffee and green Tabasco decaying in his wake – not merely old, old as sin. Ancient.

Clearly, being the fleshly embodiment of evil accelerates the aging process, and radio does the rest: Every moment counts, literally, and must hum with manufactured glee – or, better yet, woe – lest these poor dumb fucks stuck in traffic and trapped in a gray existence tune their ears and dials away from the unctions of the Devil.

"Hi, Jessica."

"Hi."

"Are you sure you wanna do this?"

"Um, I changed my mind. Never mind." Jessica's voice is quaking.

"Whaddya mean you changed your mind? You can't change your mind. Jessica?"

"Yeah – who's this?"

"My name is Ryan."

"This isn't Ryan."

"Yeah it is. Why don't you believe me?"

"I don't know. Because I listen to you every morning. You sound a little bit different in person."

"Well, how do I sound?"

"You sound tired. You need a nap."

"It doesn't take a rocket scientist to figure out I haven't been home in a week. All right, now listen, Jessica: Tell me what's goin' on."

"Well, I...I...I've been having an affair with my boss."

" 'I've been having an affair with my boss.' Is your boss married?"

"Well, yeah."

"Are you?"

"No."

"Have you ever met your boss's wife?"

"Yes."

"Do you take her calls when she calls the office?"

"No."

"Where have you met her?"

"Um, at the office."

"Is it worth it, what you're doing? Is it worth it, knowing all of the ramifications of sleeping with a married man who is your boss? Is it worth it?"

Jessica hangs up in Satan's ear.

"How do you not ask that question?" Seacrest's voice rises in plea. He snickers. "I have a feeling that guy's gonna be pissed at me 'cause he's not gonna get any more office action."

"Well," says Ellen K, "he shouldn't."

"That was awesome," Seacrest says. "She hung up right at the point of impact. That was great. Love it!"

Ryan Seacrest dwells in the air from 5:00

to 10:00 each weekday morning, hosting L.A.'s most popular radio show. From February through May, two or three nights per week – depending on how many feckless, talent-free wannabes remain – he hosts *American Idol*, a sewer of innocent depravity that draws thirty million TV viewers per night. Weekends find him hosting *American Top 40*, the nationally syndicated radio countdown of all the best pap that now passes for popular music. Seacrest's also the managing editor and lead anchor of E! News – his $20 million deal with E! gives him a shot, with corporate backing, to create, market, and own new shows – and he's one of Larry King's CNN stand-ins when the old fart's off being fitted for yet another new heart. And starting last December 31, he's heir to Dick Clark's drool cup on "New Year's Rockin' Eve." So you can see why Ryan might sound as if he needs a nap.

But napping is for mortals. The Angel of the Bottomless Pit has souls to harvest, a mission demanding as much science as art. Seacrest's voice – full of wiseass pep – has worked on radio for more than half his present incarnation, dating to his high school days in suburban Atlanta. It is not a versatile or interesting voice – expunged of all traces of any but the most generic middle-American accent, it is the aural equivalent of a bag of fast-food fries – but it is quick and, in a familiar sort of way, engaging. From a studio on the fifth floor of a faceless, nameless office building in Burbank, surrounded by soundless TV and computer screens, tiers of digital-editing equipment, and a knot of assistants, Seacrest connects to the masses. He says "You know I love you" ten times each hour to folks he wouldn't piss on if they were in flames, and invariably they reply, "I love you, too." They are no less precious to Old Scratch for their facelessness. Names and faces mean dick; hell needs numbers.

Cutting Room Floor: Seacrest

THE PITCH: Only a grizzled slob of a magazine writer could hope to explain the bizarre appeal of America's most popular and primped TV androgyne.

SCENE: On the wall by the door to his production office, down the hall from his radio studio, Ryan Seacrest has hung a framed 2004 *New York Times Magazine* profile of himself headlined "Bland Ambition" and devoted to the premise that he is devoid of talent and personality. It's not hanging there ironically. He's just thrilled to be noticed.

BACKSTORY: A four-day business meeting with an ambitious junior executive. Seacrest has both talent and a personality, but he has spent most of his life in a radio or TV studio and, by nature and choice, his talent and personality are stunted. Funny, smart, well-spoken, he's focused only on building an empire of pop crap. Even an off-the-record dinner with an E! exec – the same schmuck who greenlit Anna Nicole Smith's reality show – consisted entirely of Seacrest laying

"Five-, six-, seven-, and eight-o'clock hours, we program the show differently," he explains as a Mary J. Blige tune spins. Some hours, Seacrest somehow finds enough time between traffic reports, gossip, promos, and ads to play as many as three songs. "The five-o'clock hour, people are waking up, people are going home from the overnight shift, so we're a little bit more adult. At the six-o'clock hour, kids are getting up, getting ready for school, starting to listen with their moms and dads. As we get closer to seven – this is the 'mass-cume' hour – everybody's in their car. You've got the carpooling, you've got the commuters, and so we do a very mainstream hour. After 8:15, we get into more of the provocative-relationship thing, because school starts right about 8:30. The mission is to get the moms to come back after they've let their kids go."

Mass-cume?

"Young kids, teenagers, moms, dads, singles – it's our biggest listenership hour."

Cume?

plans for world domination, or at least that part of the world ruled by Jessica Simpson and Lindsey Lohan.

CONFLICT: The gay thing. Not that I think Seacrest's gay – although much of the world seems to – or that I care, or that anything's wrong with it. But considering the fact that everyone from Jay Leno to my rabbi questions his manhood, I couldn't avoid the issue altogether.

WISH I'D WRITTEN: My Seacrest interview transcripts and notes ran 30,000 words. I talked to Simon Cowell. I spoke with Kathy Griffin (who has worked with him, mocks him in her standup act, and told me that she knows "for a fact" he's not gay). I phoned the dean of Syracuse University's Center for the Study of Popular Television. I asked Ryan's people – his two personal assistants – for contact info for his mother and sister; I'm still waiting for them to get back to me.

I tried, in other words, to find a way to write a straight-up profile of a young TV host/mogul on the make. So why did I wind up portraying Ryan Seacrest as Satan? For laughs, and to see if he'd hang my story on his wall, too.

"Cumulative. We have the biggest cume in the city in morning drive – over two million. So we sell our advertising as mainstream. I don't try to be too controversial, too dirty, too this, too that. It's fun and it's real, but it's kind of right up the middle."

And with the punch of a button, Seacrest slides directly from this tutorial live to air: "Hey, if you missed our conversation about Britney Spears and is she preggo or not – there're rumors that she's having another baby – we'll try and get to the bottom of it before we get outta here at ten o'clock."

It turns out that there is no bottom to get to. Britney's publicist, on line 1, informs the Great Smog Basin, "To my knowledge, Britney is not having a baby." But, of course, knowing anything is entirely beside the point. Ryan Seacrest's job, in his own words, is "content provider" – Lucifer's gum-ball machine – and at that level of abstraction, the being or non- of a fresh Spears zygote matters not a whit. The preggo question is itself the content; any answer, or no answer, will do just fine. The gum-ball machine doesn't care what shiny, sugared ball of goo rolls down its chute.

He bolts from his stool at 9:57 A.M. and hustles down the hall to his office, where one of his two personal assistants hands him a sheaf of paper, printouts of yesterday's Google Alerts.

I myself have read thousands of Google Alerts for Ryan Seacrest. He is either feuding with Idol judge Paula Abdul or he is not. He is either feuding with Idol judge Simon Cowell or he is not. He is either canoodling with the Desperate Housewife Teri Hatcher or he has dumped her. And he is either a hetero, homo, metro, or shmetrosexual, or not.

"There was an agent I worked with who said, 'You should really try and curb that innuendo,'" Seacrest says. "I thought, Why? Who cares? I know what I'm attracted to, and that's a female. It's somehow become a stripe in the Ryan Seacrest business; it somehow takes on a life of its own just because I'm not the stereotypical guy. A friend of mine has a house with a basketball court and a pool. The guys go over and play basketball; I lie by the pool and nap in the sun. That defines me. That's consistent with who I am. I don't pretend to play basketball because I wanna feel like one of the guys. I wanna lie in the sun and relax.

"Never believe people in this business who say they don't read what's written about them," he says, thumbing quickly through the stack. Then he has to run. Literally. Running, he says, clears his head. Five drive-time hours of radio are done. Soon, he's due at the *American Idol* studio, where four innocent children with stars in their eyes and songs in their hearts will be primped for sacrifice tonight.

I can't prove the guy is Mephisto, but this

I know: When Belial lands on planet Earth, he won't be sporting horns and bare hooves; the Tempter don't roll like dat. Seacrest's Bentley – his other car is an Aston Martin – is black, with tinted windows, and yet it shines in the gloom. I tailed it late one morning through a March thunderstorm from the underground garage of the Burbank office complex, through the Cahuenga Pass, into the bowels of Hollywood, and not a drop of rain touched it.

And I'll tell you something else: If Ryan Seacrest wants your gig, you'd better check your pulse and hide your fingernail clippings. Ask Dick Clark, or what's left of him. Ask Casey Kasem, who used to host *American Top 40* until a mysterious swelling left his tongue permanently clamped to his upper palate. Ask Rick Dees, who had the KIIS morning show for twenty-two years, until a few days after Rosemary's Baby bribed a janitor to swipe one of his hankies and Dees suddenly, simultaneously was struck with incurable hives and hiccups, essentially ending his radio career.

Or ask the ghost of Brian Dunkleman, the sad-sack comic who was Seacrest's *American Idol* cohost during its first season, back when nobody knew *Idol* would grow a huge pair of creamy tits and Seacrest wore golden highlights in his flatironed hair. Poor Dunkleman just disappeared. You'd have an easier time finding Jimmy Hoffa.

Hannah Arendt had it right: Evil doesn't puke green soup. Evil puts his nose to the grindstone and his shoulder to the wheel. Evil drops out of the University of Georgia in 1994, at the age of nineteen, and heads for L.A. in a Honda Prelude with $2,000 in Christmas cash he stashed over the years and a job cohosting *Gladiators 2000*, a Saturday-morning kids' show, sharing duties with a thirteen-year-old girl.

"I auditioned for it, and they offered me the job at $200 an episode," Seacrest says. "I got that audition because I was actually hosting a show for ESPN while I was in college, *Radical Outdoor Challenge*. The production company was based in Atlanta, they needed a host for cheap, I did it. On ESPN, who cares what you're doin'? I couldn't believe it was on ESPN. I sent the tape to the *Gladiators* people, got the *Gladiators* gig, said to my mother, 'I've got a job. It's not gonna be able to pay for much, but I've got a job. We're gonna do thirteen episodes at two hundred bucks a pop, and I wanna go.'"

Over the next several years, Seacrest hosted every two-bit TV extravaganza this side of Robert Blake's perp walk – everything from *Wild Animal Games* and *Ultimate Revenge* to "Disneyland 2000: 45 Years of Magic and America's Party: Live from Las Vegas" – all while he kept working his way up the FM dial.

"I've conditioned myself to go to work every day at a studio," he says. "I have gone to a radio station every day of my life since I was fifteen years old. It's just a part of who I've become. I was not born to dunk the basketball, I was not born to play an instrument, I was not born to hit all the notes. I was not born to do any of those things. What I've figured out how to do is make people feel comfortable on television and on the radio, which enables me to have access to them, which is key for what I do. And I think more than anything else, I know when I go to bed that no one's working harder doing what I'm doing, and I think, quite frankly, simply that hard work at some point was gonna pay off."

Seacrest's talking while he's getting his hair done and his face made up for *Idol*, which goes live in an hour, at 5:00 P.M. PST, twelve hours after his radio show began this morning. He has a post-*Idol* dinner meeting with an E! VP, and a predinner *Extra* interview at the restaurant. He's an investor in the restaurant, too – in six restaurants, actually, three in L.A. and three in Las Vegas, steak joints and sushi houses. He has a line of clothes. He's also fixing to buy Kevin Costner's palazzo, a ten-thousand-square-foot, $11.5 million home in the Hollywood Hills with a tennis court and movie theater. But all of this is small potatoes beside the billion-dollar empire Seacrest plans to build.

"I learned a very important word just after I turned twenty-one. I learned the word equity. That was a very important word. That is the home run. I got the chance to shadow Merv Griffin and spend time with Dick Clark – guys who had done it in the broadcast world – and I realized what I do, what the public gets to see me do, isn't even a fraction of what I really want to do. What these guys did, they used all those shows – *American Bandstand* and *Pyramid* and *The Merv Griffin Show* – as sales devices to get in the door to sell other projects that they owned. Because Dick Clark was coming, they'd take a meeting with him. But he didn't want to talk about being a host; he wanted to talk about selling a show. And that's the model we've set up through the E! deal."

Seacrest's voice is hushed, full of ravenous determination. Tonight, his *Idol* dresser has chosen a dark-blue suit, with a dark-blue shirt and tie. All dolled up, his eyes blank gray, Seacrest looks exactly like a man primed to provide content to thirty million Americans who will spend the next irretrievable hour ingesting a long ad for Coke, Ford, cell phones, and the twisted illusion – thanks to a viewer voting process generating more than forty million phone calls during the two hours immediately after *Idol* airs – that talent and democracy are somehow compatible.

But give this devil his due: His hostmanship is masterful. Seacrest seamlessly shepherding eight "singers" and three bickering, babbling "judges" through a sixty-minute maze of plug-ola is the only subtle aspect of *American Idol*. I watch him on the TV set in his dressing room, because *Idol* doesn't allow "journalists" on the live set, and the man on the screen in the dark-blue suit and shirt is a perfect traffic cop, genial and efficient. Each ticking second pivots upon his glad-handing, bantering, and breaking for commercial while milking the "drama" – and yet he seems not to be there at all.

It is nothing to sneeze at, this hard-earned gift of his. Moments after the show signs off, when he returns to the dressing room, he still seems not to be here.

"Okay," he says, removing only his necktie. "All rise. Movin' on."

At the restaurant, on Sunset Boulevard, the *Extra* crew greets him with lights and cameras as he leaves the Bentley for the valet to park. Inside, the interview commences immediately in a spot near the bar.

"Fortunately for me," he tells the woman from *Extra*, who has been oohing on camera over his success, "I'm in this unique business of not singing, not dancing, not performing – just kind of being there...."

Suddenly it's clear who and what Ryan Seacrest is: Chance – Chauncey Gardiner, Jerzy Kosinski's passive, sexless, tube-addicted cipher, whose own TV debut in *Being There* finds him "drained of thought, engaged, yet removed.... Television reflected only people's surfaces; it also kept peeling their images from their bodies until they were sucked into the caverns of their viewers' eyes, forever beyond retrieval, to disappear."

Seacrest's alarm rings at four the next

morning. An hour and a half into the radio show, he is on the phone with Donald Trump, who's in L.A. to cast the sixth season of *The Apprentice*. It's a pleasant chat – Trump is about to spawn again, Martha Stewart is a whiny loser, the lineup for auditions to get fired by the Donald starts tomorrow morning at six – between two of our nation's premier pimps.

"You know I love you," Seacrest says to Trump before hanging up.

"I love you, too," Trump answers.

Afterward, during a stretch of commercials and the traffic update – "The northbound 5 is whimpering along in slow motion," Commander Chuck Street, pilot-poet of the Pepsi Jet Ranger 1 helicopter reports – Seacrest scarfs his take-out egg whites. Mondays and Wednesdays, the egg whites are doctored with a few drops of green Tabasco. Tuesdays and Thursdays, he mixes in some crumbled feta. Fridays, a yolk.

"So I don't have the same thing every day," he explains.

But that's the rotation?

"That's the rotation. It's actually written up in the cubicle back there for Crystal so she can order the right one on the right day."

How many egg whites?

"Like, six egg whites."

Azoy.

One of Seacrest's junior producers has a segment idea: His dork of a roommate has a hard-on for a medical receptionist and an appointment at the doctor's office this morning, so Seacrest can fly along as wingman via cell phone and help Mr. Hapless score a date.

"I love it," Seacrest says. "Let's create awkward moment after awkward moment."

Which is precisely what he does. The ninny gets nowhere, and the receptionist gets in hot water with her bosses for yakking on the phone while she's at work. "Would you call yourself hot?" Seacrest asks her. "I'm the typical brunette in glasses at the desk, basically," she tells him. It makes for good radio, and Seacrest's brain starts storming.

"You know what would be a great show? Get a guy – like Wilmer Valderrama – and his posse, his entourage, right? So his entourage, they all struggle with the girls, let's say. He does essentially what I did, not on the radio, but on TV. You have him try and hook his buddy up, and then you cover the date. And you roll on all of it. That's funny, right?"

"That's great," says Ellen K.

Thus inspired, Seacrest plays a Shakira tune and phones an E! development executive while she's still in her car on the way to work.

"I had this idea," he tells her. "And I want you to bake it a little bit."

"Okay, I'm baking."

And he makes the pitch – a guy like Wilmer Valderrama and his socially inept posse, all of that – and adds, "You get to kind of cover celebrity and dating."

"Exactly," she says. "Which is always a good thing." She pauses. "Do you want to hear something funny?"

"Someone just pitched it," Seacrest says, disappointed.

"No. Well, yeah. Someone has pitched it. You know who it was, about nine months ago?"

"Who?"

"Stephen Baldwin."

"He pitched that show?"

"Yes."

"Shut the fuck up."

She just laughs.

"Dammit," says Seacrest. "Well, there are no new ideas in this town. We just did it on the air, and it was great."

"Was there a celebrity on the air or no?"

"No, just me. But, it worked. Actually, it didn't work. The girl almost got fired. Which is great."

"Well, there you go. Where are you right now?"

"I'm on the air. I got ninety seconds, then I gotta go back on."

"All right. Well, call me later."

Crestfallen, Seacrest neglects to mention that he loves her. Could be he doesn't, or maybe he's tired. Unshaved, harrumphing his throat clear, he signs off quickly – "It's 9:53, thank you for havin' us on, Seacrest out" – and bolts the radio station, bowlegged in his boots and jeans.

Billboards, bus signs, pop-up

ads: Seacrest is everywhere. His E! deal runs for three years. He has three more years to go on his KIIS contract. *Idol*'s ratings this season – its fifth – are higher than ever. It could go on without Randy, Paula, and Simon – two potted plants and a smug prick – but not without the Dark Lord of Hosts. Not that he's going anywhere.

"If they said, 'Hey, you're gonna be charged $10,000 a month to host *American Idol*,' I'd pay $20,000. This is something that I would pay to be a part of, to drive everything else I'm doing. It fuels everything else. It allows me the exposure and the access to the public and to the executives in our business. But it's not my baby. I'm a hired hand. No equity."

Tonight's *Idol* costume is a black suit-and-shirt combo, which goes nicely with the stubble.

"It's a good suit, right?"

Indeed it is.

In a few minutes, Seacrest will appear on the TV set here in his dressing room and thirty million Americans will hang on his every word.

"These contestants are so close to the finals, they can taste it," he will say. "But there is only room for twelve. The country has voted, and the results are in. The drama is about to unfold, and anything can happen. This – is *American Idol*."

His pacing and inflection will be perfect.

I will get gooseflesh sitting here listening to him, and I'll wonder for a moment if I'm getting sick.

Tomorrow morning, at the radio station, I will do something I have never done before as a professional: I'll ask Seacrest to sign a photo for my six-year-old son.

YOU ARE MY IDOL, Seacrest will inscribe it.

Next week, back in New Jersey, we'll sit on the living-room sofa to watch the show, and my boy will see Ryan Seacrest and say, "I bet he's thinking of me."

Get thee behind me, Seacrest.

"Maybe so," I'll tell my son, and silently pray for his mortal soul.

Chapter Five

Ewan McGregor

Twit

I've got a bad feeling about this.

For weeks I have girded myself, but the Jedi refuses to show. First he's spotted by a spice miner in L. A., filming Michael Bay's latest extravaganza, *The Island*; then the Bay shoot wraps and poof! Ewan McGregor's gone. I miss him completely. Well, not completely. I see the son of a bitch on Leno, pitching *Robots* on his way to Tatooine or wherever the fuck.

Enough is enough: I ring Yoda. I don't like calling Yoda – last time we spoke, goddamn Yoda told me to buy Cisco at 132, right before it split and plummeted into the Death Star – but I don't have much choice. The kid could be anywhere on the planet – McGregor makes movies in such profusion that his buddy Jude Law seems idle by comparison – and my time is short.

"A terrible connection," Yoda says, "this is."

Where are you, Master?

"Laurel Canyon Boulevard. To the Valley I am headed. A man about a horse to see."

Fine, fine. Where's Ewan?

"Ewan?"

Obi-Wan. Where the hell is Obi-Wan? I need to find him quick.

"To London you must go. What up?"

He's on the June cover.

"Which movie? A ton of dreck that Jedi does."

Your movie. This Sith thing.

"*Vey iz mir.* A screening did you get?"

You're breaking up, Master Yoda. You I'm losing.

I haven't seen it, and I don't want to get into the whole *Star Wars* thing with him. Yoda's bitter, and I can't say that I blame him; you try sitting around with your long green thumb curled up your crinkled, three-cheeked ass for almost twenty years while George Lucas fingers his pupik and tries to figure out what to do with the franchise.

"Clear your mind must be," croaks Yoda before the "end" button I hit. "The press thing Obi-Wan does not enjoy."

Obi digs the Starbucks. I bring two

grande lattes to the photo shoot, one for Ewan, one for his publicist. If you want to sit at the feet of a Jedi, come in humble. And don't show up empty-handed. Make an offering.

He smiles, open-faced, a boyish grin. His hair is tipped with blond, a leftover from the Bay shoot. He fairly exudes the Force, a visual musk. It's in his bright blue eyes and small square teeth – not bad for a British subject – and the way the cleft in his chin, his filtrum, and the worry crease between his eyebrows form a strong center line, a heroic vertical. Yet he's no pretty boy; see the off-center mole on his forehead, the wee burnt-umber De Niro mark high upon his right cheek? A spot of malevolence, a bit of mischief. A worthy foe, aye.

Plus, God didn't stop there – oh, no. The wardrobe folks have poured him into jeans so tight that Ewan's fleshly light saber bulges forth like a Reek's horn.

"I feel like I've been staring at his crotch for weeks," I tell his publicist.

"You cahn't really avoid it," she chuckles, both thumbs massaging her BlackBerry.

Indeed, a serious perusal of Ewan's oeuvre will bring the viewer eye to eye with the McGregor man-root, an uncut link of Scottish sausage that even in a state of flaccidity would make a Wookie yelp. It first shows up – barely a cameo, really – in *Trainspotting*; in *The Pillow Book*, it truly merits costar billing; by 2003's *Young Adam* – as close as noir may ever come to outright porn – McGregor's anaconda boasts its own dialogue coach and gaffer.

Which ain't to say the kid can't out-act his wang. Even as a twenty-year-old villager from Crieff, Scotland, plucked out of drama school in 1992 to play one of the leads in a six-part BBC series, *Lipstick on Your Collar* – written by the genius of the Dark Side, Dennis Potter – Ewan was a pip, with enormous range and kineticism onscreen. His performance as Renton, the lead junkie in *Trainspotting*, made him an international star at the age of twenty-five. In 2001, he starred in *Moulin Rouge* AND *Black Hawk Down*; in '03, in addition to the soulless lout in *Young Adam*, he was the Dixiefied youth in *Big Fish* and the early-1960s Manhattan playboy who woos and wins Renée Zellweger in a frothy botch called *Down with Love*.

But McGregor's career arc – he's thirty-four now, with more than thirty movies already in the can – seems odd, at least for an actor who once said, "To do a crappy event movie for a lot of money, like *Independence Day*, I would never taint my soul with that crap."

Ah, well. Like Yoda always says, impossible to see, the future is – and that's no crap. You go from slagging Hollywood to donning the pigtail, poncho, and knee boots as Obi-Wan for three dorkfests to becoming one of Michael Bay's hand puppets to being mentioned as the next James Bond, and before you know it, you're just another $10-million-per-picture hack with a bagpipe burr and a bad haircut.

I ask Ewan's publicist if he ever turns a job down.

"Oh, loads," she says. "He turns down loads."

What he turns down this morning is getting photographed in a T-shirt *Esquire* had printed up with

I DID THREE STAR WARS MOVIES
AND ALL I GOT
WAS THIS FUCKING T-SHIRT

across the chest. He won't even try it on.

"But it's not true," he protests.

Ach. Much to learn you still have, my young apprentice.

He wouldn't wear the T-shirt.

"Pity. Where will you battle do?"

He wants to meet at the London Zoo.

Silence.

Yo, Yoda, you there?

"Pain, suffering, death I feel."

Me, too. I think I've got the flu. And a wink I haven't slept.

"Go I will let you. On the other line Carrie Fisher I have."

But Master, how shall I defeat him? He is younger, quicker, and more stalwart than I, not to mention better hung. Master? Master!

Late on a warm weekday afternoon, the zoo, which first opened back in 1828 and looks like it hasn't had a paint job since, is nearly empty of Homo sapiens, except for a few small knots of uniformed schoolchildren on a class trip. I arrive early, armed with my tuna sandwich and tape recorder, but I have blundered stupidly: new

Cutting Room Floor: McGregor

THE PITCH: Amazing how quick a "serious" young British thespian's disdain for Hollywood can vanish when he gets his hands on a light saber.

SCENE: London, March 16, 2005 – my eighth wedding anniversary, by the way – in a basement photo studio. Skinny Brits everywhere – all of them, except for Ewan McGregor, chain-smoking – plus Ewan's busty publicist, which I note solely because her tits are spilling from her blouse. Plus me – and if the writer is at the photo shoot, where nothing of any interest ever occurs, something has gone very wrong.

BACKSTORY: What's wrong? Well, after agreeing to be *Esquire's* June cover boy, Ewan hasn't managed to find any time to be photographed or interviewed; given the lead time a monthly magazine needs, we're already past deadline. And all I have, besides a disgruntled wife (this is twice in three years that I've been on the road working on our anniversary) and a nasty flu, is the vague promise of an hour or so with Ewan later today, a promise I can't afford to trust under the circumstances. So – on the off-chance that Ewan comes to blows with the photographer, or finally declares his manlove for Jude Law – here I be.

CONFLICT: I get my hour or so – ninety minutes at the zoo. Ninety pants of heavy corduroy and no belt; the belt back at the hotel is, and down my pants are falling. I am fat, jet-lagged, sweating with fear and fever – in short, doomed.

McGregor materializes out of nowhere. One moment the walk is empty, then suddenly he's in front of me looking like the most ordinary bloke in the world. But his powers are apparent despite his tatty brown cardigan and work pants: Clouds race across the sun, the wind rises, carrying a hint of rain, and high above us, birds wheel – dipping, crying, generally acting like clumsy metaphors of the phylum Fallacious Patheticus.

"What's the best thing to do?" the Jedi asks. "Walk and talk? Do you want to sit down or just wander around?"

minutes of the dullest conversation ever put on audiotape. Ewan sounds earnest but glum; I sound as if I'm on another planet. No interesting scene, no snappy dialogue, no chemistry, and no do-overs. Just a big hole in the middle of the magazine to fill, and no time to fill it.

WISH I'D WRITTEN: *Portnoy's Complaint. Ulysses.* Hell, *Tuesdays with Morrie.* But like Don Rumsfeld said: You go to war with the army you have.

I had next to nothing. I had an anecdote about the late Dennis Potter – author of, among many other scabrous, brilliant things, *The Singing Detective* – sitting with a 21- year-old Ewan and warning him about choosing his next film too quick, but nowhere to put it without braking the story to a stop. I had plenty of Ewan bitching about the paparazzi shooting him with his young daughters, and a lot more about his zest for motorcycling. And I had this exchange: "I have a very romantic idea about being a Cambridge student, reading literature, where for a couple of years it's your job in life to read amazing books and discuss them and write about them."

Seriously?

"I fantasize about having the room and the maid and everything, y'know? Not really about the maid. Well, a little bit."

I'd rather sit.

"You would? All right. That's a good way to start. We can look at some animals as well, which is nice. Do you like animals?"

Yeah. Outside of humans.

"They're the next best thing really, aren't they?"

Disarming bastard, he is. Buys us coffees at the zoo cafe' and we grab a bench in a greensward nearby. Time was, McGregor drank his way through interviews – and much else – and coffee was never his beverage of choice. That's over, not that he wants a big deal made of it.

"You tell someone you've been quietin' down, and the next thing you know, you were a raging alcoholic who needed to change his life or was gonna die. I drank a lot when I was younger, and I got to a point where I didn't want to anymore and felt like it was out of place in my life, and I stopped. It's a hard thing to do, but it's really as simple as that. I was trying to be a great dad, a great husband, a great actor, and a great drinker. I had to lose one of 'em, and the only one I was prepared to lose was the fourth."

McGregor gave up smoking, too ("I don't
think about drinking," he says, "but I still miss cigarettes"), but has found the compulsion to chain-act – he has been known to wrap one of his films on a Friday, attend the premiere of another on Saturday, spend Sunday catching up with his wife and two young daughters, then start a new shoot Monday morning – a harder habit to quit.

"I recently had some quite heated arguments in the States, specifically about my friend Jude Law, who people were railing about having done so many movies, how ridiculous it was. I went, 'Can you tell me why it is ridiculous for an actor who's working to work a lot? Why is it?' The idea that Jude had done too many, or that I had – I was told years and years ago that I had made too many films that year – I think that's ridiculous.

"There was all kinds of shit coming out of people's mouths, mainly agents and lawyers, people who weren't actors. I love working, and if you're lucky enough to be in a position to make six movies, why not? It's such a blast, why wouldn't you want to?"

Um, to avoid being mocked by Chris Rock at the Oscars?

"Yeh," he says. "I was really uncomfortable with that. I thought it was really upsetting. I could only imagine what it would've made me feel like if he was using my name. It was probably devastating for Jude. It also didn't make sense to me, because he's a good actor, Jude. The actors that

[Rock] chose to herald as true movie stars, in my view, weren't the greatest actors that have ever walked the planet, y'know?"

I don't think the joke was about acting ability so much as pure star power. . . .

"Yeh, yeh."

He hugs himself inside his cardigan. The temperature is dropping, rain is coming, and Ewan looks downright forlorn. Jedi, shmedi: It's easy to forget how sensitive, how needy, how hungry for approval and afraid of being humiliated actors can be. I'd better change the subject.

I don't suppose now would be the right moment to ask you about your penis.

"Uh-uh. No, 'cuz I won't tell you. I'll just show you it."

I've seen it. And I must say, it's an impressive penis.

"I like my penis. There's no question about that. Yeh."

I've never said that to any other actor.

"Oh, really? 'Nice cock, by the way,' Thanks."

I think I'm gonna call it your "man-root."

He laughs. "Sounds like something you put in an herbal tea."

Harvey Keitel's the only other nonporn actor I can think of whose pecker has had much screen time, and it's really no contest.

"I was quoted a long time ago as saying I was doing it for the sisters; I felt like I was doing it as kind of a feminist act, to be showing my penis onscreen. Because it was just turning the tables round. I've been in films where my penis has been onscreen and there weren't any tits or anything onscreen, which is the opposite of the way it's normally done."

Would you still do it?

"Yeh, yeh. One of the things about doing the Bay film, in a way, is that for many years I've had no self-imposed barriers, no limits, no boundaries. Maybe you have to be naked because it's right for the film. If movies are representative of life, then a huge part of life is nudity and sex. I'm naked half the time, so why wouldn't I be naked in a movie? Why shouldn't a character in a movie be?

"So there's no boundaries, right? The Michael Bay summer blockbuster – why would I say I won't do a film like that? If you like it when you read it, fuckin' do it. The boundaries – they're just not there, so you allow yourself to do anything you want, from *Young Adam* to *The Island*. Fuckin' bring it on.

"My attitudes have changed since I was young. It would be very bizarre if they hadn't, y'know. I've recognized over the years that it isn't any different anywhere else. Hollywood doesn't own the monopoly on being horrendous in a business sense to actors and to talent. It is the same everywhere. I thought the British film industry was godlike and the American industry was horrendous; I've realized that they're both the same. Ours is fueled with less cash, but the same despicable behavior goes on in both."

Does that mean you're ready to become the next James Bond?

"I don't know. They haven't approached me. I don't think they've approached anyone. The easy part is wanting to be James Bond. Fuckin' everyone wants to be James Bond. I would love it, but the worrying part of it is that they're really long shoots, and then you have to do a very great deal of publicity for them. I don't think I could do it. And I like to make a *lot* of movies – and if you were shooting for six months and then you had three months' publicity tour, you're not able to do an awful lot of other stuff."

So who's got the bigger light saber, you or Liam Neeson?

"You'll never get that out of me."

It turns out that we have met at the London

Zoo so that Ewan can pay a call on an old drama-school friend.

"In my first year, we had to choose an animal and study it for an hour every weekend. We would have movement classes where we would become this animal. I was a slow loris."

What?

"Well, I'll show ya. It's over in the nocturnal-mammal area. It's a nighttime animal that moves in almost slow motion. It's got huge eyes. And it's just a beautiful thing."

I find that if I summon all my power, I can keep my pants up using only my mind – not unlike Yoda in the climactic battle with Count Dooku in *Attack of the Clones* – as we walk to the dowdy building called Moonlight World. Here the zoo has managed to re-create the loris's native habitat, the dense rain forests of Sumatra, Java, and Borneo. It is dark. It is steamy. It is the dankest basement I have ever not seen.

"This is the adjustment room," Ewan whispers from the gloaming. "It's where one's eyes adjust."

Sweat pours down my brow, my neck, my asscrack.

"There's one."

Peering into a glass enclosure, I can barely make out a plump, huge-eyed primate not even a foot in length – a creature more Spielberg than Lucas, with monkey's paws and a scrunched face like a bear's – stock-still along a narrow tree limb, doing nothing.

"This is a pygmy slow loris. Mine was just your straightforward slow loris."

My lips tingle with fever; I feel close to fainting. We shuffle along from case to case, straining to read the signs.

"It may be over here, I think. *Ahhh*, this looks to me like – this is a slow loris. This is them."

I see nothing but leaves.

"They're so fuckin' slow, though, there's no movement to draw the eye, so I cahn't – they're like in another digh-mension. There he is up there climbing."

Yes. And I see another coming. I think.

My voice is a hoarse echo. Goddamn Yoda was right: I'm gonna die.

"*Mmmm*. What's kind of interesting about them, as I recall, is that they seem to be constantly in motion. Of course, as soon as I say that, he stops. They've both stopped now that I've said that, so that's bullshit. This is slightly another plane of time, don't ya think?"

Someone, or something, grunts. Could be me.

"I wonder how long they live. It might be that one of these slow lorises is the slow loris that I chose."

McGregor stares at the nearest slow loris. The slow loris stares back at McGregor. I stare at the red light on my tape recorder and silently vow never to write another celebrity profile if only Yahweh – the hell with Yoda – will deign to get me out of here alive.

"Look how this one lies – really flat in front there. Aye, he's brilliant, idn't he? All right, mate. All right."

He says he really dug *Young Adam*. He's very proud of you.

McGregor laughs. "You've come a long way since I saw you last," he says in what I presume to be a slow-loris impression. His voice is up an octave, quavering.

"Good, aren't they?"

Grunt.

"Shall we go?"

Yes. By all means.

I don't recall him putting me in a taxi, although I know that he did because my tape recorder is still running when I get

back to the hotel.

Upstairs, I rewind the tape.

"They're nice, the lorises, aren't they?"

Yes.

"I'm glad you liked them."

Yes.

"And a little London mist to cap it off."

Yes.

A car door opens. I speak the name of my hotel in a voice that sounds like a man at the bottom of a deep well. The door slams.

"Take care. Nice seeing you."

Yes. Thank you.

I sit staring at the tape circling the spools for a while, then turn it off.

The phone next to the bed rings. Yoda. With a load on.

"A prayer," he says, "you never had. Jewboy."

Hey, a word of advice from you couldn't have hurt. Anything. A little tip.

"Your little tip right here I've got: With a Jedi never fuck."

Yoda thinks he knows it all, but he doesn't. Sure, I took a Jedi's whipping today, but I also heard a Jedi's vow, and goddamn Yoda ain't gonna like it when he finds out what it was.

I search the tape to find the exchange, back when Obi-Wan and I are still on the bench, drinking coffee.

I have a hard time with these *Star Wars* movies.

"Yeh, yeh. That's fine. You're perfectly, completely at liberty to have a hard time with those movies. You're not alone."

Okay. But I want you to stop making them.

"Yeh. Well, I'll tell you what: I will now. I promise never to make another one."

He was laughing, but I could tell he meant it.

Chapter Six

Nicolas Cage

Wack

EXT. STREET: DAY

These modest ranches side by side by side – white clapboard, pastel stucco – their eave-shadowed door fronts bearded with the shrubbery of perpetual spring; these short-trimmed rectangles of lawn, edged down their tidy, wide driveways to the abrupt, empty sidewalk; these treetop aeries where the chirping power lines and buzzing birds meld with the insects' thrum into the eternal song suburban: this perfect block – anywhere, to look at it, but exactly *here* – tucked away in sunny desolation, walled in by normalcy.

Here, *exactly.* Each home has its number, each family its name, each square of turf its history behind the whitewashed door: tides of war and conquest; crusades for honor, freedom, love and gold. But this is not our script today. Today, Nic Cage comes home – a morning jaunt, wistful yet lighthearted – exactly here, to Hackett Avenue in Long Beach, California.

Then Cage sees the house where he grew up, and his nostalgia curdles into skittish silence. He paces the empty street beside his shriek-yellow Ferrari, fretting, his hands jammed into his pockets, his narrow face pointed eyeless at the ground. The onscreen Everyman of a culture constantly attuned to the whispering in its head, Jimmy Stewart yanked inside out, every nerve end aflame in the raw air. Where else could he have come from but this perfect block?

"What are the rules," he asks, "of, like, knocking on people's doors and saying hi, but having a reporter from *Esquire* magazine with you?"

Rules? We don't need no steenking rules. They'll be thrilled.

"I don't even know if anybody's still here, I just thought it'd be an, an experience. But what a surprise attack, though – I mean, I haven't been here in, like, twenty years."

Nic, Nic – folks do this all the time. This is supposed to be fun.

"What do we do?"

Uh, walk up and knock on the door? This, after all, is only life: no script, no storyboards, no soundtrack, no severed ear decaying in the grass, no extraterrestrial stashed in the closet. It'll be nice.

He stands, hands on hips, puzzled. "It doesn't look the same at all. There used to be this beautiful jacaranda tree right in the front – it had periwinkle blossoms. They chopped it down. Yeahhh. It's a little, a little, a little – it's unsettling. I gotta tell ya. Why would they chop it down?"

Maybe it fell down. Was the house always pink?

"No. I think it was green. I'm not sure. I don't know. We can't just go in."

He seems genuinely nervous, ready to bolt. At the door, he knocks twice, quickly. Off-camera, to our left, a woman from the next house down opens her door and comes toward us, yowling her delight. She stops in her tracks a few feet away, staring.

"I'm Maggie," she calls out. "You're a big movie star."

"I guess, yeah. That's me. I grew up here."

"The neighbors told us about you coming by and dropping in."

Cage looks dumbfounded. "I never did that before," he says.

"You haven't? They said you did. They said you came by one time."

"How long ago?"

Maggie shrugs. From a nearby backyard, a dog begins barking; another, a few houses away, answers.

"I came by here once," Cage murmurs. "I came by here with my brothers once, a long time ago."

"She may not answer," Maggie says. "She may not come, with you being a man."

"Oh?" says Cage, his voice lilting in dude-ish befuddlement. "I'm sorry?"

"She may not come, with you being a man. Two men."

"Oh. Oh. *Oh,* I see what you're sayin'."

Maggie cups her hands around her mouth and yells at the door where we're waiting. *"Ellen! Ellllllennnn!"* she shrills, then steps right past us to her neighbor's door and begins to rap her knuckles excitedly on its tiny square of glass.

"That's okay," Cage says, edging away slowly. "That's fine – we'll let her be. I might go walk around the boulevard."

"I'm telling you," Maggie says, reluctant to let him vanish into the ether, "one of the neighbors told us that you came by here one night."

"Okay, well, that must be who it was."

"My brother came by. Maybe she's thinking of my brother."

Suddenly, Maggie is jumping up and down. "She's coming to the door!" she shouts "She's coming to the door!"

Yes, Ellen, fortyish, pulls open the door. her hair is undone. She's wearing a flowered blue housedress, what my mother used to call a duster. Though she smiles brightly to see the winner of the 1995 Academy Award for Best Actor on her stoop, she looks as if she has been asleep until a minute ago.

"Hi," says Nicolas Cage shyly. "Hi, I used to live here."

"I know," Ellen says dreamily. "One day I guess a few years ago, you were pounding on the door, and I got--"

"I don't think it was me," Cage says before she can finish the sentence. "Ahhh, d'you remember meeting me before?"

"Noooo," says Ellen. Was it a dream? Is this? How do you mistake another man, even his brother, for Nicolas Cage?

"But it's nice to meet you now," he says, waving one ivory hand. "I'm Nicolas. Hi."

Ellen laughs, sagging a bit, her leggs rubbery. Speechless.

"Well, I just wanted to say hi," says Nicolas, eyelids aflutter. "I, uh, wanted to come back. I love it here. There used to be a big tree, a big jacaranda tree, in the front of the house, that had periwinkle blossoms on it. Do you remember that?"

He ducks his head, pauses a beat, and, raising it again, strains to compose his doe-eyed face into something like a relaxed and winning grin. It winds up as a small boy's smile, touched with rue, adorable and yet uneasy with itself. This isn't acting – this is life; but then, too, I am here watching him, listening to him stammer as he culls the surge and tingle of apparently unbidden emotion for the world he needs, noting the fey black-and-white shoes worn with his old blue jeans and navy T-shirt, seeing all of it – even the veins cording his sleek neck, his ropy forearms and well-tuned biceps – as theater, as character, as Method, fallen blossoms of the missing tree, proof of what once happened on this spot to young Nicky Coppola.

Cut to Ellen, shaking her head. "It wasn't here. Our neighbors had

Cutting Room Floor: Cage

THE PITCH: America's oddest leading man leaps from *Leaving Las Vegas* to – POW! – *The Rock*, BAM! – *Con Air*, and BOOM! – *Face/Off*, thus becoming America's oddest action hero.

SCENE: The interior of Cage's screaming-yellow 1967 Ferrari 275 GTB-4, a low-slung two-seat speed machine perfectly built for a lean, limber actor, not for a fat scribe from Cleveland. My knees are level with – also not so far from – my eyes, my right shoulder is pressed to the door so Cage can shift gears, and my tape recorder is gripped in my left hand as near to Cage's head as I can hold it – because his voice is so soft, I'm afraid it won't be audible over the angry hornet's buzz of the engine.

BACKSTORY: We got off to a lousy start when I drew a rough parallel – I was only trying to be clever – between porn and action films and Cage took umbrage. Things got worse when he recalled that I'd dissed him in a *GQ* Sean Penn profile the year before – "where you said that Tom Cruise and myself had become more like vehicles (than actors)." But it really got weird when Abel Ferrara's name came up.

Ferrara's a renegade New York City film director – *Bad Lieutenant* is his nasty masterpiece – who wanted Cage to star in *The Funeral*, which Abel was preparing to direct back in 1995, just as I was profiling him. My story ended just as Cage backed out of doing *The Funeral*, and one of the last lines in the story quoted Ferrara thus: "If (Cage) was here right now, there's about nine people that would put a bullet in his fuckin' head."

one, and I used to love it. I remember they cut theirs down."

"Yeah... yeah," Cage says. "Well, listen, I don't wanna take any more of your time."

"Oh, God," says Ellen.

"That's all right," Cage says. "No, no, please. Thank you for..."

"Want to come sign a wall?"

"If you, if you, if you want me to, I will. Yes."

"We never had a deal, you know," Cage tells me now. "There was no deal. No deal was broken."

He sounds far more worried than angry.

"I heard he was tryin' to put a hit on me," Cage says.

Seriously?

"That's what I heard."

CONFLICT: It was a bad blind date, and while I knew I wouldn't get a good-night kiss, I thought maybe I could lighten things up when we got back to Cage's production office by offering to arm-wrestle – something I've done with a number of subjects just to change the mood.

Cage was unamused. "No, I'm not gonna arm-wrestle with you," he said, "because arm-wrestling really isn't about strength – it's about leverage and mass. That's an honor I'm not gonna let you have."

WISH I'D WRITTEN: His father was a literature prof, but I was still surprised to find myself talking about Kafka with Nicolas Cage. He talked about *The Metamorphosis*, about how Gregor Samsa, man-turned-cockroach, would scuttle out of his room to listen to the violin music in his family's parlor.

"That story made me literally cry," Cage said.

"Yes," Ellen says, right on cue. "Yesyesyesyes."

INT. CAR: EARLIER THAT DAY

We've had a long and tortured trip from Hollywood, thirty miles north. Cage wouldn't, couldn't, make it any other way. "I took the Ferrari," he's warned at his production office on Sunset Boulevard. "But on the way down, I noticed smoke." Shrug. "So I guess it'll be even more of an *adventure.*"

The smoke turns out to be nothing more than the oily residue of two months sitting idle while Cage was on location; the adventure proper consists of finding Hackett Avenue in Long Beach. No sooner have I squeezed into the '67 Ferrari than Cage says, "I brought us a Thomas Guide," and thrusts into my hands a binder of maps as thick as the Pentateuch.

No actor of our time can match the range or sound the depths of Everyman's psychoses like Nicolas Cage – from the infant-snatching sad sack of *Raising Arizona* and the deranged, roach-scarfing yuppie of *Vampire's Kiss* to the homicidal asthmatic of *Kiss of Death* and the suicidal sot of *Leaving Las Vegas* – but still this is a puzzlement: a thirty-four-year-old man of normal wit who has lived in southern California and nowhere else and who cannot find his way to the house where he spent the first twelve years of his life.

Driving, he talks. I turn the tape recorder on and putter with the maps. Long Beach. No problem – we take the 405 south. But Nic Cage, like all So-Cal natives, suffers the dread of exiting the freeway. "So, so when do I have to – when do I have to get off the road?" he asks, a catch in his voice.

I thumb through the guide, deep into its Deuteronomy. Culver City begets Hawthorne. Hawthorne begets Gardena. Gardena begets Torrance. Torrance begets Carson. The four-hundred-horsepower Ferrari – a twelve-cylinder, two-seat hardtop – is snarling like a bottled hornet, and Nicolas Cage's voice drifts over the noise of the engine as if out of a dream.

"I remember when I was a kid," he muses. "We used to have to drive through this factory. We're gonna pass a factory, and we're gonna smell it." I look up to see him smiling, warm and absent, at the windshield.

This is special. This is a marvelous example of what the great acting teacher Stanislavsky, in his seminal *An Actor Prepares*, terms an emotion memory. Unfortunately, I can do nothing with it, routewise.

Is Hackett Avenue an exit?

"It's not an exit, no. Palo Verde is an exit, maybe – I don't know. Palo Verde or Atherton. We gotta figure out how to get to that."

Palo Verde is indeed an exit, a major artery. Hackett Avenue runs parallel to it.

Is it close to Cal State Long Beach?

"Very close. That's where my dad taught."

August Coppola was a professor of literature when the family lived on Hackett. Cage's mother, Joy Vogelsang, was a dancer of some renown. Of their three sons, Nic was the youngest by two years. It was not the happiest home, nor is it a subject Nicolas Cage talks about anymore.

"I feel my family has in some ways been the victim of my publicity," he says, closing the discussion as soon as it begins. What he's said about it in the past makes it clear that behind the Coppola door on Hackett Avenue – as behind many another carefully closed door, anywhere – everyone was, in some sense, a victim. Nic's mother, harrowed by severe clinical depressions, was hospitalized for long periods, beginning when Nic was six years old. While the boy sought refuge inside the family TV – "I was trying to figure out how to get inside," he says, "literally, physically"– August and Joy struggled to keep the marriage going for six more years. After the divorce, August took custody, feeding his youngest son a steady mix of culture – cinema, fine arts, Great Books – and moving to the edge of Beverly Hills so that Nic could attend a better high school.

He dropped out in his senior year to study acting. "I broke my father's heart," he says, wincing even now. "He wanted me to become a writer, because to him writing was – and I agree with him – the root of all creativity."

Absolutely. Still, the fact that August had ferried Nic to San Francisco to spend summers with his cousins there – oh, yes and with *Godfather* and *Apocalypse Now* director Uncle Francis Ford Coppola, August's Oscar-winning brother – surely must have cushioned the shock, if not the heartbreak, of Nic's decision.

He changed his name in 1983, weary of being asked about Francis at every audition and of the assumption that his last name would light his path. As Nicolas Cage, he scored big with the critics the next year as a wounded vet in *Birdy* and made his starry bones playing a lunatic baker with a wooden hand and a love-roiled heart opposite Cher in 1987's *Moonstruck*. He was all of twenty-three years old then. Take away the money, the awards, the fame and what's left of Nic Cage is an artist whose reach and power transcend genre and script, a risk taker whose bravura and control are perpetually warring, an ad-lib mannerist who has learned to play it straight. "There's a very fine line," he says now, "between the Method actor and the schizophrenic."

I ask him why he chose acting. "Acting for me is this incredibly sacred hero that came in and saved my life," he says. "To me, it's been like a therapy – it's what's kept me balanced, kept me with a sense of purpose. I could get all the stuff out of me that I had, all that fire – anger, or love or lust. Anything." He pauses, then goes on. "All actors are wounded birds – we couldn't really be doing anything else. I've done scenes with five extremely talented actors all in the same room – one guy's barking, another's shouting profanity, the other's in a trance, one's asking to be hit. It looks like we're all in a nuthouse. We take our afflictions and we transform them into a place where they can be, be glorified. When the fact of the matter is, historically, we're all street urchins. Gypsies. We came out of the gutter. We've become so glorified in the movie-star system that it's become this artificial royalty, which if you look at the roots of it, is completely preposterous. The truth is that we're circus clowns."

Cage has made movies half his life now – more than thirty films in seventeen years – working steadily, at times constantly, with directors as wildly disparate as David Lynch and Norman Jewison and even Uncle Francis; Cage can currently be seen in Brian De Palma's *Snake Eyes*. Word is that Woody Allen wants Cage for a lead in his next film--"I can't really talk about that," he says – and he's working for the first time with Martin Scorcese on a project called *Bringing Out the Dead.*

Cage onscreen remains a treat – quirky, soulful, alive – even when the movie stinks, which most of his don't, although since, oh, 1993, say, with *Amos & Andrew*, through 1994's *It Could Happen to You, Guarding Tess*, and *Trapped in Paradise* and his post-Oscar triptych of action-thriller slag – *The Rock, Face/Off, Con Air* – they've been largely box-office gold and cinematic dreck.

Those last three films in particular strike me as a waste of Cage's time and talent. Watching them on video as preparation for our time together, I was stunned by how closely even the best of the action genre hews to the rigid structure of hardcore pornography (not that I've seen any, but I've read about it), from the redundant fantasies of ludicrous plot and the plodding, inane explication of the dialogue to the wallpaper of lousy music and the too-brief intervals between the choreographed spurting of blood and cum.

Nic Cage ain't buying it. "You can parallel anything to anything if you want to, but I'm not goin' there. I don't think it's crap to go to a movie and get your mind off of your problems. If you just wanna get stupid, that's not crap. Why not see if it's possible to give all the explosions and whatever it is that stimulates people and gets their minds off their problems – which I think is cogent and nothing to be ashamed of. We're in an entertainment industry. It's not just putting on the beret and smoking a Gitane and saying, 'I'm only going to do foreign films because I'm erudite and I'm so cool.' I don't buy that. I think it's a matter of doing every kind of movie you can possibly do."

He's got the Ferrari wound to

about eighty-five miles per hour, passing a line of semis on the right. The heat in the passenger compartment is basting my legs. On the map, Hackett Avenue looks like a series of short dead-end blocks.

"I can go from one universe and bounce to the other. I can make – I *will* make – another small, independent movie; I'll make another dark film. That's why I have a production company – so I can continue to make smaller, edgy films.

Edgy? I'm not sure I've heard him correctly over the engine. Itchy, maybe?

"Edgy."

We like edgy.

"We were thinking of calling it Edgy Films."

I want edgy.

"You'll get a lot of edgy. A lot of edgy's coming out of me, man."

I feel a sense of edginess filling our space right now.

"It's what we call edge. You've heard of wall-to-wall carpet? This is wall-to-wall edge."

You cut yourself just breathing the air.

"It's that edgy," agrees Nic Cage.

It's also time to leave the bosom of the 405. I go back to the maps while the tumblers inside Cage's head conitnue to spin.

"You think Buddy Hackett lives on Hackett? I mean, George Lucas lives in Lucas Valley – why doesn't Buddy Hackett live on Hackett? We gotta find this place, we really do.... This, this return, the homecoming, as it were...that was the other high school – I didn't go there." I look up and see the school flash by. They're putting on a performance of *A Streetcar Named Desire.* "That'd be fun to do, to go to a high school play. That'd be amazing. What time are they putting that on? I would love to do that. I mean, hell... But we gotta figure this out.... There's Atherton. A right on Atherton?"

Yep.

"This is looking good. I'm feeling a sense of something here. I could be wrong."

We're roaring up and down empty, sunlit streets, all of which are utterly identical.

"We're gonna make the move now. A right? Here we go – we're goin' in. It's changed a lot, I have to tell ya...I'm not recognizing much. This is twenty years ago...."

After a few minutes, I realize that we should've gone left on Atherton. Cage nods and turns us around. He hits the brakes when we finally reach Hackett. "That's it. That's it. Oh, man. How; how; how cool."

Until he notices the missing jacaranda and walks through his old front door.

INT. LIVING ROOM : LATE MORNING

Whatever comes to him once he's inside the house has blunted Cage's edge and rendered him mute and wary.

"You can tell I don't have a housekeeper," Ellen says, laughing.

"This fireplace," he says, entranced. "Yes, and that's where the TV was, up against the wall, and I used to sit on this round, red carpet and try to get inside. Right there."

It is a small brick fireplace, open on three sides, in a small, low-ceilinged living room. The television stares back from the far wall, close to a sliding door that opens to a patch of green outside.

"You mind if I look at your backyard? Is it okay? I am sorry to just drop in on you. I am sorry."

Too sorry: How strange is it, really, for someone to cruise by the old house and decide to ring the bell? Ellen is rapt, beside herself with glee: It's Nicolas Cage, in her living room. But Cage himself seems to resonate with the guilty child's inchoate fear that anything he may say or do – has said, has done – may not only be wrong but shatter a family's peace.

Out in the sun, he smiles to himself: "I loved this backyard. This backyard is so great for kids."

Back inside the house, he wants to go. "Which wall would you like me to sign?" he asks. Ellen points high on the kitchen wall to a small over-hang where the living room begins. "I hate to mar your house up," Nic Cage says. "Is there a paper or something I can sign? You seriously want me to write up there?"

"I seriously want you to, yes." She pulls out a dinette chair for him to stand on. "I seriously want you to."

"All right," says Cage, stepping up.

At Ellen's prompting, he writes, "To Eric, Shannan, Steve, and Ellen – I love this house," and signs his name.

"So you have good memories here?" asks Ellen.

"Yeah. Well, I have memories, yeah." His voice trails off. "Well," he says, "that was very kind of you, to let us come by. All right. God bless you."

He edges out the door. he wants to walk. We walk up the block and around to an alley that runs behind the house.

He seems pensive, distant. I ask if he's all right.

"Yeah," he says. "It's kinda sad. It's hard. It's draining. I mean, just, you know, you know, there's an overwhelming kind of combination of things I'm feeling right now. Sort of a melancholia and sort of a release, a freedom. It looks better than I thought it was gonna look. I'm not talking about the house – the whole area, the whole neighborhood, everything. It looks charming. All this stuff that I've tried to do, this drive, the desire to make it – when I see what my life could have been, the simplicity of it, the charm of just not trying so hard. And I wonder – if I'd just stayed here, somehow."

This is the danger of wading too deep into nostalgia, into that ocean of a child's feeling memory: to be swept under and out of sight by the tow of illusion, of what-might-have-been. The happy family intact, the tidy life becalmed by sanity. But real life, terra firma, is a struggle. Divorce, depar-ture, insanity, the ferocity of drive, the burning desire to get out, move on: That, sometimes, is life. And sometimes art.

What drives Cage now? What can he be afraid of anymore?

"I fear in some way losing balance. I know that my ideas and feelings are applicable to the nature of the work I do. I'd rather that they go some-where productive than explode on myself; in other words, it seems that I'm avoiding some kind of insanity. That's why I work so hard."

We're coming back around the block now, back to where the Ferrari is parked. Word of his return has gotten out, and suddenly Cage is surrounded by old neighbors whose children he grew up with. They shake his hand; they go to get their cameras.

"Yeah," says one, a skinny old man in a red-and-white gimme cap. "I was sittin' there, just startin' to mow the lawn, and I saw that Ferrari. Boy, that's a beautiful thing. And I thought: That's ol' Nic."

"Yeah," says Cage, standing in the street, palms out. "I came back, just sort-of-feeling nostalgic about where I grew up. It really looks good, you know. It's really peaceful here."

"You're doin' rather well," the old man says.

"Oh, I guess so."

"Gettin' along."

"Yeah," says Nicolas Cage, standing in the sunlight, the echo of mourning in his voice dredged up from the bottom of some far-off well. "Yeah, I am."

When Cage moves off to chat with a couple on the sidewalk, I sidle up to the old man. What does he remember of young Nic?

"Very little, to tell ya the truth. I was always workin'. If my wife was here, she'd talk your leg off. Several years ago, on the Fourth of July, he stopped by – him and his mom and his brother."

I turn and see Cage standing beside the Ferrari, his right arm looped around the shoulders of a woman, her left arm looped around his waist. Her husband is snapping a picture, preserving the hard evidence of his return.

Chapter Seven

Sheryl Crow

Pill

God, I feel like hell tonight
Tears of rage I cannot fight
I'd be the last to help you understand
Are you strong enough to be my man?

No. Sorry. You are not strong enough to be her man. Maybe once upon a time, after that summer when your voice and your balls dropped and anyone seemed possible, you thought so. Surely you hoped so – her soft blond-brown hair, her fine cheerleader legs, her wide, toothy smile, her cracked voice and sly cackle. So you took your very best shot, and one beery night when lightning sliced the sky, with a sweet, sad smile, she said maybe. But she never said yes.

Years later, you ran across her, a woman who was winsome and tough, even while heaving tequila in the parking lot at 3:00 A.M., but her answer then, too – to breakfast, to a next time, to maybe settling down and working it out together – was no. Thanks, but she'll just grab her things and hit the road. No hard feelings.

Oh, it's not that you're not strong. You're heap-big strong. You're just not strong enough to be Sheryl Crow's man, not nearly as strong as she is. She's that homegirl, that woman, almost forty years old now, more tough than winsome, more sad than sweet, as strong as steel. She sings the blues, scornful and scorned, steeped in the Stones, drenched in Dylan, butt deep in country mud. She lives the blues, touring hard and long, sweating out the songs, away from home so goddamn long, there ain't no home no more. And, sweet Jesus, she has the blues; eight Grammys and all the money in the world can't snatch 'em away.

But the fame and the cash wail a blues all their own, and Crow is stuck right there right now, solemn about the future of her "artistry," worried about the mainstream and the market, hoping to meet a man strong enough to save her from herself.

The first time we sit down – we meet in coffee shops; she doesn't want to visit the Vermeer exhibit at the Met, doesn't want to go bowling, doesn't want to go to the Central Park Zoo – something is amiss. Something in her eyes, her crooked smile, her ragged voice.

"I have to go running," she says, bolting the dregs of her coffee, rising from her chair. And she's gone. She was sitting there for four minutes, four minutes by the clock. Most of her songs run longer than four minutes.

She has to go running: It is her gratitude jog, the forty minutes each day when she counts her blessings, no matter how careworn and blue she feels. Even the stuff she truly isn't all that grateful for – singing backup in a slinky black sheath for Michael Jackson, say, or that mope in the front row one night, back when she was opening for Dylan, who kept shouting, "Show us your tits!"– is on her gratitude list, because it's important for Sheryl Crow, who has a tendency toward depression, to remember that she has had some incredible experiences.

Once upon a time, she was a cheerleader, yes, the daughter of a piano teacher and a lawyer who also played the trumpet. She was a good girl who graduated from the big state college and then became an elementary-school teacher in St. Louis who also played in a band. She got engaged to a nice Christian boy named Mike. "If you stand up in front of the Lord," Mike warned Sheryl, "and say you are going to be my wife, and then you sing in bands every weekend, we're not going to make it."

Crow didn't sing in the band that weekend. She went home to Kennett, Missouri, instead, kissed her family goodbye, and left for Los Angeles, the wilderness of glory. She wept during rush hour on the freeway, waited tables and sold some songs, sang backup, lugged her demo tapes from producer to producer. She chased the blues and she fought the blues. There were six-month depressions, stretches of time when she wouldn't leave her apartment, long bouts of drunkenness.

After four years, she made her first album, and it wasn't *Tuesday Night Music Club*; her first album was a glossy piece of shit that never was released. That's when she hooked up with the musicians who became the Tuesday Night Music Club. They were beautiful, talented, smirking losers, and that's exactly how they saw themselves. They were too gifted to succeed, too smart to sell out, night creatures loping through the basin of smog, and when the tapes they had made together of the songs they had written together became a Grammy-winning, $85 million smash in 1994, Sheryl Crow already had moved on down the lonesome trail, alone.

> *Nothing's true and nothing's right*
> *So let me be alone tonight*
> *You can't change the way I am*
> *Are you strong enough to be my man?*

Our next coffee shop is only a few blocks

from the first one. We were going to meet at the first one again, but at the last minute Sheryl decided this coffee shop would be better.

It must be the food that draws her here. She orders three eggs, scrambled, home fries, whole-wheat toast, a side order of beans, coffee. Her face is smiling, seamless, her eyes as clear and blue as a newborn's, but her grin is lopped, turned inward at the edges. Rain pounds the street outside; inside, over one tinny speaker, opera unspools.

She has seven songs left to record for the new album, she says, and three weeks to finish them. "Which seems like an impossibility," she adds, "but I'm gonna do it. This album is just kind of gravitating toward a sense of the last couple of years – this bizarre holding pattern. And it's kind of about that."

Crow has been working on the new album for nearly a year. The problem with getting her work done isn't so much that she is feeling gloomy – show me the talent who isn't fighting the undertow on any given day and I'll show you Zamfir, master of the pan flute – but that she has reached the point in her career where the trappings of success and the fear of failure are getting in the way of what she was born to do. And she knows it.

"I really had a hard time with being what I consider to be successful, because the capacity for failing is so much bigger the more successful you get. You get to a point as an artist where it can be to your detriment to have money and to be hanging out with a pretty heavy crowd of people who are famous and who talk about being famous. It has no bearing on

Cutting Room Floor: Crow

THE PITCH: How to make a best-selling album in only two or three years. Wait – make that four. Co-starring Kid Rock and Keith Richards.

SCENE: Downtown, New York City, April, 2001. The club's name is Shine. Sheryl Crow, currently stuck near the end of Year One of trying to self-produce *c'mon c'mon* – finishing the album will take yet another year – is playing a word-of- mouth show to a cavernous room packed with upscale white people. Six weeks – and counting – I've waited for Crow to sit and talk to me, so that I can write the story she and her management people said they were gung-ho to do, and all I have to show for it is an invite to this yupfest. Then Keith Richards suddenly appears onstage – his smiling skull hung with braids, his guitar miked to stun – and what's left, even for an angry Jew, to complain about?

BACKSTORY: I generally avoid raising tabloid issues with profile subjects, but Crow and Kid Rock have been all over Page Six, and he spent too much of the Shine show onstage, bellowing off-key. Sheryl won't speak of romance, preferring to talk about how he's helped her "artistry" – her word – to my mind, a far more embarrassing subject.

reality whatsoever. And for me, it's been not good for my artistry. It's made this record a very difficult record for me to make."

Reality is also the weight of years piling up as life's other, unmade choices slip away. These days, Sheryl Crow's belly is grumbling with another hunger, one that no royalty check, no statuette, no Denali of beans can ever satisfy.

"I want a family. I want a husband who wants to be a part of a team. And it's hard to find people that want to be with somebody who's in the public eye and who is gone a lot and, hmmm . . ." She catches herself and looks out through the window, out through the steamy rain.

"I don't know," she says finally, and there's a sixty-miles-from-Memphis drawl in her voice now. "I mean, honest to God, I can't even know what it's like to have kids. I don't know. But I'm sort of up for that. I'm a little bit burned out on everything being about me in my life. Not

CONFLICT: When I finally do sit down with Ms. Crow, she orders a breakfast big enough to choke a trucker and checks her pager just as I ask her my first question. "Okay – so fire away," she says. "What was it again?"

"Do you compare yourself to anyone?"

"Joan of Arc," she says, and breaks up laughing.

It occurs to me at once – and again, listening to the meandering interview tape; and again, when she jokes about nicknaming her band Fine Young Cannabis – that Sheryl might want to lay off the herb and focus on getting the album done.

WISH I'D WRITTEN: A gentler, kinder piece. It was clearly a rugged time for Sheryl Crow, as a human and as an artist – and I got word later that she was "devastated" by the story I wrote. Not that it hurt her career, nor that I felt I'd done any kind of hatchet job on her, but rereading such lines as "How many more tunes can she write and sing about good loving gone bad while her sweet jelly roll dries into biscuit?" makes me feel like a real bastard now.

that I don't think I'm a fascinating topic, but lemme tell ya . . . ."

There is rue in her laugh. Weary self-regard. Hope – the belief that if she managed to spin this magic web of stardom for herself, she can also settle back down, leave the road, hang a glider on the old front porch, and knit a pair of pink booties.

"I'm gonna enter a second phase of my life, where I really want to have kids," she says. "I think that will happen. In fact, I know it's gonna happen. Because I'm *willing* it to be."

Meanwhile, three years have passed since her last album of new stuff. That one – *The Globe Sessions* – was like a heart scraped raw. Nothing glib, no spunky hooks – hell, she even brought off a Dylan song that never made it onto *Time Out of Mind* with wry, rollicking ease. But in 1999, she put out an album, *Sheryl Crow and Friends Live from Central Park*, that also was a Fox TV special, and, oh, it was very much an Event, a tour of the wax museum – there was Sheryl with Eric Clapton, with Keith Richards, with Chrissie Hynde – yet artistically it was, ah, not good. After only three albums, Crow seemed too young, too vital and strong, to be hiding away in the tombs of classic rock.

Three years is a long, long holding pattern for a popular musician, and that silence is all you need to know about the conflict between Crow's yearning for a home, for a family of her own, and the momentum of her career. How many more tunes can she write and sing about good loving gone bad while her sweet jelly roll dries into biscuit? Seven more? Follow the lyric line back to Bessie Smith, to Molly Bloom, to Mother Eve – that crawling king snake done bit; now I need me a good, good man – and there she sits, still pushing her home fries around in her ketchup, humming a few bars of "Leaving Las Vegas" while the last bus to Mayberry wheezes past the coffee-shop window.

Oh, Sheryl, Sheryl. Say it won't be so.

I have a face I cannot show
I make the rules up as I go
It's try and love me if you can
Are you strong enough to be my man?

The studio has become tedium, an

endless excursion to the mall, a marathon casino junket to the Atlantic City of the spirit. It began so new and shiny; now it might be day or it might be the middle of the night, it might be winter or summer, it might be better if you put a six-string to it or just left it alone. Can we try hearing that with the six-string?

We can indeed. There is nothing we can't do with the help of Pro Tools and the lovely Trina at the knobs and the fellow behind her with the computer keyboard. The technology is our friend – if not for the technology, we could not record the music – but it's the friend who brought all his shit with him, took over the house, and never left. The technology now is the music; we can try hearing it with the six-string plus a zillion other ways and never finish the album at all.

"Take the drums and fuck with them," Sheryl says. She is yawning, her pale hands on her hips, wearing a stitched-leather coat against the air-conditioning, tight jeans, and pointy brown cowgirl boots. Even with a stacked heel, she's no taller than five-foot-three or -four.

"This is how I attempt shopping," Sheryl says. "I like to try everything on fifteen times and go back and buy the one I love. It's fine to go for something lo-fi, but in this day and age, what's the point of it?"

She is listening to the drum-fucked, six-string-added version now with eyes closed and one foot pumping and her biggish head shaking to the beat. The song itself is a damp ballad about losing love and getting over it, the taped vocal slurry and lush.

When the song is over, Sheryl sighs and reaches for a Marlboro Light.

"Oy vay," she says.

Oy vay? Such an enigma, this Missouri girl. Somehow, her grasp of the blues, those feelings of loss and the hope for redemption, her roots in this world, seems to be slipping away.

Two puffs on the cigarette and she stubs it out. She wants to hear the song again. With the six-string.

The song is called "Over You." I think. The album is called, um – I don't know. I'm not sure Sheryl has named it yet, and I don't wish to bother her about these details because she's hard at work and, to be frank, she seems a tad cranky. She made a cute little joke in the studio lobby – she and her band had just been invited to play at Jimmy Buffett's annual fete down in Florida, and Sheryl quipped to her bandmates, "What, did Bono cancel or something?"--but when she looked over and saw me making a note, she frowned and told me not to write that down. A couple minutes later, she said that she had come up with just the right name for the band – Fine Young Cannabis – but she didn't want me to write that down, either.

"We're just chewing the fat here," she explained.

Oy, Sheryl.

When the baffled and carpeted studio walls close in on her, when she realizes she needs to get out and just rock it really, really real for the people and blow all this Pro Tools shit clear out of her pipes, she arranges a series of small-club dates in New York – but these, too, prove somewhat enigmatic, sort of a scaled-down *Live from Central Park* redux, with "surprise" guest stars, silly cover versions of seventies chestnuts, and no new material at all.

I can see her reluctance to try out her new songs; she says she just doesn't want Napsteroids downloading them an hour after the show. The Joe Walsh, ELO, and Badfinger covers? Well, Crow was born in 1962 and genuinely gets her rocks off whanging away at their hits. And I certainly do grok Keith Richards and Steve Earle showing up to play and sing; hell,

I can even stand it when Stevie Nicks whimpers "Leather and Lace," seeing as how Mama Cass is dead.

But it's hard to shake the feeling that Sheryl Crow may not feel too comfy actually fronting a band, or singing naked leads, or putting out albums. That she may be a little too willing to cede the spotlight as her "special friends" cavort onstage and she plunks away on her bass and grins over at the VIP section behind the black velvet rope, where Sandra Bernhard and Meg Ryan and Kevin Bacon and the VH1 execs sit and sip their fancy drinks.

And then there's the skeezy riddle of Kid Rock, the latest entrant in the "Are you strong enough to be Sheryl Crow's man?" sweepstakes. The bastard offspring of one night's passion shared by Linda Lovelace and Pet Rock; ten woofing, goofing pounds of Detroit white-rap trash in a nine-pound wife-beater tee and a pimp fedora; the certified-double-platinum auteur of the timeless "Balls in Your Mouth," with its lilting refrain of "Balls in your mouth / balls in your mouth; 'U want my balls in your mouth'" – he's up there, too, yelping and mugging "Sweet Home Alabama" and, at one of her own shows, in plain view, groping Sheryl's leather-clad, sweet-mystery-of-life ass.

Oy, Sheryl, Sheryl. Say it ain't so.

When I've shown you that I just don't care
When I'm throwing punches in the air
When I'm broken down and cannot stand
Will you be strong enough to be my man?

The eggs are history. Gone, all gone: the

eggs, the beans, the home fries, even the toast. Kid Rock's gone, too – vanished, say the gossips, into the fetid jungle of Pamela Anderson.

"It's totally never my policy to ever talk about anybody in an interview," Sheryl vows when Kid Rock's name is raised, but she was the one who brought it up when I asked why she wasn't doing any new material during her club shows. It was none other than the Kid who warned Sheryl that any new stuff she did might wind up scarfed by Napster – but, hey, as long as we're on the subject, just how dumb is he in real life?

"He's not dumb. He has an overview of what entertainment is that just blows my mind, a great scope of what people want and what's considered kind of challenging to the audience. The other thing is, he's wildly talented. As he gets out and plays with other people, people are shocked at how talented he is."

Would this be the same Kid Rock who wrote "Fuck U Blind" and "Blow Me" – *that* Kid Rock?

"It's like Lenny Bruce to me – Lenny Bruce challenging the audience, saying things that are really taboo, that scare people, but everybody inside is kind of laughing about it."

(*Lenny Bruce?* Kid Rock has precisely two things in common with Lenny Bruce: He likes showgirls and getting blown.)

"I went and visited him in Detroit and got a pretty clear picture of who he is, and there is no artifice or pretense with him. He is a Detroit boy who lives outside of Detroit, who still hangs out with his buddies there, who has his friends around him, and his family pretty much works with him or for him – and when I went and visited him, I was reminded of who I am and what I'm from and my need to get back to that."

I don't know if she really believes this is what she needs, or if going home to her family and her old friends is no more than a pretty pill of a thought. You don't have to burn your bridges in this world – life and death do that for you – and what Crow has left behind is the toll you pay for pushing down the road as far as talent and ambition and luck will take you. The toll is your innocence. The toll is all of those nice illusions you had about what fame and money would mean to you. The toll also is living with the fear that nothing you'll do with your artistry will ever mean as much as all you've left behind – the love and comfort, your sense of having a safe place in the world, a home – all of what vanished in the rearview when you pulled out of the driveway for the last time, alone.

The morning rain is relentless; there will be no gratitude jog today. She checks her pager: nada. She was a cheerleader, yes, but that was a different life, another girl, who left Missouri and found herself on the 405 freeway in L. A., stuck in the middle of the evening rush hour, crying her eyes out, wondering what she had done to herself – and when *Tuesday Night Music Club* made her a name, the maw of success swallowed up that girl whole.

"That record really represents a lot of darkness and a lot of pain," she says at the coffee shop. "And it was really a blessing and a curse. We were looking back on life with a sense of defeat and a feeling of grandiosity – like, we're better, and we don't even wanna be successful, because if we're successful, we've become one of them. And then I became successful and

I became one of them. And there is no way out of that." She pauses. "I don't even know that selling out exists anymore. You can't ignore the fact that music has become more about commerce and the visual aspect."

And for some reason – maybe because of the rain – I mention Van Morrison.

"And Van Morrison isn't on the charts," she says.

Well, he's on my chart.

"But you know what I'm saying. I mean, just look at Sting: How wonderful that his record was not doing so well, and then he got a Jaguar commercial, and now we all own his record."

Oy, Sheryl, I say. Please. *Sting?* I'm leaving now.

She starts giggling. "A car commercial or a video – I'm saying it's the same thing. I mean, do I have to have like sixteen naked girls with fake tits in my videos to get my shit played? You write a song, you have a pretty clear visual of what the narrative is, but some director gets hold of it and makes a commercial out of it, and your record label goes through all kinds of political hoops to get it played however many times. It's the same thing. It doesn't say 'Coke,' it says 'Sheryl Crow.' You're a commodity. There isn't any difference."

No. Sorry. There *is* a difference, a flesh-and-blood difference, all the difference in the world, everything that matters to what comes out of the heart and lungs and into the ear. Nobody's asking you to turn into Sippie Wallace; just don't become Cher. Keep pushing down the road. You can write the bus, sing and play the bus, see if the bus sounds better with the six-string, and none of it will make a bit of difference. Sooner or later, either you get on the bus or it leaves without you.

Yeah, you wind up alone either way, but that's why they call it the blues in the first place, and it's everywhere. You can hear it and feel it back home on the front porch, too – which is why you left, which is the only reason that even the people who don't drive Jaguars buy it and listen to it. It's the sound life makes when all your special friends go home and no one on Napster cares enough to download you anymore.

Chapter Eight

Paul Newman

Hoss

He is the fierce-faced punk at the

Actors Studio in New York City in the early fifties, perched backward on a
folding chair, one leg up, glowering toward the front of the room.

The rest of the class sits back, listening, at apparent ease in their dark
suits and dark ties, their skirts and blouses.

The tough guy's wearing a white T-shirt tight enough to show the
curve of his lats, his smoke cupped in one hand, his jaws clamped so hard
that the muscles in his cheek quiver. No one in a room of sixty people
could look more alone.

You'd never guess that the tough guy's a Shaker Heights Jew, that his
father and uncle founded the largest sporting-goods store between New
York City and Chicago, that he has a degree from Kenyon and a year in the
master's program at the Yale School of Drama.

You'd guess that he'll get laid: He's rock-hard, ice-cool, gorgeous.
But you'd never guess that he'll ever amount to squat.

He has drunk, fought, and fucked his sorry way through two colleges.
He has been tossed off the football team at one of them, and he has made
the front page back home in Cleveland after duking it out with the cops.

He has survived three years of World War II in the Navy Air Corps – two as a radio gunner on a torpedo bomber in the South Pacific – and he has exhausted his GI Bill tuition benefits.

He has managed a golf range.

He has sold encyclopedias door-to-door.

He has been a bane and a grim disappointment to his father, who has died.

He has failed at the family business, which has now been sold.

He has a pregnant wife – his first wife, an actress he met doing summer stock in Wisconsin – a two-year-old son, a sixty-dollar-per-month apartment, and $250 in the bank.

The first time he goes up in front of the class to do a scene in workshop, the tough guy gets creamed. Basted. Slammed.

Not that he doesn't know a few things. He knows that James Dean, six years younger than he is, is out in Hollywood already. He knows that Brando, one year older – Marlon, the conquering hero, visits the Studio once in a while to hone his chops and pluck some city chicken – has already been anointed a god of stage and screen.

He knows that he's not so quick a study, that he has neither their emotional equipment nor their savvy, that he can't gnash and explode like Brando or melt down glistening like Dean. They are astonishing actors, those soft boys.

He knows that he was very good, very smooth, selling encyclopedias. He can do that. Or maybe he'll finish at Yale Drama and teach.

He knows that he is out of other options.

He is a fuckup – this, too, he knows. He has made aimless failure look easy, which it's not – not if you're from Shaker Heights. It took a dogged lack of commitment and a tenacious aversion to hard work. It took a whole lot of beer and fuck-you. It took a tough guy.

And this – the sum of his feckless boyhood – *this* he can use. He will use it. He will use what he has. He has nothing left to lose or to hide, nothing and no one to hide from – himself least of all.

Doomed to failure? Okay, boys. Let's fail as gracefully as we can.

The future? Fuck it.

This, it turns out, is his first gift to the craft, what he can reach for at the bottom of the trick bag of his soul, what's left when everything else has turned to dry suds.

Look, Ma, look, Pa: I don't give a fuck.

An epiphany of sorts, and a paradox,

because, in fact, he gives a fuck. He does not want to be a lightweight, which is what he knows he has been so far. He remembers his father during the Depression, when the store was out of cash, taking the train to Chicago and returning with the promise of hundreds of thousands of dollars' worth of sporting goods from Spalding and Wilson, because his father was a man of integrity and the companies knew they'd get their money. His father was not a lightweight. His father traded newspapering for the cold hell of retail to put a house around his family, to secure a future for them.

When his father died in 1950, at the age of fifty-seven, the son went back to Cleveland and took his place behind the counter, selling roller skates and baseball mitts and sleeping bags, and he felt a stone in his chest where his heart had been.

Behind the counter and in the account book, the tough guy found more shadows and ghosts than he could bear.

He didn't last a year before deciding it would be better just to go, to go and keep going.

He's going to be an actor.

He's going to pay the price of seeming not to give a fuck – about the future, about success, about what anybody else thinks of him.

He's going to live alone within himself, pretend to care deeply about nothing, to be past caring, especially about the things he cares deeply about.

He's going to act, and act as if he's not acting.

He's going to be Hud. Cool Hand Luke. Fast Eddie. Butch.

He's going to be a beautiful loser, a self-made orphan, adrift and misjudged, as scornful as he is scorned.

He's going to be the adolescent fantasy of a man's man, a cocky, gritty, hungry motherfucker, tough inside and out, all smirk and sinew, opposed – not by choice but by the helpless purity of his nature – to the laws that govern everyone else.

He'll get laid, all right, but he won't win the girl. Hell, odds are he'll be pushing up daisies by the time the credits roll, but he'll have won his immortality. Anchored in no bedrock but his wild spirit, alive forever in a land beyond giving two shits what anyone else sees him as or wants him to become.

Ah, freedom. He has no other choice. No past – his father's shade floats dark behind him, knowing that his pretty boy couldn't cut the mustard. No future – he looks a lot like Brando, but without the inner mounting flame, and a little like Dean, but without the quenchless, sullen anguish. No wizard, just a tough guy hidden, alone behind the curtain.

He's here now at the Studio: husband, father, fuckup. This is his last, best shot. Now.

Now was all he had.

"I don't know what I've learned," Paul Newman growls in a voice smoked and cured by seventy-five years, many of them spent inhaling Marlboros, scotch whisky, and high-octane exhaust.

Then comes the pause. Long pause. *Loooooong* pause. It's a by-God-vintage-Actors-Studio pause, a quiet billowing like fog, a hush that gathers, waiting, falling like the dark. You can hear the tape recorder whirring.

He looks like Paul Newman. That sounds moronic, I know – he is

---

Cutting Room Floor: Newman

THE PITCH: Icon. Idol. Titan. And the coolest 75-year-old ever to wedge himself behind the wheel of a Porsche at Daytona.

SCENE: Walking the dog. Literally: Newman and I are walking his dog, Lovey, briskly – and silently – through the bare woods of his estate in Westport, Connecticut, on the sort of breath-snatching winter day that no one in L.A. will ever admit missing. It's kiss-off time – after we return to the house, he and I will part ways forever. Newman knows it – I think that's why our pace is so quick. Our interviews have been a tooth-pull for us both. I can't tell if he's half- deaf or just deep, whether he's relaxed or catatonic, if he's pissed off or tired or bored or all of the above. Lucky for him, I'll be gone soon and he doesn't have a story to write. And lucky for me, I'm here walking the dog under the cold sun with Paul Newman.

BACKSTORY: Your heroes don't always disappoint you, but Newman – once upon a time, an angry Jew from Cleveland who went to Hollywood and struck it rich enough to head back East on his own terms – sure puzzled the hell out of me. I had read, and I'd been told, that he doesn't like

---

Paul Newman, jag-off – but that's still the first thing you notice. Fast Eddie and Hud, Butch and Luke. No gut, no dewlaps, no fancy pants. Loafers, cords, and a crewneck sweater.

His wrinkles are creases now; vertical seams stitch his lips. He is an old man, yes . . . and yet unbent. He is lithe, well oiled, loose – a sleek old tom. He takes smallish steps, but with a quick, athletic grace. He may have been five feet eleven inches tall, as he used to claim – his height was once a matter of hot media dispute – but he's no taller than five nine this evening. The pale wisps remaining on his pink, perfectly formed skull are sufficient to convey the impression of a full head of hair. The eyes, *those* eyes, are blue, yes, but a blue washed of depth. He seems tired, a little beat. Hell, he's seventy-five, it's after five: Maybe he's just hungry.

What the fuck is that on the left side of his nose? A bolus, a mass, too large to be a pimple, purple and swollen with blood. It's not huge, but it's

---

doing press and won't talk much about himself. True.

CONFLICT: *Esquire* got a letter from Newman's brother, Arthur, after the profile ran. "I thought it would be about a man I've known for 75 years," he wrote, "but this story seemed to be about an entirely different person." He ended by recalling "an ancient society where disgraced scribes would hold pens before their eyes and fall forward onto their faces."

WISH I'D WRITTEN: About his politics. In terms of post-WWII American liberalism, Newman has seen and done it all: He went to the South in '63 (when Barack Obama was hardly 2 years old), he was a delegate to the Democratic convention in '68, he helped fund *The Nation*. I asked him, early in 2000, what he thought of the men running to replace Bill Clinton.

"It doesn't matter with this Congress," he said. "I mean, it's irrelevant. They should detonate the whole bunch of 'em. There would be a half-dozen good men lost in the procedure, but I think they would be brave enough to say, 'It's worth it – we're willing to sacrifice, throw ourselves on the sword.' Their actions are just short of criminal."

a presence, something you can't avoid looking at.

He just sits there on the couch, hands clasped behind his neck, looking up at the ceiling. He's in no hurry.

You want him to open and spill himself? He won't. He doesn't think of himself like that, as a subject. Long ago, he decided that his inner life would stay that way ("This is the great age of candor," he told *Playboy* in 1983. "*Fuck* candor."), that celebrity was another, lesser role, empty of meaning and not to be trusted, that the jabbering media and the panting women and slick men fawning and pawing and thrusting themselves upon him – that fame itself – had come to him for stupid, superficial reasons. He does not gaze at the mirror and say, Holy shit, look at my beautiful eyes.

His right hand lifts his sweater and scratches absentmindedly; his belly looks flat, taut, tanned.

"Maybe that's the problem: I don't know what I've learned that's going to make these golden years golden."

He laughs, laughs to himself.

"It just seems like burnt umber."

We're in a large, overheated sitting room, part of an office suite that takes up the first-floor corner of an apartment building on upper Fifth Avenue in Manhattan. Forty-five years of framed movie posters fill the walls. I'm staring at the one touting *The Long Hot Summer*, vintage 1958, starring Newman and Joanne Woodward – they married in '58 – and big ol' Orson Welles, dead now fifteen years.

Summer did all right – Newman was named Best Actor at Cannes for his work in it – but it wasn't that year's box-office sensation; that would've been *Cat on a Hot Tin Roof*, for which Newman got the first of his eight Best Actor Oscar nominations. And although *Summer* was a strange bit of business, a dark trio of Faulkner stories slapped silly by a Hollywood ending, it wasn't the weirdest major-studio release of 1958, not by a long shot; for that, see *The Left-Handed Gun*, the story of Billy the Kid via Gore Vidal, all bruised psyche and blind, weeping vengeance, starring Paul Newman channeling James Dean.

By 1963, with twenty films and three Oscar nominations for Best Actor, Newman had become the most versatile and bankable movie star on planet Earth – and that was six years *before* Butch Cassidy vaulted him to hero status for yet another generation. One degree of Newman knits nearly a whole century of cinema: He has been directed by Hitchcock and

Scorsese, acted with Fred Astaire and Tom Cruise, directed Henry Fonda and John Malkovich; for God's sake, this guy lost Oscars to, among others, David Niven and Tom Hanks.

In a debased celebrity culture that rams cow shit down every goose's craw and calls it pâté, what does it mean to be a star? If Brad and Leo are icons, what does that make Paul Newman?

Lucky.

"Think of the torrent of sperm out there," he says softly, so softly that I find myself bending toward him, "and that yours landed here. Stunning."

"Long odds," I say.

He nods.

"Entrepreneurs in Silicon Valley – if their sperm had landed in Papua, New Guinea, where would they be today? They would have a lock on the abacus industry, but that's about as far as they could go."

This is textbook Newman. He is an ancient mariner, a survivor of a generation of tough guys, a stranger to self-congratulation and self-parody, a man who busted his nuts and yet found it unnecessary to seek release and affirmation in moshing with hotel furniture, punching pencil-necked photographers, or dancing the Watusi when he hit the end zone. Rarer than a virgin in Vegas is a Paul Newman interview in which luck, whimsy, and serendipity don't get the credit for his success.

"It is luck. It is . . . *stunning*. I didn't think very much about the future. I never felt like a leading man, never *felt* it. You've gotta *feel* like a leading man in order to be a leading man, and I never had that kind of confidence."

The first time he actually saw himself on a movie screen, in 1954, he was shit-faced drunk, a blessing. *The Silver Chalice* was the title, a costume drama, the kind of crap that is laughable kitsch even when done well, which this wasn't. Jack Palance, playing the pagan magician, was lucky enough to be disguised by an evil goatee; Newman, wrapped in a mini toga, played the slave turned sculptor whose task was to craft the goblet Christ would use at the Last Supper.

At a movie house in Philly, slumped down with a case of brew, he watched himself, a cigar-store Indian in ancient Rome, turning slowly to deliver his first line of film dialogue.

"I hope these hands never again have to perform such a sad duty," he said, his voice as flat and dead as dirt.

Surviving that dog took luck.

James Dean dying and bequeathing to Newman his first plum role, as Rocky Graziano in *Somebody Up There Likes Me* – good luck, too, at least for Newman.

Meeting Woodward, not just a great actress but the daughter of a publishing executive, a Georgia peach who not only could live with Newman's obliquity and rough edges but could also share her passion for literature, for politics – and who was willing to set aside the meat of her career to raise their kids: That was lucky, yes.

Butch Cassidy? Luck. Brando had the role, with Newman cast as the Sundance Kid. But Brando had no time for acting – he was too busy trying to solve what they used to call the Negro Question – so the producers switched Newman to Butch and tried to get Warren Beatty. Then Steve McQueen. They finally settled for Newman and Redford.

But he had something beyond the luck. It was Newman who refused when Warner Bros. suggested that he change his name to something that sounded less Jewish, who bought out his first and last studio contract in 1959 for half a million dollars he didn't have and became one of the first movie stars of his time who would control his value and his work, who said goodbye to Hollywood and bought a home in Connecticut in 1962 and lives there still, who marched in Alabama in '63 and campaigned for Gene McCarthy in '68, who spoke his beliefs in public and backed them with deeds and dollars at a time when most citizens sat mute – especially those dolls whose earnings were based on an image of insouciant glamour – and who refused to mail in the same tired, smirking, tough-guy, buddy-buddy shite in movie after movie, choosing instead to grow as an actor and as a man.

Luck?

Sure.

Great good luck – and the will to work and the stamina to endure.

Luck, heart, and a pair of big stone balls.

Brando? A lunatic, an island.

Dean? Dead.

McQueen? Dead.

Monty Clift? Dead.

Little Sal Mineo? Dead.

Tony Curtis? Um, you tell me.

Newman? *Loooooong* pause.

"Let me retire to the john," he says. "This beer has gone through me fast." He has consumed one seven-ounce pony of Bud.

He comes back rubbing his cheek. He has seen the fireball on his nose.

"I go to the doctor once a year," he explains, "to have my face scraped. All the rough edges – it's sore as hell. It's what they call a precancerous growth. One of those choice things that come with age."

He is seventy-five years old now. He has seen his colleagues come and, most of them, go. He doesn't kid himself about the future.

"You can't be as old as I am without waking up with a surprised look on your face every morning: Holy Christ, whaddya know – I'm still around. It is absolutely amazing that I survived, survived all the booze and the smoking and the cars and the career.

"I'm at that age when you really start thinking about what the end is going to be like and how gracefully you're gonna do that. That becomes almost a – if I would have to say I was preoccupied with anything, it would be that: just wondering how graceful that exit is gonna be.

"Is it just gonna be *non compos mentis*? Is it gonna be whining and screaming? Is it gonna be graceful? Is it gonna be quick? Is it gonna be one of those long, drawn-out . . . you wonder about it. It doesn't occupy my day, but you wonder about it."

Suddenly, Joanne Woodward enters the room.

"This is my lady," Newman says, introducing us, and the gravel in his voice is gone. His voice is rich and warm and full of joy.

Lucky, yes. She is seventy years old, more rounded now than curved, and more beautiful for that. She smiles at him with that look that women have who have stuck it out, who have come to cherish the boy in their man.

"Don't believe any of it," she warns me on her way out to dinner. "It's all one big joke."

But this much is no joke: He *has* slowed. He retired from auto racing in 1995, after winning the GT-1 championship at the Daytona Rolex 24 at the age of seventy, and the movie work is sparse, redundant, cued by his creases and old white head and dusty pipes. *Since Nobody's Fool* in 1994 – a fine job, garnering him his eighth Oscar nomination for Best Actor; he lost, of course, to Mr. Box o' Chocolates – he has played a creaky shamus in 1998's pat but watchable *Twilight*, and he did his level best as Kevin Costner's pop, crusty and wise, in *Message in a Bottle*, the purest celluloid tribute to nausea since Mickey Rourke died. His new film, *Where the*

Money Is – he plays yet another cranky *alter kocker*, a bank robber who fakes a stroke to get out of prison and into a nursing home, where Linda Fiorentino, playing the hot 'n' nasty nurse, cajoles him into one last heist – was shot two years ago.

And since?

"Lean stuff out there. It's dry, a dry season." His voice, solemn to begin with, trails off into a grunt.

I ask about *The Homesman*, a project he's talked about the past few years, a character-driven western he's written and rewritten. He has said that he'd like to direct it and star in it with his wife – they've done eleven pictures together – and then call it quits.

"I can't seem to get anybody interested," he says. "I may have just run out of steam on it."

Hard to believe, I say, that no one's interested.

He squints, frowning. Tell him you love his popcorn and red sauce and salad dressing and he'll thank you kindly with a twinkle in his eyes, but don't blow smoke up Paul Newman's bony old ass. Don't even try.

"You think you can just *muscle* anything through?"

Muscle? I'd think being Paul Newman would be enough.

"Not true," he snaps, and falls silent for a while.

"One swan song," he says softly. "Just something . . . memorable."

Loooooong pause.

"What is," he says, "is."

A shrug.

"No complaints," he says. "I've had a pretty good run."

Behold the man. Listen to him. *No complaints.*

A pretty good run. *My lady.* Bud in a pony bottle.

Pally, you can argue that Newman was not all *that* fine an actor – although the only men with as many Oscar nominations are named Nicholson, Olivier, and Tracy. You can belittle the car racing as a rich man's hobby – as long as you give props to the dude for *huevos grandes*. Hell, you can keep the charity stuff out of it, too; he won't mind. Besides, that began twenty years before Newman's Own, with the No Sutch Foundation in the 1960s. The name was a cloak and a joke, a guarantee that the checks he wrote would be cashed right away, but the money, hundreds of thousands of dollars, was real. Then came the Scott Newman Foundation. Then the Hole in the Wall Gang Camp for terminally ill children.

But even leaving all that aside – and stowing, too, the old-codger-facing-the-horizon, the living-legend hagiography – answer me this:

How can you *not* love the man?

He's going back to Daytona to drive in the Rolex 24. He swore that he'd return at seventy-five. If he's drawing air, he'll be there. More than ever, now is all he has.

So, if the scripts he sees these days are few and far between, if the directors now come from MTV and NYU, if the writers are fresh from Harvard, and if the actors are from the San Diego Zoo, digitally enhanced planks of pine who piss and moan about the emotional agony, the soul torture, of playing a part in a fucking movie – if he never acts again, so what?

They were merely roles, anyway. He shot a decent stick at best; he never ate those fifty eggs; he didn't die in Bolivia. He was a working actor, the kind who took his script and broke it down scene by scene and beat by beat, who worried about having enough rehearsal time, who'd show up on location a week or a month in advance of shooting to ground himself in the reality he hoped to capture. He was not a confident actor. He never could stand to watch the movies everyone else adored. He saw himself up there sweating to create, forcing things, working too hard: the *Un*natural.

In 1961, when his *Hustler* costar George C. Scott told the gossips how unimpressed he was by Newman's work, they went to Newman for a piss shot back. He agreed with Scott and kept working. A box-office hero with his pick of any script – and nearly every one asked him to puke up another Fast Eddie, another Hud, another Luke, another Butch – he took roles in films that no one wanted: a Mexican outlaw in *The Outrage*, a Western version of *Rashomon*; a disc jockey turned freedom fighter in WUSA; a union-busting logger in *Sometimes a Great Notion*.

He began to produce and direct his own films; the first, *Rachel, Rachel*, starring Woodward, earned a Best Picture nomination in 1968. It lost to *Oliver*!

In 1969, he formed First Artists Production Company with Barbra Streisand and Sidney Poitier; later, Steve McQueen and Dustin Hoffman joined up. The idea was that they would produce quality films, films they cared about. The reality was that the lunatics couldn't run the asylum, and he himself was bored, frustrated, sick of playing Paul Newman playing Paul Newman.

"I'm running out of steam," he said in 1968. "Wherever I look, I find parts reminiscent of Luke or Hud or Fast Eddie. Christ, I played those parts once and parts of them more than once. It's not only dangerous to repeat yourself, it's damned tiresome."

It had come full circle: He was back behind the counter at Newman-Stern Company, retailing skates; hell, he was up there on the shelves himself, a product. *The Towering Inferno*: This they went to see him in. *The Sting*: This won Best Picture.

Fuck the work, fuck the industry, fuck the money. Fuck the fucking eyes especially. Worse than toting Jayne Mansfield's rack, worse because he had worked hard to become a solid, versatile actor, had taken the craft seriously, and wound up candy on a stick.

Besides, he had discovered racing. This circle he liked – fast and faster, no thought beyond the screaming cockpit, no introspection, no box office. You won or you didn't. He kept his filming schedule clear from April to October – racing season – and turned pro in 1977. He was fifty-two years old, and acting was now something he did on the side.

And *this* – fuck it, just fuck it; just drive the bitch like you stole it and pass the fucking Scotch – this he could use to become the actor he'd always wanted to be, free of all the smirking boyo shit and freeze-framed machismo.

The transformation began in yet another movie no one saw, 1976's *Buffalo Bill & the Indians, or Sitting Bull's History Lesson*, in which Newman played the living legend as a drunken buffoon and a showbiz fraud. Then *Slap Shot*: Newman on skates, playing a muff-diving hockey lifer who sports a brown patent-leather leisure suit off-ice and isn't above diddling a teammate's wife. And when Redford pulled out of *The Verdict* because playing the boozehound shyster wouldn't gloss his image, Newman took the part, pouring himself into a raw wound of a character and – stripped of all mannerism – bared the soul and spirit of the man, coming out on the other side in the flat-out best ride of his career.

He's the codger now, dressed in a Sarah

Lawrence sweatshirt and chinos, bi-focals perched on the tip of his nose, at home in Westport, Connecticut. He's the country gent with rolling acres of trees and a river, and a big red barn fixed up as a screening room, and a pool, and an electric gate with a sign on it that says *chien bizarre*. He takes his cup of coffee into the den and sits, surrounded by books and pictures, facing the window that looks out across the yard, sits in an old wooden desk chair that squawks like a dented cornet, sits and watches his wife tote a basket of wash up the walk to the house.

He reaches into the bottom drawer of the desk and fishes out a chocolate bar. Newman's Own – he buys them at the grocery. Another circle closed, another arc of life returned to earth. He is what his father was: a businessman, a brand name.

He breaks off a small piece and lets it melt in his mouth.

He is what his father was, a family man. Five daughters. His first child, Scott, his only son, overdosed and died at the age of twenty-eight, in 1978. Scott had tried to become an actor, had tried stunt work, had changed his name to William Scott and tried to become a singer. It had been bad between them for a long time before the pills and alcohol carried Scott away, worse than it had been back when he himself was his father's son and a fuckup.

When the phone call came, he was not surprised to hear that Scott had died. What shocked him was the anger and the hurt. What enveloped him then was the length of the shadow his own father had cast, and the darkness of the shadow now belonged to him. He can't act it away, can't drink it into light, can't outrace it or out-tough it.

He can't even name it. Not grief. Not guilt. It is past naming, and he is long past trying. It is always there. But sixty yards away stands another house, where one of his daughters now lives with her family. That is where he goes to try to close the circle – to play with Peter, his three-year-old grandson, who takes him by the hand into the playroom and bids him to sit on the floor.

"Okay, Pop-Pop," Peter says, trailing his hands down the side of his grandfather's head, "wipe your mind. Wipe your mind."

And he will wipe his mind of everything, and it will fill again with the color of winter light and the smell and sound of the little boy on the floor pretending with him.

Then a line of dialogue drifts back to him from twenty-five years ago, from when he played Buffalo Bill for Robert Altman:

"The last thing a man wants to do is the last thing he does."

He's the codger at home, in the old stone house built in 1736, in the sunlit kitchen, grinding organic coffee beans for a fresh pot. The Scotch and the smokes are a long way behind him now.

We have split a small piece of the Newman's Own chocolate, and we have walked the dog. The chocolate, laced with orange, is organic, too. The little dog – Peter has named it Lovey – is certainly organic. Everything seems to be organic but the talking.

"That chocolate," I offer, "was damned good."

Loooong pause. He's sucking at the chocolate in his gums, I think.

"Ah," he says, "it *is* good."

Forget the films: Movies are movies, food is life. I eat this guy's salsa, his popcorn, his Sockarooni sauce – and if I had any use for salad, I'm sure I'd use his dressings, too – and not because Newman's Own is the only corporation in this country that gives every post-tax nickel of its net to charity, more than a hundred million dollars to date, but because the stuff is so damn tasty.

I figured it would be easy to get him talking about his good food, his good works, his giving.

It isn't – not with Newman. It makes him uncomfortable.

"I don't ask any questions about it," he says. "I'm afraid that if I ask any questions about it, I could come up with the wrong answer. It's the act in itself that is the important thing, not seeking out the motivation for it. Every donation that I ever made to anything was always anonymous. Now I have to broadcast it. I really don't like it."

He is now a spokesman for the Committee to Encourage Corporate Philanthropy, whose goal is to increase the total annual amount of corporate donations from $9 billion to $15 billion by 2004. He spoke late last year at the kickoff banquet to a gaggle of CEOs – Chase Manhattan, Kmart, Citibank, Xerox, America Online: more than two dozen of the lucky bastards, all self-made, rugged individualists who weren't born in Papua, New Guinea – and told them, "Wipe your minds," and asked them to commit 2 percent of their annual after-tax profits to charity.

Well, they said, they'd have to think about it. They'd have to consider their responsibilities to the shareholders.

They thought about it. They discussed it. They voted no.

Loooooong pause.

"With all the questionable things we're capable of doing," he tells me, and this clause is followed by a pause so long that a bunch of skinny Europeans could plant a net on either end of it and start a soccer match, "it seems that all entities should participate in holding out their hands to people who have less than they have."

Frankly, I could go for another piece of chocolate, but I left my wallet in the car. So I figure it's a good time to ask him something – loooong pause: two can play that game – deep. Something about Paul Newman, the man sitting here with me, being more than the sum of the parts he has played.

If he ain't Hud, ain't Fast Eddie, ain't Cool Hand Luke, ain't Butch, who is he?

Who is Paul Newman?

"I don't know," he says, sipping the dregs of his coffee. "You can't not absorb some of those character traits into your own personality. You try to separate those little fragments you've created. You don't know. The only time you'll know is when you're on your deathbed, and then you'll say, 'Okay, now we're down to ground zero.' That's when you separate what's real and what isn't real."

Help me out, buddy.

"You peddle me, I peddle you," he tells me, shaking his head. "It's just that."

See you at Daytona?

"I'm not going to have much time," he says.

He nearly runs out of time altogether a week

later, behind the wheel of a Porsche 996GT3R during a practice run down at Daytona. The Porsche spins out on a cold set of tires and whips hard into a tire barrier, blowing the windshield and crushing the nose and rear bumper. The paper says that he walked away with bruised ribs.

I put a call in to his office: I don't want to waste a trip if he's not going to drive.

A couple of days later, my phone rings.

"Scott?"

Yeah.

"Newman."

Loooooong pause.

He broke a rib, he says. But he's more angry and embarrassed than hurt, and there's nothing to be done for it but to get back on the Airdyne and get ready for the Rolex 24 in a couple of weeks.

I dunno, man – if I'm your wife or kid, I'm lobbying hard for you to stay home and walk the dog.

"I've heard a lot of that," he says. "A lot of, 'You dumb old shit.'"

The kids, he says, have taken out additional insurance policies on his life.

I laugh.

"I'm not kidding," he says. "I had to sign the papers."

I don't say so, but I think he's pulling my leg. If you sell life insurance, are you going to write a policy on a seventy-five-year-old auto racer?

Maybe, if he's Paul Newman.

The day before the race, I find him in

the garage, staring into the Porsche's engine while the crew tries to fix a fuel-system problem. He has his shades on, and a blue ball cap that says No Mercy on the crown, and a jacket that I swear he wore in *Twilight*, a tan car coat with a nipped and pleated elastic waist, the sort of polyester-fiberfill garment that would be perfectly at home on any shuffleboard court anywhere in the foul and desiccated state of Florida. And, Jesus Christ, maybe it's his wretched coat or the pain of his cracked rib or the sight of him standing stiffly and bent at his waist amid a clutch of scrambling grease monkeys in jumpsuits wielding screaming torque wrenches, but he looks shriveled, antique, a Methuselah of the pits.

I want to ask him about the coat, I suppose because I can't quite get over how shitty it looks, and because I don't know dick about cars or racing and I want something lighthearted to say, but he blows past me with a quick handshake and a granite game-face frown.

"I'll catch up with you later," he growls, jumping into a little golf cart. He fumbles with the key awhile before he can crank the thing, poking and scowling and pumping the pedal, and it's all that I can do to keep from shouting, *Yo, Pop-Pop, wipe your mind. Wipe your mind, you dumb old shit. You go tomorrow.*

But my guess is Pop-Pop already knows that, and that he just might shuffle over and try to kick my nuts to jelly if I remind him.

The Porsche is a black beast, a

thing of primal beauty. I don't know dick about cars or racing, and God knows I don't want to know, but if you could fornicate with metal, I'd mount this curved and panting thing and dry-hump it until the grease monkeys put their torque wrenches to my heaving ass and spun me off.

A fair portion of the body and roof of the Porsche is covered by WHERE THE MONEY IS in green script, with dollar signs trailing. Circled in white on both doors is the number 75. This is no coincidence, of course; the last time Newman raced, five years ago, right here, he drove number 70.

Back at his team's hospitality tent, the canvas is hung with plants and flowers, the tables are covered with white cloth, and the buffet is laid heavily with chicken cutlets, pasta, shrimp salad, layer cake, cookies – and a nice big vat of salad on its own table, surrounded by a phalanx of bottles of Newman's Own dressing – but the place is empty.

It's time to go.

The race is called the Rolex 24 because it goes for twenty-four hours straight, one of two such endurance races in the world, the other being Le Mans, which, to my befuddlement, the slack-jawed, beetle-browed rednecks here pronounce with very adequate French accents--"Leh Mah"--even as they rinse down their fried pork rinds with Old Milwaukee. Many of them are crowded behind the fence in back of the Newman team's pit for the start of the race, their women – and if you ever wonder who besides exotic dancers gets all the tit jobs, check out this track – standing on tiptoe and craning their necks to catch a glimpse of . . . him.

Fast Eddie.

Luke.

Hud.

Butch.

And someone else, some tough old coot no one really knows.

He sits with his back to them, sits in a lawn chair in his quilted, black-and-white, fireproof jumpsuit, his feet dainty in blue suede racing shoes set squarely on the concrete floor of the pit, his No Mercy cap planted on his head. Strips of electrical tape cross his ears, holding his earplugs and his sunglasses in place. He sits, at ease, his red-gloved hands on his thighs, staring at his shoes.

No one could look more alone.

The women mock at fanning themselves when he turns his head and they mark his profile, not because they're warm, but because it's . . . him.

He looks even older today than yesterday. He is. One day older, one day further along on his ride to the near horizon, and each sun seems to have carved itself another, deeper seam into that lodestone of a face.

You might guess that he's a movie star, a cocky, gritty, hungry motherfucker.

You might guess that he's exactly where he wants and needs to be.

You'd never guess that he has ever, for one second, felt that he could cut the mustard.

He is one of four racers who will take turns at the wheel of number 75 from Saturday at 1:00 P.M. until Sunday at the same time – or until the car dies.

It is a race of attrition more than speed – the winner will average a bit over 107 miles per hour – and engines will die in handfuls: By the time

Sunday afternoon rolls around, only twenty-nine of the seventy-eight cars will finish. And forgive me, but number 75 will not be among them. Where the Money Is will blow its engine at 9:35 P.M.

It doesn't matter now: Saturday at 1:00 P.M. is all he has. He rises from his lawn chair and moves to the front of the pit to watch the race start, then comes back to the lawn chair and stares into space.

He's going to drive the second stint.

At 2:25 P.M., the sunglasses will come off and he will jam on his mid-night-blue helmet with the planets and stars painted white on its sides and, in small block letters just behind his brain, BLOOD TYPE O+.

(He's funny, the tough guy. Dry. Fuck-ing nuts. Not that he doesn't know a few things – about luck and love, about loss and leaving.)

At 2:25 P.M., he's going to move like a lithe old cat to the front of the pit and poise himself, balancing on the riser, waiting, waiting, waiting for the Porsche.

When it comes, he will throw open the driver's-side door and unzip the webbing to free his teammate, and he will pour his flesh and bone into the driver's seat, yank down the steering wheel, and clench the shifter, his eyes flaming, his mouth a slash of desire as naked as the metal cage around him.

He knows that the last thing a man wants to do is the last thing he does.

He's going to go, yes.

He's going to be another great good man – the last of his kind – gone.

But for now, he's going to go in circles. He's going to go like stink.

Now is all he has.

Chapter Nine

Robert Altman

Angler

Director at age 78*

"I never knew what I wanted, except that it was something I hadn't seen before.

Words don't tell you what people are thinking. Rarely do we use words to really tell. We use words to sell people or to convince people or to make them admire us. It's all disguise. It's all hidden – a secret language.

Wisdom and love have nothing to do with each other. Wisdom is staying alive, survival. You're wise if you don't stick your finger in the light plug. Love – you'll stick your finger in anything.

I love fishing. You put that line in the water and you don't know what's on the other end. Your imagination is under there.

Whether it's a bad novel being translated to the screen or a good novel being butchered or how to keep the restroom clean in a filling station, it's all the same thing: You gotta entertain people.

The worst trap you can fall in is to start imitating yourself.

The only place there's a lotta room is at the top, because nobody really wants to be there.

I don't know what self-doubt is. But when I don't know what I'm doing, it shows in the work.

There's been a few times when I just realized, God, I don't think there's any real way out of this other than just to finish and see if we can slip it by.

I loved radio drama. Each audience member had his own picture. When you heard the creaking door, everybody had his own door.

I was going to Santa Fe one time, and somebody said, "It's great down there, you know – it's a real artists' colony." I remember saying, "I didn't know they colonized." Of course, they don't. That's the one thing artists *don't* do.

When people ask for advice, what they're really asking for is help.

I'll give you the same advice I give my children: Never take advice from anybody.

You can't know it all. You don't have the time.

I'm not very smart about money. I don't know much about it. I certainly don't collect it, or save it, or store it. And I might regret it one day. But I don't think so. I've always felt that I could survive some way.

I didn't mind military school; I kind of liked it. I thought it was a nice little adventure.

I was a pilot. I flew a B-24 in the South Pacific. I did forty-six missions, something like that. We got shot at a lot. It was pretty scary, but you're so young, it's a different thing. I was nineteen, twenty. It was all about girls.

Mr. and Mrs. Smith get married, they have problems, they get back together, and they live happily ever after. End of the movie. Two weeks later, he kills her, grinds her body up, feeds it to his girlfriend, who dies of ptomaine poisoning, and her husband is prosecuted and sent to the electric chair for it – but here's our little story with a happy ending. What is an ending? There's no such thing. Death is the only ending.

Jazz has endured because it doesn't have a beginning or an ending. It's a moment.

I was a pretty good golfer, and it got so that it obsessed me. And I was just pretty good. And then when I'd get a job, I couldn't play every day; I could play only on the weekends. About four strokes sneak back into your game. And finally I thought, I'm just not having any fun with it. I'm tortured by this. I hate it. And I just quit.

Every ad for every film is exactly the same.

We make too much of the good and too much of the bad.

I love gallery openings where everybody runs around drinkin' that crappy goat-piss white wine and you can't see the work at all. And you realize that the artists – and them people all *think* they're artists – they can't like anybody else's art. They can admire it if it still leaves them in the same place, if it isn't direct competition to them, and they can say, "Oh, well, of course I'm a great admirer of that." It's very safe.

I knew Sam Peckinpah slightly. We shared the same editor for a long time. But we were jealous of one another. We were all jealous of anybody who was succeeding. I've always been more openly expressive in my admiration for European and Asian directors, and I think maybe it's because they're not a threat to me. They're in a different cubbyhole.

Hot air just came in from the window. Hot air comin' that way and hot air comin' this way.

I've always had the final cut."

– interviewed by the author, New York City, fall, 2003, three years before Altman's death

Chapter Ten

Will Ferrell

Actorrrrrrrrrrrrrrrrrrrrrrrr!

The toughest part of talking to Will Ferrell is getting past his mustache. Ferrell's head is huge – not actually oversized like the well-carved pumpkins atop many of Tinseltown's tiny marionettes, because Ferrell's a big man, six feet three and two hundred pounds, easy, but it's still a massive head – and the mustache has much ground to cover. The first time I mention the mustache, we're eating a late breakfast at a place off Sunset Boulevard.

Heck of a mustache, I tell him.

"Okay – good," he says, warm, friendly. I don't think he actually heard me. he's talking about running the Boston Marathon last April and how, thanks to *Old School*'s success, he spent the whole twenty-six miles listening to dudes chant, "Frank the Tank"– his *Old School* character's nickname – as he plowed on past.

"Kids were running next to me, snapping pictures, Ferrell says. "Runners were running up ahead and then having their buddies stand next to me, snapping. It was insane."

Blah, blah, mustache, blah. Mustache. I'm across the table trying to focus on something – *anything* – except the mustache. No dice. He grew it for the comedy he's filming now, *Anchorman*, starring Ferrell as a lovable pig of a 1970s local news stud. So the mustache has an obvious, Dabney Coleman-esque machisomo, but there's more to it than that. Way more. It's lush yet disciplined. It's cruel yet not haughty. It's – ah, fuck it. I can't take it anymore.

Will? Your mustache. Will – it's, it's... frightening.

He stops. Smiles wide. Cackles quietly, an almost silent laugh.

"Isn't it?" he asks, his voice soft yet proud. "It's a monster."

It looks like it wants to jump down and start crawling up my leg. Some sort of gay-porno thing going on there...

"And you know how it all started?" he says. "Just the subtle difference of shaving this"– the tip of his index finger traces a clean-shaved strip I hadn't really *seen*, maybe an eighth of an inch of bare skin between his nose and mustache – "somehow gives it that extra sleaze-plus-cheesy effect."

He's absolutely right. You can have big talent, good fortune, a sunny, sweet, and sane disposition, but sometimes the ineffible quality that we mortals sense as stardom boils down to no more than this: Will Ferrell is blessed with acreage between his upper lip and nose spacious enough to hold a full-sized – nay, a *Magnum, P.I.*-sized-'stache *plus* an insinuating, all-nude band of flesh, stubbled yet creamy. Jesus.

The whole effect is pretty arousing, I must say.

"Very much so," he muses. "Very much so. Even when I look at myself in the mirror, I'm completely aroused. I think part of it is this," and again he fingers himself softly on the naked square of his philtrum, the indented furrow of skin under the nose.

"Engorged," he says, nearly whispering now. "It becomes...*engorged*."

Now that you mention it, Will, it does look a little...swollen.

"Should I put a napkin over it?"

It takes swagger and pluck to balance on the

thorny cusp of fame, to dwell in the Hollywood Hills and drive a Toyota Prius, to jump from playing Frank the Tank jogging bare-assed down the street in *Old School* to playing Buddy, the soul of innocence, a North Pole elf traipsing in yellow tights and a white fur collar to New York City at Christmas in search of his human father in *Elf*. Hell, it takes pluck and swagger merely to have survived costarrring in *A Night at the Roxbury*, in which Ferrell was forced into a black thong and close proximity with the Darwinian question mark called Chris Kattan.

But John William Ferrell, all plucky swagger, is nothing if not a survivor. In his thirty-six years of life, he has survived a comfy childhood in Orange County – in coyote-ravaged Irvine, no less. He has survived the rigors of the University of Southern California, huddled with his fraternity brothers around the draining keg, waiting for the pizza man and the last check from home to clear. He has survived a vicious curriculum, emerging with a degree in sports information and a gaudy 2.97 GPA. And thus emboldened, tempered by hardship, he cast his fate to the wind, trekked back south upon the rugged 405, and moved into his old room at his mommy's house for a couple of years to gather his strength and decide what to survive next.

What molds, what drives the man? What flames roar beneath the laughter, the balls-out comedic stylings, the mustache? What inner demons forced Will Ferrell to finally cry out, Yes – yes, I can!

Kay Ferrell knows. She's Will's mama, and she's visiting the Anchorman set today, watching her boys work. Will's little brother, Patrick – not little, really, just younger, Pat stands six feet five, which a big, plucky plumber's gut swaggering over the belt of his jeans – is here, too, working as Will's personal assistant. Kay, with her quick smile and honeyed voice – she grew up in North Carolina – has a mother's knowledge of Will's murky soul, and she lays it bare.

"He was born like that," she says. "Very even tempered, very easy going. His father and I kinda went, 'How'd he get like *that?*' You know those little Matchbox cars? Will would line up his Matchbox cars by himself, and be totally happy. You'd say, 'You wanna go to Disneyland today or line up your cars?' and he'd have to think about it."

Adam McKay, an ex-*Saturday Night Live* writer who's directing Anchorman and is good buddies with Ferrell – they wrote the script together – sings a different tune. When I mention interviewing Ferrell, McKay frowns.

"One-on-one with Will?" he says. "I would not do that if I were you. What you don't want to be is in a contained, closed room with him. That's the worst possible situation to be in. I'll be honest: He's bitten people."

Paul Rudd, the actor who plays one of Ferrell's news-team sidekicks, overhears this.

"Talkin' about Will?" asks Rudd. "He bit me."

Where?

Rudd undoes his belt and starts to pull down his pants.

"No, Paul," McKay says. "Just point to it over your clothes."

Rudd's hand waves over his crotch. "He bit me in the hip," he says.

"He bites you in weird places."

We're past the mustache now. Our

eggs are cold. Ferrell's reminiscing about moving back home after USC to try comedy and acting classes and regional theater. Ferrell caught his big break not long after he joined the Groundlings, L.A.'s version of Second City, when Lorne Michaels came west hunting fresh *SNL* meat. Ferrell made it past the first audition and got ready for the callback, which began with a meeting with Michaels in New York.

"I had read how Adam Sandler, in his meeting with Lorne, had humped a chair and had him laughing so hard, he signed him on the spot. So I thought, I'm gonna go in there and be funny. I had a briefcase full of fake money, and as Lorne starts talking, I was gonna open it up and start

Cutting Room Floor: Ferrell

THE PITCH: Sure, you've seen his naked butt in *Old School*. But is there more to him than that?

SCENE: Wandering backstage and upstairs through the ancient New York City theater where Conan O'Brien's taping his 10th-anniversary special. Ferrell's in his leprechaun suit; Abe Vigoda, older than the theater, walks by and nods. Andy Richter's in some sort of Viking loincloth and fur helmet. And Jack Black has just arrived from Los Angeles, looking like he flew in without a plane, eyes pinwheeling, cackling non-stop.

BACKSTORY: Ferrell's making *Anchorman* when I visit; *Elf* hasn't come out yet, and he's fretting about it. I saw Elf at a screening and thought it would be a smash, but a screening – sitting alone or with a claque of insiders in a small, plush, private theater – can be deceptive.

"Is it too sappy?" Ferrell asks.

I tell him hell no, that it's a Christmas movie, after all, adding, "You're on the cusp of wonderful things."

stacking piles of money on his desk. 'Lorne, you can say whatever you want, but we all know what really talks. And that's cold, hard cash. Now, I'm gonna walk outta here. You can take the cash if you want. Or not.' And then just leave and not come back.

"So I walk in with the briefcase, and I can tell right away the atmosphere is tense. It's just all business. Lorne's there, Steve Higgins, the producer, is sitting there, and I'm carrying this briefcase, thinking, I don't think the money thing's gonna work.

"Lorne goes through everything, and he says, 'Steve, anything you'd like to say?' And Steve just goes, 'Nice briefcase.'"

Ferrell laughs that almost silent cackle of sheer delight.

"What I recognized when I started doing comedy was that I'm probably not the wittiest, not the fastest on my feet, but the one thing I can guar-

---

"That'd be fine," he says, looking serious. "That'd be great."

CONFLICT: Ferrell, the cover boy, had committed to an *Esquire* party commemorating the issue – or maybe he hadn't, at least in his mind. But the magazine thought he had, his name was on our invites, and he was in New York City to work on Woody Allen's *Melinda & Melinda*. He called from JFK Airport the afternoon of the party and said that he was sorry but he was heading back to L.A. shortly to be with his pregnant wife. It was big of the bastard to apologize and explain. Like my mom always says, "He didn't have to do that."

WISH I'D WRITTEN: At our last interview, Ferrell was nervous about meeting (and working with) Woody Allen. "I might just come up and give him a hug and not let go – just get it over with and just give him a bearhug and make him really uncomfortable."

He'll fire you, I say.

"Wouldn't that be funny, though? I got fired by Woody Allen – because I wouldn't let go."

---

antee is that I won't hold anything back. It was just funnier to me, and it played funnier, when instead of just yelling at someone in a scene, you're yelling to the point where you're losing your voice – the one extra step. If that's what's called for within the context, isn't that our job as comedians?

Thoughtful and intelligent, sure, but what Ferrell's really talking about now is his ass, which gets far more screen exposure in *Old School* than the complete filmography of Harvey Keitel's cock. And while it's evident from his clothed work in *Old School* and *Elf* that Ferrell's much more than a sketch comic, that he's a strong big-screen presence and an actor ripe for grown-up roles, not to mention a huge back-end chunk of change if he does *Old School 2*, the real question is –

Did they have to shave your ass, Will?

"No, no. It was just ready to go."

No makeup?

"I don't think there was, and now that you bring that up, I think I missed an opportunity. I should have requested powder."

Did you have an ass double? You know, a stunt ass?

"There might've been. I bet there was a stunt ass standing by in case I chickened out and lost it. They must come across that, where someone's like, 'I can't do this. I didn't realize you meant *totally* naked.' So I think they did have someone."

The critics loved you, Will, but they dissed your ass.

I know, I know. I got beat up a little bit. I didn't think it looked that bad."

No, not bad. Maybe a trifle doughy.

"But I got comments from the actresses. I mean, maybe they were just being nice, but across the board they were like, 'You got a cute butt, Will.' So that's the only critique I need to hear."

Here's the truth: He's sane, this guy. And *sweet*,

the sort of square who met the woman who later became his wife – Swedish bombshell/actress Viveca (she's really an art house auctioneer, but Will asked for a favor: "There was a picture of Viv and me in *People* at the *Old School* premiere, and it said, 'Will Ferrell with his wife, Swedish actress Viveca.' *Wow*. A one-name Swedish actress. I want you to perpetuate that")--dated her briefly, and then actually stayed pals with her for six years before their romance bloomed.

I knew when I met her: She's the one. I'm just gonna wait. I'm just gonna wait for her to come around the bend."

Nowhere in Ferrellville do you sniff the self-loathing and nervous narcissm that fuel a standard-issue funnyman. *Anchorman* is six days from wrapping, and the cast and crew have been working twelve-hour days all week, but you don't just visit the set – built inside the shell of an old vacated furniture store in Glendale – you *hang out*, along with family, friends, and producers' kids so young, they've yet to sprout their horns.

"Usually, six days out, everyone's really intense and stressed out," says Christina Applegate, who plays Ferrell's love interest. "*This* job – not one day of yelling. No one has raised their voices. It's the best job I've ever had. Will's surrounded in okayness. He's just grateful to be able to do what he wants to do."

Fine, but what's it like kissing the mustache?

"It's gross and exciting all at the same time. It's horrible. It's *so* disturbing, I've had nightmares about it."

Ferrell and McKay waited years to shoot this script. When their chance finally came – due in large part to *Old School*'s box office success and Ferrell's burgeoning star power – they didn't want to spill a drop of fun.

"I think some people put so much weight on it that it becomes overbearing," Ferrell says. "We always had the philosophy that if we ever got to do this ourselves, we wanted to avoid creating an atmosphere of pomposity. We just can't believe that these things we thought of three years ago – now we're actually gettin' to do 'em. Hopefully you're creating stuff that will make people laugh, but we're not changing world history – and now that I've said that, I'll probably be driving a UPS truck two years from now."

Unlikely. Ferrell's heading to New York City soon to star in Woody Allen's next movie. After that, he's starring with Ed Harris in a small, dark film by off-Broadway playwright Adam Rapp. He's also being mentioned as the lead if the latest attempt to film a version of *A Confederacy of Dunces* ever gets off the ground. And he has read that Sofia Coppola's a big Ferrell fan.

"But I won't work with her," he says. "I'm just letting you know, I will *never* do that."

And, of course, DreamWorks would like to churn out an Old School sequel, but Ferrell's not sure that reincarnating Frank the Tank is what he wants to do.

"It'd be great to be in a position where you can make choices regardless of money. My tastes are always gonna lead me to go for the amazing project where I'm being paid in Turkish cantaloupes. So now that I'm in the back of some peoples' minds as maybe having the potential to do other things, we'll see. You know, it's tough, a comedian saying, 'Yes, I would like to cross over and do this other thing.' You run the risk of sounding obnoxious. That having been said, *Yes.* I would. I would *love* it."

He's sane. He's sweet. And he loves his

dogs. He and Viveca have three – a Lab, a boxer, and a pointer – and he breaks the news that they're expecting a human baby, their first, in March.

"We didn't want to do a press release or anything," he says, half-apologizing.

And that, along with work, just about covers it. He's too busy working to plan another marathon. He isn't returning his trainer's phone calls.

No other hobbies? No interests?

"I don't have the humidor or an antique-pistol collection. Not yet. You know what? I swear to God, you know what's fun for me? To go through my pile of bills and statements, put a game on and shred documents."

Shred documents?

"Yeah, shred documents. That's a great afternoon for me."

What are you shredding? Scripts?

"No – bank statements, those sorts of things. I love shredding documents."

What kind of shredder?

"It's not high powered. We've gone through about three of 'em."

Is it one of those that sits on the wastebasket?

"Sits on the wastebasket, yeah."

Then what?

"You throw it out."

No special steps between shredding and throwing out?

"No, it goes right into the recycling. So that's a hobby."

C'mon, Shredding documents is not a hobby.

"Well, it's *like* a hobby."

The last time I see Ferrell, he's in

New York City to do Conan O'Brien's tenth anniversary special. He's talking about the pleasures of working with Bob Newhart, who plays his North Pole papa in *Elf*.

"We would wrestle every day during the shooting – full body, Greco-Roman. Don't let Bob fool you; he's spry. He'll get you in a headlock quicker than you'd think. I would just jab him in the eyes. That's not fair, I know, but Bob is similar to a wolverine---pound for pound the fiercest animal on the planet. You don't wanna get down on the ground with him, so I would disable him that way."

It's late afternoon, and he's having a bite to eat, sitting alone in a dressing room wolfing a plate of take-out chicken. The good news is the mustache is long gone. The bad news? He's dressed as a lap-dancing leprechaun: black shoes, green kneescocks, an emerald green satin shirt, a matching Speedo, and – thank God – a robe. Although he happily flings it open to prove that he's still wearing the Speedo.

Ferrell's bit for the show – reprising a former appearance – consists of humping Conan's leg and sliding down it to shine Conan's shoe by rubbing it violently with his ass crack.

Seriously, Will, is there anything you won't do?

"Absolutely. The photo shoot we just did for you guys – the photographer had the idea of doing The Thinker, but totally nude. I was like, 'Sam, it's a great idea, but I just don't wanna do it.'"

Dude, you just dry-humped Conan O'Brien's shoe for an audience of millions.

"I don't know why there's a difference. I guess because it's a lasting image in a magazine, and this just seems more fleeting."

By the way, I saw the Ping-Pong photos. Nice camel toe.

"Ah," he says with a wicked grin. "I didn't know that I had one going. But it's not a bad thing. That's kind of the essence of who I am. That's good. That's okay."

Chapter Eleven

Drew Carey

Clevelander

In real life, he's not that fat; I myself would go no further than "husky," although when he tilts back his head, a thickish roll of adipose tissue forms on the back of his neck, a stubble-dotted crest that I recognize as the distinctive marking of a native of Cleveland's west side. He is light on his feet – we are bowling, as Cleveland men must – and full of vim. Still, by the criteria of Los Angeles and prime-time network television, where a granite ass is only slightly less de rigueur than a development deal, he's a ZIP code.

He *feels* fat, surely, or he wouldn't keep saying he wants to drop some weight. Drew Carey announces a diet nearly as often as Sean Penn threatens to stop acting, and with equal credibility. He has just signed with Disney to play the role of Geppetto in a telemusical version of *Pinocchio*, and this has inspired reform. Somewhat.

"I quit drinking because I want to lose weight for that," he says, although, given the three beers he says he drank the night before, a few beers in New Orleans over the past weekend, and some beers in Las Vegas the weekend before that, the meaning of "quit drinking" is not quite literal.

When the lane wench asks if we'd like anything to eat, Carey orders two hot dogs with fries and a Coke.

"I'm hungry," he explains with a shrug.

We are bowling for a buck a pin. Carey brings his own ball, with DREW etched above the finger holes. His bag also holds a chamois cradle to blot the excess oil from his ball, a spotless pair of shoes – ivory, to match his bag – and a little hand cushion. He could have a leprechaun in there to jump out and fellate him between games and it wouldn't help much: His approach is a stuttering mince, his hook is a spin, and, besides, his luck is bad.

Down forty dollars going into the third game, he is scowling, all business. Off his feed, even.

"You can have that other hot dog if you want," he mutters.

The hot dog is awful, and the fries suck, too. Worse, a fed and focused Carey blasts a 180 to drop his debt down to fifteen smackers. Suddenly, I'm down twenty-eight pins going into the final game.

"You're not doing this on purpose, are you?" he asks with a grin.

No way.

"Because I've *got* the money," he cackles.

"Two knights are walking through

the forest" – Carey loves this joke, but stopped telling it onstage: Nobody laughed – "and they come across a milkmaid. One lifts his visor and says, 'Pray thee, fair maid, have you seen a black knight with a red cross on a white shield and a crimson banner?'

"'No, my lord.'

"'Very well, then. Go about God's business.'

"They go another mile down the road, and they come across a blacksmith. 'Pray thee, stout smithy, have you seen a black knight with a red cross on a white shield and a crimson banner?'

"'No, my lord.'

"'Very well, then. Go about God's business.'

"They go about a quarter mile down the road, and one knight lifts his visor, looks at his buddy, and says, 'Where the *fuck* is Frank?'"

He *does* have the money: After our

fifth and final game he changes a Ben Fathead at the cashier's desk and forks over eleven clams to pay off his losses. Then we hike to the deli next door, where he orders up a bowl of chicken noodle soup and another

Coke. All this – even with the bowling-alley tube-steak and french fries – is at least a minor improvement over his routine interview fare, a double cheeser at Bob's Big Boy. And there is moola where his maw is: He had a two-year, million-dollar deal with A&W Restaurants to purvey grease to the masses in regional commercials, until a company weasel saw an episode of his sitcom last November featuring Carey cavorting at a McDonald's in Beijing, whereupon A&W announced the deal was off.

"I was really sad about that," says Carey between spoonfuls of soup. "But I didn't eat at the McDonald's on the show. I grabbed a fry off a kid's plate, but I didn't get any of the food. When I was in China, I ate at A&W almost every day – there was one around the corner from where we were staying. I like the company. I thought we had a good relationship."

Carey is forty now; his father, who died when Drew was eight, had heart problems, as did one grandfather. "I think about that a lot," he says. "I don't want to die like my dad did. That's one reason I want to lose weight and start eating better after this."

What he means by "after this" – this lifetime, this TV season, this bowl of soup – I have no idea. In his book, *Dirty Jokes and Beer*, Carey promised to lose forty pounds. "I'm going to lose the weight," he wrote, "get a light tan, and get my back waxed." His visible skin is still Oreo filling, and, though I haven't got the stomach to ask for a peek at his back, I'd wager he's tufted. Small wonder, then, that after a decade of sitcomedy dominated by that Nike-shod paragon of anal retention, Jerry Seinfeld, the prim and bloodless *Frasier*, and the latte-lapping phantasmata of *Friends*, Middle America has come to embrace this eminently flawed yutz.

But a gut, a crew cut, and a dorky pair of glasses hardly explain Drew Carey's rise from a $300-per-night stand-up to a $200,000-per-episode TV star. In 1986, Carey was fresh from six years in the Marines when he started to work as a comic. A couple of *Star Search* gigs got him some notice, but the big break came on *The Tonight Show* in 1991, when Carson waved him over to the guest couch.

"I felt like I was in show business," says Carey. "Nobody would ever ask me again, 'What are you gonna do after the comedy thing dies down?' I wouldn't have to hear that bullshit anymore. I was a comic, and no one could take it away from me."

He moved to Los Angeles, living in motels and storing his books and clothes in a Datsun sedan while he waited for the next best thing. "Then I bought a station wagon, because I could put more stuff in it," he says.

Cutting Room Floor: Carey

THE PITCH: You can take the homeboy out of Cleveland, ply him with money, fame, and women, and mentioning John Elway will still make him bawl like a baby.

SCENE: A bowling alley on Ventura Boulevard in Encino. It's a midweek evening, crowded and loud, and Drew Carey and I are bowling – and the fact that this feels like the most natural thing in the world to be doing strikes me as strange. He's got the top- rated show on TV, he's impossible not to recognize – a few folks come up for autographs or a handshake – but Carey's just a guy out to roll a few lines and grab a bite to eat, normal as toast.

BACKSTORY: Everybody's from somewhere, but being from Cleveland is different. The mix of pride and shame fuels a rage that knows no bounds, and when two Cleveland sports fans meet, that wrath can reach a boil at the drop of a name – John Elway's, say. Some of this I put in the story; what's not there is the pure sadness.

When I asked Carey if he ever cried after a loss, he said, "Yeah – 'The

"Stand-up I only did because I was good at it, and I wanted to do something that I was good at, but the sitcom thing – I'd look around and see other people get sitcoms and think, 'Fuck, *I'm* as funny as they are. *I'm* as talented.' A lot of it was just me having this chip on my shoulder."

Ah, the chip. Unmasked in the spotlight, the stand-up comic has the Freud-baffling task to *kill*, to goad and revile without mercy and with glee, to detonate into laughter the bleakest fear at the dark center of the soul. *Look at me*, says the stand-up, I am ridiculous and pathetic, but not nearly as ridiculous and pathetic as my wife, my mother, Bill Clinton, the Polacks, that faggot, airline food – and not nearly as ridiculous and pathetic as *you*, who need me to do this for you. Without the chip – without that undoable knot of yearning and fear and rage – you simply won't endure the work, much less go out there and slay them. Without the chip, you won't outlast the hecklers and the bookers and the people who came to

Drive'" – the 1986 AFC Championship Game. "I wouldn't cry at regular games," he added, "but games when you could've won, should've won..." and his voice trailed off and we just sat there. "We were the better team," he said finally, with a hurt fury any Clevelander would know in an instant.

CONFLICT: Larry the Cable Guy makes a cameo at the end of the story, long before he became a household name, if your house is a trailer. His agent called me after the story ran, mad about how I portrayed Larry. For one thing, I was told, he doesn't drink, and I say he had "half a load on." And I said he had long hair, but he doesn't. I had the wrong guy, the agent said, or I'd done an awful injustice to a struggling comic. They were considering some kind of legal action, the agent said, but suggested that maybe I could square things by writing a profile of Larry the Cable Guy."

WISH I'D WRITTEN: Beyond the untellable joke – trust me: You really don't want to know – I wish I'd had a crystal ball. Who could've guessed that this lovably foul-mouthed comic, a man whose passions included porn and strippers, would one day succeed Bob Barker as host of *The Price Is Right?*

drink and chat, the bad sex and lousy food and filthy toilets, and the friends and family who ask what you'll do after you finally realize that you're a failure.

And even with the chip, and a pair of balls big enough to keep on playing it, the odds are overwhelming that you won't make it, that you'll wind up selling shoes. A thousand stand-ups die slow deaths nightly on the Chuckle Hut circuit, all thinking, "Fuck, *I'm* as funny as Drew Carey" – and who's to say that a hundred of 'em aren't? – and every one of them knows in his heart that he will wind up selling shoes.

If comedy isn't pretty, stand-up is a pit of deathless hell. But Drew Carey had two major advantages that kept him clawing to the top: He is from Cleveland, where deathless hell is part of the landscape, and he was sexually molested when he was nine years old. . . .

"Kid's walkin' down the street,

and he finds a welder's mask. He goes, 'Oh, cool – a welder's mask,' and he picks it up and puts it on, and he's walkin' along, flippin' it up and down, when a Cadillac pulls up.

"'*Pssst,* kid, get in the car.'

"Kid gets in, and he's ridin' along with this old man, playin' with the welder's mask, and the old man says, 'Kid, you know what frottage is?'

"Kid goes, 'No, sure don't,' flippin' the mask up and down, and the old man says, 'Hey, kid, you know what mutual masturbation is?'

"Kid goes, 'Naw, never heard of it' – flip, flip, flip – and the old man leans over and says, 'Hey, kid, you know what pedophilia is?'

"The kid looks at the guy and says, 'Hey, buddy, listen – I'm not really a welder.'"

If that joke offends you – his favorite

pedophilia joke is far more grim, so brutal that I'm not repeating it until after this section – Drew Carey wants you to understand something: He doesn't care.

"I'm not gonna stop making jokes because some whiner can't take it. Too bad."

The Drew Carey Show has drawn fire from groups as diverse as the Anti-Bigotry Committee of the Polish American Congress and the Ark Trust, an animal-protection organization that gave him a Foe Paw award for mocking antifur activists. He is unmoved.

"Fuck them. Every guy from Poland has to be a fucking engineer or lawyer now or it's insulting? Go fuck yourself if that's how you think. Who gives a shit if you get a Foe Paw? *Who gives a shit?* They don't make a bit of fucking difference."

It's this transparency, the willingness to speak his mind as if he had nothing to lose and no image to burnish, that separates Carey from his Kramdenesque, everyshlub persona – and from a generation of stand-ups-turned-stars who have cashed in their chips to shill for American Express or guest-edit *The New Yorker*. When Carey took a $3 million book advance, back when the doyens of publishing were still cramming cash up the crack of every stand-up with a TV show, he didn't hire a ghostwriter or fill pages with his old routines; he actually *wrote* the thing, including one chapter titled "101 Big-Dick Jokes," a handful of semiautobiographical short stories, and a matter-of-fact discussion of his molestation, his depressions, and his two long-ago suicide attempts.

Even as a touring comic, Carey battled the darkness. "I'd lie in the hotel room all day," he has said. "Eating pizza, watching TV. My whole day was to prepare for those forty-five minutes onstage. Sometimes I'd eat a meal and think, 'Oh, that cheese isn't exactly right. What else would you expect from this lousy world?' After my act, I'd go to the hotel bar and cry." Carey never saw a therapist or took an antidepressant; he used nothing but self-help books and affirmation tapes to turn his life around.

Today, Carey may be the hottest star in television comedy. In 1998 alone, he made $45.5 million. With the half-hour improvisation show *Whose Line Is It Anyway?* – Carey is host and co-producer – following his sitcom, ABC has deeded him an entire hour of prime-time Wednesday real estate, and, with three seasons left to run on his seven-year contract for *The Drew Carey Show*, he's calling his own shots.

"If I do an eighth year," he says, "I know how much I want."

How much?

"A *shitload* of money."

Now that he knows he'll never have to sell shoes, Carey worries instead about losing his chip, about ditching the absurd struggles of everyday life for the airless sphere of celebrity.

"I noticed that when different comedians got famous and successful, they quit being funny. What they talk about isn't stuff I relate to. They quit going to buy their own food, they don't walk the dog anymore. I was always guarding against that. You can't live in your own world just because you're making money."

Then I hear him talk about "key demos" – as in "men eighteen to forty-nine."

Key demos? That's fancy talk from a west-side stand-up.

"It is weird. It's not something I saw myself doing years ago, but I'm doing it, so I might as well learn about it," he says. "I did this all for the money, you know. I think it's to my detriment. I think I've changed in certain ways I don't like. I used to think I liked practical jokes. I think I can take any kind of joke. But somebody played a practical joke on me at work – I had to go do stand-up at Caesars in Vegas. So this is a Friday, and I had my carry-on bag, and somebody put a ten-inch dildo in my bag – they stuck nails under the surface of it so it would show at the X-ray machine. So I go to the Burbank airport, and they bring my bag back to take a second look. I don't know why they're doin' it, but it doesn't bother me.

Then I'm walkin' away and I hear the guy goin', 'Isn't that the guy from the TV show?' But I'm used to people talking about me when I'm right there. I get to Caesars Palace, and I'm in my room with my date for the weekend, unpacking, and that's what I find at the top of my bag. I have to explain to her that this was not mine. 'Honey, look what I happened to find in my bag.'

"At first, I kind of laughed it off. Then I thought, 'What if I did get caught with it?' I don't want that in the tabloids – that's the last thing I want. I was pissed. I really was pissed. I went back, and all day Monday I didn't talk to anybody, all day Tuesday I didn't talk to anybody. I was waiting for somebody to come up and apologize. I just carried this anger with me the whole next week.

"I ended up having to apologize to them for being so angry. I should've never acted like that. They were just playing a joke. Five years ago, that would've been the funniest joke. I would've thought, 'Oh, what a great prank.' I would've planned to get 'em back. Just because I'm on TV and I'm worried about how much I'm worth and what'll affect the ratings – I got even madder at myself."

What's the worst thing about – no. I'm sorry, I can't. The other joke is just too grim.

Does the term "Red Right 88" mean any –

"Oh, my God," Carey gasps before I can finish the question, a forkful of fettuccine Alfredo frozen above his plate. Tonight, we're in the upstairs dining room at the Improv, where Carey takes the stage each Thursday night to hone his improv chops with assorted friends and castmates from *Whose Line Is It Anyway?*, but I did not come here to eat or see the show: I have a job to do. I need to determine whether Drew Carey truly is the ur-Clevelander he portrays on his TV show.

The test has three parts; Red Right 88 is the easy one. Even a half-assed Cleveland Browns fan knows that Red Right 88 was the pass play called by Browns head coach Sam Rutigliano on second-and-nine at the Oakland thirteen-yard line with less than a minute to play and Cleveland down 14-12 on January 4, 1981, in a playoff game still known back home as the Ice Bowl – the windchill factor at kickoff was minus-35 degrees – when a *fucking field goal* would've won the game and quarterback Brian Sipe wobbled a duck into the end zone and into the waiting arms of a Raider with forty-nine ticks on the clock.

Carey puts down his fork – you know he's hurting – and recalls precisely where he was the moment that Rutigliano's brain and Sipe's arm went dead: in a betting hall in Vegas, where he lived at the time. "Union Plaza," he says, hollow-voiced. "I could point to the exact spot in the corner of the room where I was standing."

Not bad, but not enough. Hell, you mention Red Right 88 to my mama and she'll tell you the expiration date on the box of the Entenmann's coffee ring she was eating that afternoon, and then she'll slap you red. You can come from Cleveland and not *be* a Clevelander: It's too easy, however bizarre the choice may seem to an outsider, for a man to wear the seal-brown-and-orange chip of yearning, despair, and impotent rage as a mere accessory. But to be a true Clevelander is to suffer deeply and without surcease, and to suffer thus is to be a true Clevelander.

As excoriating as the interception was, the true Clevelander is more nauseated to this day by what Sam Rutigliano – fired not long after and last seen coaching football at Jerry Falwell's Liberty College – said to Brian Sipe after the interception, as eighty thousand heartsick fans pried their frozen asses from their seats and headed into the dusk of another endless winter. Hence, part two, which I repeat now to Carey:

"I love you, Brian. I love you."

"Shut *up*," he pleads. "I've got a comedy show to do in an hour."

The last part of the test is three syllables: John. El. Way.

"I hate Elway. Hate him. To this day, I've never played Denver – fuck 'em. If they want entertainment, let 'em watch the Broncos. I hate myself for sayin' it – it's really horrible – but fuck him. Fucking Bucky Bucktooth. I'm sure he's the nicest guy in the world. It's not his fault he's playin' for Denver and he's competitive. In reality, I really don't wish anyone any ill will. But fuck him. I hope he breaks his leg. I hope he has grandkids, a long life – oh, *God*, I hate him. And Michael Jordan.

"I don't like Michael Jordan, either. Fuck him, too. Him and 'the Shot.' Beatin' the Cavs every time. I'm glad he's retiring. I don't like Terry Bradshaw, Ahmad Rashad – he made that catch in Minnesota – I hold it against all these motherfuckers, anybody who ever beat Cleveland in a game. I hold it against you. I take it as a personal thing. Fuck you all."

Supper is done, the test finished. We are silent awhile, the Lake Erie wind howling through our hearts.

When Carey takes the stage, the full house

roars. He machine-guns through five vintage minutes of his stand-up act –
with two TV shows, he hasn't written any new material in a while – and
brings up the rest of the troupe. Carey participates, but it's clear that he's
an improv apprentice. After years of commanding the stage alone, Carey
has to work at sharing space, at listening, at trusting his mates. His biggest
laugh comes when he lifts his shirt while standing in profile, displaying
more belly in one second than most southern Californians see in a lifetime.

After the show, out on Melrose Avenue, Carey is just hanging out,
greeting fans and giggling with his cronies, when a long-haired guy with half
a load on wanders up to him. His name is Dan Whitney, and he's a comic,
too, working out of Florida at small clubs as a doofus character he calls Larry
the Cable Guy. He and Carey go back a ways, and they shake hands and
share the one about the hillbilly who meets a professor at the local college.

"Whaddaya teach?" the hick asks.

"Logic."

"*Logic?* What the hell's that?"

"Perhaps it would be better if I demonstrated it for you. Tell me, sir,
do you own a Weed Eater?"

"Sure do."

"Well, then, logic tells me if you own a Weed Eater, you have a yard
and, therefore, a house. Furthermore, if you have a house, it's logical that
you have a family, including a wife. Indeed, proceeding by means of logic,
the fact that you own a Weed Eater means that you are, in fact, a hetero-
sexual."

"Gawd*damn,*" says the hillbilly. "That logic of yers is sump'n."

Back home, the hillbilly's talking with his neighbor about the professor of logic.

"*Logic?*" the neighbor asks. "What the hell's that?"

"Lemme show ya," says the hillbilly. "You got a Weed Eater?"

"Nope."

"Faggot."

When Carey heads back into the club, Whitney turns to me. He
wants me to know that he's booked for a week in Albany, New York, where
Larry the Cable Guy is apparently huge.

"Fuck," he mutters, shaking his head, shouldering his chip. "*I'm* funnier than Drew Carey."

I don't have the heart to tell him that he's probably not, and that I
take a size 12.

Chapter Twelve

Ann Coulter

Heartthrob

"Pick me up at 7," she said.

Late summer, New York City, and I'm out on the town with Ann Coulter, ultraright queen of spleen, the bosomy scourge of liberals everywhere, and the one person in America who feels that maybe the Swift Boat Veterans for Truth went a bit easy on John Kerry. Ann's the sassy gal whose tenure as a *National Review* columnist ended in 2001 after she suggested that the proper U. S. response to September 11 should include forcibly converting the Muslims – not *every* Muslim, mind you, just the naughty ones – to Christianity.

I like Ann. Not because I agree with her on much, but because she's a good writer, fearless and funny. She wields words like a shiv, and she doesn't give a shit who gets spattered by the blood. Coulter's easy on the eyes, too; that counts, of course. You won't see me asking Phyllis Schlafly out – or, for that matter, Maureen Dowd.

I like her also because Coulter is the Ultimate *Shiksa*, a species of which I'm inordinately fond, a yellow-haired, God-fearing, mom-and-pop-hugging Wasp from patrician New Canaan, Connecticut. She graduated from Cornell and the University of Michigan law school, then practiced law until the publication of *High Crimes and Misdemeanors*, her best-selling Clinton-must-go screed, in 1998. She's the kicky, self-confident sort of girl who'll wear a purple miniskirt to give a speech on the evils of late-term abortion. She's a nonfiction, star-spangled version of Alexander Portnoy's Thereal McCoy, and tonight she's all mine.

So I've hired a limo. I've showered, shaved, and shat. I've brought a single pale-pink rose for her. And I'm nervous as hell.

"A rose!" she squeals. "Oh, thank you!" She seems honestly tickled. Her voice is girlish, her smile wide, her eyes bright and blue-green. She's wearing tight jeans, a light top not far from the shade of my rose, and a small cross on a chain 'round her narrow, well-scrubbed neck. Into her forties now, she looks a smooth ten years younger.

"Thank *you*," I reply. "It's so nice of you to join me."

"No, thank *you*," she insists. "A ball game! I'm so excited!"

"Me, too!" I squeak. "It's gonna be *great!*"

Too loud: I see the driver glance at me in the mirror. My mind goes dim. I feel myself blushing. I am a dolt.

Why I'm so nervous I don't know. This isn't a real boy-girl date, after all, so I'm not worried about trying to dip my wick. And I'm hardly cowed by female beauty; in the line of duty, I've dallied with four certified supermodels – five if you count Yogi Berra. Besides, Coulter's politics don't enrage me as they do my wife, friends, and colleagues.

True, I'm a lifelong lefty – I voted for Nader in 1996 and 2000, and I'd love to see a viable third party born in our land – but I'm also a fifty something dad in a leafy north-Jersey suburb, paying property taxes out the ying and fretful about the next shoe bomb dropping. In any case, I'm not debating her; I just thought it'd be cool to see a Mets game – the Yankees are on a road trip, and I'd rather eat dirt than put a penny in George Steinbrenner's pocket anyway – with a pundit so deeply loathed by nearly everyone I know that they've never bothered to read a single word of her work.

"I was at the office earlier," I say, "and when I told some of the folks there about going out with you tonight, they were, um, ah..." I can't manage to end the sentence. I'm thinking about what one of them asked me: What are you planning to say to that *bitch?*

"Hopping mad," she says, finishing my sentence.

"Yep. They were furious."

"You know, if I wrote about how all sex is rape, if I were Elizabeth

Wurtzel writing about Prozac, or Naomi Wolf, I would have been on the cover of every one of these magazines. They pretend to write about serious things while putting chicks in short skirts on their covers. I've written three nonfiction best-sellers *and* I'll put on a miniskirt for them. But no. No. I don't exist."

She laughs – low, throaty, a lovely, vampish laugh – and crosses her long legs.

"One of the magazines – it may have been yours – after 9/11 compared me to Osama bin Laden. And my publisher was shocked. It was the first time they had to deal with publishing a right-wing loony, and I really thought it was adorable watching their reaction to the press I was getting. Because it's all I ever get."

That was *Esquire*, all right, but I don't tell Ann that. Instead, I mention that the Left's venomous disgust for George W. Bush sounds much like what the Right felt for Clinton.

"I've thought about this," Coulter says, "and I think it's different. We thought Clinton was pretty funny. It was a more lighthearted approach. I mean, he was a horny hick in the Oval Office; you had to laugh about that. I really didn't mind his policies. He was about as good as Bob Dole would've been. With Bush there is something more angry. The hatred of Bush I think goes back more to the Nixon era in '72. They see him as the focus of evil, and I can't say I ever really thought that about Clinton. I don't think he had enough energy. He was getting too many blow jobs."

That wicked, wanton laugh again. Too many blow jobs – a tough concept to grasp, and I can't think of anything to say. Must. Not. Think. About. Blow jobs. I hated Richard Nixon – Reagan, too, come to think of it, although I had a big lump in my throat and tears in my eyes watching his funeral on TV. Blow jobs. No. Think about Michael Moore. Jeez, I miss the Cold War. Blow jobs. Try Noam Chomsky – ah, that's better. BLOW JOBS.

Man, it's quiet back here.

"I'm very confused right now," I say. "Politically," I quickly add.

"Come to the dark side," Ann Coulter says, grinning, her voice husky, tinged with mock drama, her reedy fingers caressing the air like a mesmerist's.

I laugh. But I'm beginning to see why I'm so nervous: I've already been skulking – quietly, cautiously, guiltily – down the dark-side backstreets, just me and my knuckle-dragging inner Zell. Oh, I'll bad-mouth the Bush tax cuts, but I don't mind more money in our retirement and college funds. I'll admit the Iraq war is a horrific botch, but I'd secretly love to see

Cutting Room Floor: Coulter

THE PITCH: A limo. A single rose. Two great seats at Shea to see the Mets. A blind date with a pit viper.

SCENE: Me and Ann walking from our limousine to our entry gate Shea Stadium. Heads turn in her direction; not because she's Ann Coulter – how many hard-core Fox News viewers are also Mets fans? – but thanks to her long blond hair. And her legs. At the Shea gate, Security searches her little bag; I get wanded. "I don't think there's a better sight in life than a ballfield," Ann says as we head inside. "I'm so happy."

BACKSTORY: One month each year, *Esquire* devotes itself to a Women We Love issue. It embodies, at least for me, some degree of institutional shame, like Black History month; it is more about lust than love anyway, or surely we'd have run a Ruth Bader Ginsburg profile by now. My Ann Coulter pitch to the boss was plain: Let's have a good time with a woman we fear and loathe.

CONFLICT: My wonderful, hard-left wife was mad before, during, and after my date with Ann. I quickly had to get rid of the Coulter doll who appears at the story's end; I hung on to a book or two of hers, but even that feels as if I'm hiding porn. And there were at least two Esquire editors who were deeply, vocally upset that we were putting Coulter's name in the magazine without attacking her.

WISH I'D WRITTEN: What no one who despises Ann Coulter can see – or admit – is that she's more of a comedian than a polemicist, and she knows that. When I said I thought her work was funny, she said, "That's the most important thing. I've told my editor – if we have to cut words, if it's a choice between an important factual point and a joke, we're going with the joke."

the lessons we learn there put to use in Tehran and Pyongyang. And due process for the detainees? Yo, fuck the detainees. String 'em all up – and make room on the gibbet for the moral-equivalency crowd moaning about how any abrogation of civil liberty means Al Qaeda has won.

None of this comes out my mouth, but it's crackling like a Klan bonfire inside my head. I feel faint. Woozy. And a little dirty. No more politics for me tonight, I decide. Stick to baseball.

It's a beautiful night for a ball game. The weather is perfect, our seats are great – ten rows behind the Mets dugout, club seating, meaning they'll bring us food – and the Mets have chosen this fine evening to play as if they cared about winning.

Ann's a Yankees fan. "I was at game seven of the playoffs between the Yankees and the Red Sox last fall," she says as we settle in. "Other than the night Clinton was impeached, it was the greatest moment of my life. I didn't even care who won the World Series as long as we beat the Red Sox. That was unbelievable."

I despise the Yanks – it's tribal: I'm from Cleveland – but I can't hold this against Ann Coulter, especially when it turns out that she knows the game of baseball. As the Mets pound out six runs in the first inning, Tom Glavine, the aging southpaw, chops an RBI single off the third-baseman's glove.

"Glavine can still hit," I muse. "Not great, but better than the average pitcher."

"That's like being the tallest building in Skokie," Ann says. "I'm against pitchers hitting. I know it's not pure and conservative, but it's really hard being a pitcher. It's not like any other job. You have to have an incredibly powerful arm; they ruin their arms after a few years. To expect somebody who's really good at that to also have this other skill – besides the fact that I like a lot of hits. It makes it a fun game. On the other hand, pitchers have told me it's good to have the other pitcher up there so you can get back at him if he's someone who hits yours. Which I must say is a good argument."

I know guys who fancy themselves baseball cognoscenti who couldn't discuss any aspect of the vital, highly charged DH debate with such clarity and concision.

"You've never been married, have you?" I ask.

"No," Ann says. "I want to, but it has to be the right guy."

"And even then," I say, "it's never a walk in the park."

In the glum, awkward silence that follows – unless you're either Dr. Phil or planning to propose, talking about marriage with an unmarried forty-year-old woman is *not* a good idea – I fish a Commit lozenge from my pocket and pop it.

"Nicotine," I explain.

She fairly shrieks. "I have two patches on right now – and Nicorette gum in my purse! I quit last October and I don't feel any better – no better whatsoever. Plus, it's like a miracle drug. When you're upset, it calms you down."

"That's the fundamental problem with the war on drugs," I say. "They work so well."

"I keep *haranguing* doctors, demanding that they admit to me that this is just another Alar scare. Remember Alar on apples? This is going to pass, and then they'll admit it was never bad. I keep cigarettes around – in case there's a nuclear attack and I know I only have a few days to live, I'm just gonna sit there and smoke."

The nicotine peps me up, maybe too much. When we decide to order a bite to eat—"I've been looking forward to a hot dog all day," Ann says – I can't restrain my inner Zell.

"Freedom fries?" I ask.

"Definitely some freedom fries," says Ann. "I smelled them. It was a delightful smell."

But Zell wants more. "Shall we order?" I ask. "Or must we consult first with the French?"

She giggles. "I know it's an old joke now," she says, "but I laugh every time I hear it. The levels of terrorist warnings they have in France: run, hide, surrender, collaborate."

Yeah, baby. The Mets are still knocking the ball around the yard; Glavine's still painting the outside corner. By the end of the seventh, the Mets are up 9-1, Ann and I have put away a footlong each, an order of fries, an order of sushi, and two big Diet Pepsis, and I'm admitting how embarrassed I am to live in a state whose governor has just simultaneously fied the closet and resigned for fear of a lawsuit threatened by his Israeli boy toy.

"We thank you, New Jersey," Ann cackles. "That is the greatest scandal ever."

"Did you watch his press conference?" I ask her. " 'I am a gay American' – what the hell does that even mean in that context? With his wife standing there next to him? And his parents?"

Ann arches a thin eyebrow. "I was pointing out to everyone that John Edwards has had no comment," she says.

Whoa. Now I get it. Not that Edwards is gay – he's only an Ashley Wilkes – model retrosexual – but I now see precisely what I'm doing with Ann Coulter tonight.

I should've realized it while we were wolfing our franks – Ann's a mustard *and* ketchup girl, by the way – when I was confessing how sick and tired I am of feeling guilty for driving an SUV and making a decent buck and how the Democrats are just like the Arizona Diamondbacks now – a bloated, stinking corpse of a ball club – and yeah, the First Amendment's lovely, but the Second is very, very underrated, and I've got a pistol-grip Mossberg 12-gauge in a cabinet at home that'll fuckin'-A back me up on it. Hell, I should've grasped the ugly truth about the right-wing dog in me right then:

Some guys can't get what they want at home. Could be the little woman won't give it to 'em. Could be they're ashamed to ask for it. Could be they're simply the breed of hound that every now and then needs to sniff some strange. Could be lots of things, but one thing's for *damn* sure: I'm out here tonight for the sole purpose of talking some nasty, back-alley politics with none other than Ann Coulter.

And, God help me, I'm getting off. I'm loving every second of it.

I'd like to tell you – or myself – that I pulled

out in time. I can't, because I didn't. I wish I could say that I didn't really mean those terrible things I was saying, that it was all Coulterish voodoo, but that isn't true, either. I meant every word, and I would've kept banging away all night.

Lucky for me – I guess – Ann had to meet a friend.

"I wouldn't tell you this if it was a real date," she said as we headed back into Manhattan after the game, "but I'm meeting for drinks with Matt Drudge."

"Matt Drudge? I'm getting dumped for *Drudge*?"

I'd like to tell you that I was feigning outrage – abandoned for Matt Drudge, the ur-blogger who first ran with the Monica story and forever changed the course of dry-cleaning history – but I wasn't feigning, not deep down inside.

Ann, she just laughed.

I'd like to tell you that I maintained some semblance of manly dignity. Nah.

"So," I said meekly, "it wasn't a real date. But was it a good date?"

"Oh, a *fabulous* date," said Ann. "A rose, a car..."

"And would an aging, portly lefty get a second date? Theoretically, I mean?"

"Oh, yeah. A baseball game, good conversation, *and* you're on the cusp of coming to the dark side. That's really the crucial thing, you see. People always ask me if I'd date a liberal. No – you can't date a full liberal. I can't start from ground zero on this stuff. But you I could bring to the dark side."

On her way out of the limo, she reached back and shook my hand. I didn't even rate a peck on the cheek.

It's all right now. A few days later, she arrived; in fact, she's standing on my desk at home right now, a few inches from my keyboard, wearing a tight black skirt suit and black spike heels: my twelve-inch Ann Coulter action figure, complete with flowing blond hair. I ordered it from the Conservative Book Service and I put it on my expense account.

It talks, too. In her actual voice.

"Why *not* go to war just for oil?" asks Ann when I push her diaphragm. "We need oil. What do Hollywood celebrities imagine fuels their private jets? How do they think their cocaine is delivered to them?"

My wife shouts up the stairs.

"Did you call me? Do you need anything?"

No thanks, sweetie. Me and Ann, we're doing fine.

Chapter Thirteen

Phil Spector

Castaway

The moon's a thin smile on a cloudless spring night in Los Angeles. The chartered Gulfstream, sleek and dark, all bone-white leather, burled walnut, and spotless, mirrored bulkheads, sits alone on the tarmac. We leave at 12:01 A.M.; that's what the e-mail that came this morning said. I know different: This baby goes nowhere until Phil Spector boards.

Captain Bayar, fit, fresh faced, and apple-cheeked, happy as a clam, asks if I think we might have long to wait. He's got the Huck Finn freckled grin and the Billy Budd blue eyes, and the grin doesn't lose luster and the eyes never blink when I say, Oh, yeah, we might be waiting some. He's all right with VIP lollygagging: If the client has four grand an hour, young Bayar has the wide-open sky, a topped-off fuel tank, and the whole starry night ahead.

I can handle a wait, too. I've been dogging Spector for years, hoping to write his story. In 1999, he did a brief thing with *Esquire* via e-mail; after that, we kept in touch – e-mails, his post-Hall of Fame induction parties in New York, visits to his home when I was in L.A. Doing the story always was a long shot – he's nearly as famous for being shy as he is for the music he made – but I was thrilled merely to have met and thanked him. Because Phil Spector changed my life before I ever knew his name, blew open my ears and touched my soul. Yours, too.

Rock music pre-Spector was Sun Studio in Memphis, doo-wop's death rattle, and clean-cut Caucasian cats insipidly covering the work of black R&B acts whose "race records" rarely got play on the radio or bought by whites. Chuck Berry was in lockdown in Indiana on a trumped-up charge, Colonel Tom Parker had long since dealt po' Elvis, pecker and soul, to RCA Victor, and the Beatles hadn't yet replaced Pete Best with Ringo.

Then – schooled on jazz and Wagner, all brain, balls, and hustle – came Phillip. Wee fatherless Jewboy outta the Bronx via Fairfax in Los Angeles shook thunder from the heavens. Spector claimed to be creating "little symphonies for the kids": He was. He set out to make millions and millions of dollars and music that was good and important enough to last forever: He did. And he wanted to find love – true, true love: Ah, well...two out of three ain't bad, even for a genius. Not a "mad" genius and not a "misunderstood" genius: genius. Wizard. *Artist*. Just trust the tale told in mono – back then, a whole world did.

These days, he's history. He's sixty-two years old, and every year more of Phillip's contemporaries expire, and the number of people who know him as Phil *Fucking* Spector dwindles – and every year we ask if he's ready to plunge ahead with an *Esquire* story, and now, at last... ahem... now...

Aw, shitfire, hoss, *now* we got us a corpse in the foyer – and not just any old standard-issue dead body, either. Her name was Lana Clarkson, and she was a chronically aspiring buxom blond B-movie actress/model/comedienne/hostess – a type always common in Hollywood and not unknown at the castle. She died of a gunshot to her head, and though she hasn't yet become a corpus delicti – whatever happened, it happened on February 3, and nobody's been charged with any crime at all, not yet – she did wind up dead, which is one heck of a kicker to the Phil Spector story, which wasn't exactly lacking Gothic before that.

It was screaming news for a couple of weeks – even Dominick Dunne, the ghoulish old biddy sucking and spitting out the marrow of the bones of the still-warm dead to make his living, managed to shoehorn it into a piece about Robert Blake – and then it just sort of went away. Spector was released from jail and has been charged with...nothing. The L.A. County Sheriff's Department has been investigating ever since, and it won't say when or if any charges will be brought.

Now it's April. I've spent six days in a hotel on Sunset Boulevard, blasting John Lennon's *Plastic Ono Band* and George Harrison's *All Things Must Pass* – both Phil Spector productions – waiting for a word with Phillip, until this morning's e-mail; now young Bayar and his copilot are up in the cockpit running their cross-check, and Roger, our steward, has loaded the deli platters, the fruit trays, and the cheesecake and is just now brewing our first pot of Starbucks when the airport van pulls up to the steps of the plane and the rest of the party climbs on.

There's Phillip's assistant/mother hen, Michelle, beautiful, flame-haired daughter of Spector's old drummer, Hal Blaine, toting a wee cage; inside sits Helmut, a miniature schnauzer, who was Michelle's until she gave him to Phil. There's Bill Pavelic, in his mid-fifties, a midsized ex-cop, a tough nut, smooth but a little gristly. Ask Bill what he does and he says, "Consultant"; inquire further, he says, "Human demographics." He has a smile; it just takes time to find it. He's paid protection, working investigation and security for big-ticket lawyers and their clients.

Then Phil. Small, halting steps. Jeez, he don't look so good. I mean, he's a slight, pale man anyhow, but he's *always* had that presence that comes with him knowing precisely who he is. He'll dress with gray Edwardian elegance or nightshade carelessness – either way, his threads are dark and expensive – but he seems frail now, lost in his clothes, a tired, ancient elf whose face is seamed with pain. His shoulder-length black hair – too long, too black to be his own – is matted, damp, tangled, as if someone snatched him out of bed, stuck him in the shower to wake him up, then rushed him here. His eyes are slack, a clouded, muddy brown.
I want to take him in my arms and hug him, and so I do. I kiss him on the cheek and, still holding his narrow shoulders, I say, "Phillip, how are you?"

He brightens, grins his wicked grin, his eyebrows raise and waggle, and he cocks his head and looks up at me as if I must be slightly slow.

"Yes, Mrs. Lincoln," he snickers. "Other than that, how was the play?"

Me, I was eleven in 1963, in sixth grade and
voiceless love with a girl who wouldn't even go bowling with my fat, shy ass, and each night I'd press my fevered head to the pillow, flick on my pissant transistor radio beneath it, and, sooner or later, the pounding thunder of "Be My Baby" would drown the pulsing in my ears:

Boom! Ba-boom!!
Boom! Ba-boom!!

Like God's horned fist thumping the muscle of my heart, it hurt so good. It hurt *so* good – to be bathed in perfect yearning for two and a half minutes; to find romance, mysterious and distant in my waking life, so real and near; to feel, if only for those few moments, that love so rich and wide, so deep and high, surely would someday, some way, come to me – *even to me* – else how could a sound touch me there and ring so powerful and true?

Phil Spector gave all this to me, to us. In two and a half minutes. Hey, you needn't be Schopenhauer or Lester Bangs – only alive enough to hear and to feel – to know that music doesn't show or tell: It simply is. It is as close to raw, unmediated human emotion as art can get. Not the lyric – yo, I'm not denying that Ronnie Bennet's *Whoa-oh-oh-oh* was a siren shivering my tenderloin; I can hear her banshee wailing even now – but what pierced me to the core, what stabs me even after forty years, is the wall of sound.

Except, dammit, it is *not* a wall; it's a window. *Listen* to the echo, to

Cutting Room Floor: Spector

THE PITCH: The mad genius of rock 'n' roll genius seemed in danger of being forgotten. Until the night Lana Clarkson came home to his castle to die.

SCENE: A spyware shop on Sunset Boulevard. In a few hours, I'm flying from L.A. to NYC on a private jet with Phil, and Phil doesn't do formal interviews, so I can't pull out my tape recorder or a notebook. I also know Phil goes nowhere without a bodyguard, so buying a pen or button recorder at the spy shop is a risk if I get patted down – not to mention ethically shaky. I wind up going with a mnemonic I devised years ago: I build a house in my head, and store quotes in various rooms. Still, it's a very cool shop – a good place to pretend you're Anthony Pellicano instead of a mag hack.

BACKSTORY: My story editor and I had begged Phillip for years to agree to be profiled. Now he was a murder suspect, so we were going to run a Spector story with or without him. Phil's assistant, Michelle Blaine – she and Phil are now suing and counter-suing each other, even as his the quiet spaces framing the pumping, massing beat and chords within a translucent tissue of desire – the pure love-burst chamber of a young heart torn and twisted.

Not *my* heart: Harvey Phillip Spector's, the asthmatic, nebbishy kid whose papa killed himself when Phil was only eight, who wrote and produced his first number-one song at seventeen, who subverted every aspect of the music biz and invented the *my-way-and-screw-you* rock pose, who coaxed, battered, and willed sheer sonic brilliance from unknowns, Ramones, and half the Beatles, then vanished into myth.

Myth? Vanished? Puh-*leeze*. I've read everything ever written about the bodyguards and the guns and the insanity, all the campfire tales of the recluse-zombie-maniac-dwarf self-imprisoned behind locked-around-the-clock gates, dragging his chains and howling at the moon – but I've also been to the castle. And I'm here to tell you: He's a very nice man.

Sure, it was spooky enough that first time, because I'd read all of that

murder trial nears – gave us the go-ahead; Later, after the in-person reporting was over and I was trying to tie up the loose ends via e-mail or phone, Phil wouldn't reply or let his photo be taken, while Michelle made noises about stopping *Esquire* from publishing the story. All bluff.

CONFLICT: Besides being a lifelong fan of his work, I like Phil Spector. I couldn't pretend away the corpse, or his long trail of alleged spouse abuse, drunken disorderliness and random mayhem – including literally holding the Ramones hostage in the castle when they were making End of the Century – but I was determined not to do what several other writers were doing for other magazines at the same time: indicting both Spector and the ghost of Lana Clarkson in the guise of "investigative" reporting. I knew Phil Spector, at least a little bit, and although I couldn't help being compromised by that fact, I wasn't going to pretend to a detachment I didn't feel.

WISH I'D WRITTEN: The profile I had hoped to write before the gun went off – about the greatest rock 'n' roll producer, and one of the strangest men, who ever was. The guy I met in January, 2001, was a sweet, sober soul who seemed then to have left all the demons behind.

secondhand crap, and because Phillip likes to spook you some. He sends the limo at 10 P.M., the driver says not a word, it's a stormy, wet winter evening in L.A., and a couple of obscure freeways later, when the white gates open and you climb *slowwwly* up the winding drive, it sho' nuff is a fucking castle atop a fucking hill.

Then the bodyguard steps from the dark holding a big, black umbrella, and he opens your door and says, "Mr. Spector likes his guests to use the front door," which means taking the umbrella and hiking up six, seven, eight wide flights of slick stone steps with trees dripping mist and rain and Spanish moss, and the bodyguard – the son of a bitch got in the limo and rode around to the back entrance – opens the front door, and you step through the foyer, and inside stand a couple of suits of armor and big paper-thin vases and huge, muted, medieval-looking tapestries, and the brown-skinned maid brings you coffee. And you sit on a plump settee and wait ... and wait. And there he is suddenly at the bottom of the big staircase: Phil Fucking Spector. All in black, a careful mess with a crooked smile. Myth, genius, all that, but still just another swinging dick – a wealthy man, growing old alone. A nice man: funny, horny, smart. Sure, he wants to make an impression with the limo and the steps and all that stuff, but here's the deeper impression: He's very shy and lonely. He's tiny, fragile. Timid. Happy to have company.

He doesn't want to be nagged about the old days or written about or photographed – but he also doesn't want to be forgotten. He doesn't want to die friendless. He wants to talk about the Lakers and swap stories about Ike Turner and crack wise and discuss current events. He made it too rich and too famous too young, and he grew more frightened, not less – scared to fly, leery of the music-industry thugs whose toes he stomped to jelly, afraid that he was only a mama's boy, a mayfly, a fluke. And true love turned out to be yet another tug-of-war, but worse than making hit records, because love didn't yield to insomniac obsession or the will to control and perfect each note and nuance.

The next time I visit, I drive myself to the castle and skip the hike up the steps. Phil has a few people over and orders out for pizza – Papa John's. There's a tossed salad in an enormous crystal bowl, and we eat off white banquet platters with gold-plated utensils, and it's a fine time. There's Phil and me and palimony lawyer Marvin Mitchelson and four women. One is Michelle Blaine and the other three, as far as I can tell, are more or less bimbos. Two of them have never been to the castle before, and they ask for a look around.

"No," Phil says.

"It's okay," says one of the bimbos, "we'll just guide ourselves."

"No, you won't," Phil says in a firm, quiet voice that ends that segment of the conversation.

And that's about as weird as the evening gets – not weird at all, really, unless you count Phil's bodyguard, who sits by himself on a chair near the door. Although when I later look at the third bimbo's business card – she's a "Host · Reporter · Anchor · TV/Radio" – it's mainly a photo of her holding a martini and reclining on a purple pillow with her little black dress hiked up to her ass and a pair of spike-heeled leopard-skin boots on her upthrust legs. She belongs to SAG and AFTRA, says the card – another ambitious, willing twist, aging fast but still looking to score, chum in a sea of sharks.

On the Gulfstream, Phil tells a joke: Two

Japanese businessmen are enjoying a geisha bath when one says to the other, "Akido, I regret having to say this, but I must tell you that your wife is dishonoring you. Worse – she is dishonoring you with a gentleman of the Jewish persuasion."

Akido calmly finishes bathing, and over dinner that night he says, "Honorable wife, I have heard that you are dishonoring me with a man of the Jewish persuasion."

And Akido's wife lowers her eyes and says, "Ah, honorable husband, who tell you that *meshugoss?*"

I laugh, he laughs, and gosh, it's awfully nice up here on the Gulfstream, very rock 'n' roll and yet very *haimish*, at least for a while. The coffee is strong and hot, served by Roger in white china. Phillip trades his Diet Dr Pepper for Diet Coke. The deli-sliced turkey, peppered and plain, tuna salad, cheeses, and a side platter of olives and pickles and peppers and mayo – is fresh and tasty. There is the perfect cheesecake, fresh fruit, and a lox tray in the fridge in case we feel like another nosh before landing.

Excess, I'll grant you – the smoothest, sweetest cross-country haul money can buy – but there's nothing wretched about it, not at all. A man could grow accustomed to this quick and never, ever wish to go back to first class, much less coach. Much less prison.

Captain Bayar is humming along toward Teterboro, New Jersey, at 550 miles per hour and 44,000 feet, and all is still, nearly silent, save for

Spector's hushed, boyish voice. Michelle is napping. Pavelic dropped an Ambien and is sprawled on a sofa seat back near the pantry, fast asleep. Helmut's water bottle is hooked upside down to a gizmo on his cage, with a plastic tube running through the wires for him to sip from; he hasn't made a peep since we took off.

Phillip pulls a digital camera out of a small leather case and asks me to shoot his photo. His shirt is a black tunic, untucked, buttoned up to his collarless neck, embroidered with "PS" in gold Gothic script. His black jeans are tucked into buckskin mukluks that rise to midcalf. His hands are small, with soft, tapered fingers. The only jewelry he wears is a silver ring snaking down one finger in a loose letter S. Odd? Nah. Hell, he looks like any withered old rock 'n' roller.

But after I snap the photo – he doesn't try to smile – he takes the camera and switches to a different pair of glasses and squints long and *hard* at his own face captured in the tiny screen on its back. Long, hard, sinking into some tar pit of gloom – until he rises as if hypnotized and walks slowly away, stopping square in front of the mirrored cockpit door, no more than six inches from it. And there he stands, staring through himself, blank faced, as if he had been planted, had grown from a seed embedded in the gray carpet a hundred years ago.

Then his right hand floats up to pat down a knot of hair and freezes. He's lost, devoid of himself.

The hand drops to his face and slowly strokes his cheek. Once, twice. Stops.

His mouth droops and falls open.

Time grinds to a halt, hanging with us in midair.

It is the image of a man who...ah, fuck it, hoss. There is no man there. It is an image, a shadow, a ghost.

Of the thousands of photos I've seen of him at

various stages of his life, two show Spector smiling. One's a publicity shot of Phil and the three Ronettes; leaning way back, nearly off his feet, he's laughing behind bulbous sunglasses, stopped from toppling by three comely, dusky gals with foot-high bouffants. Veronica – Ronnie, soon to be his wife, then ex-wife, then bitter foe in battles over child custody and alleged unpaid royalties – has her right arm hooked around Phil's ribs and her left under his knees. Her look isn't a smile; it's a grimace.

The other shot is unstaged: Spector and his team, his boys, his brothers-in-arms – they called themselves the Wrecking Crew – with Phillip at the center held aloft by Hal Blaine and trumpeter Roy Caton. Phil's wearing dark pants, his striped vest is dangling down to his thighs, the neck of his white shirt is open, and what looks like a cigar stump is sticking out of one side of his mouth, which is smiling from ear to basset ear. You can actually see his teeth.

Besides Phillip, twelve guys are visible – they're in the studio; the mike stands are set up behind them – and each of the men has one arm raised high in triumph. Each cocked fist punches the air. Their mouths are opened in a fierce huzzah you can almost hear today.

They have finished something. Something good, maybe great. A Phil Spector studio session could last days at a time; in an era when hit records got made in an afternoon, Spector often took weeks to match the instrumental track to the perfection he heard inside his head – before ever recording a note of the vocal. He fed steaks to the men he worked with, told them not to give up, swore to them that together they were making history. They wore T-shirts with his face emblazoned on the front. Phil was the leader, the general, their quarterback; in this photograph he has just passed for the game-winning touchdown with no time left on the clock, and the team is rejoicing. His buddies are carrying him off the field.

And *that's* the dream that never dies. Long after boy-girl love burns down to everyday ash, a man still looks back to the wars he fought and the men who stood fast with him, and those feelings – of brotherhood, the glory of toil in a common cause – are what burn forever in his soul.

Beyond his music, Phil Spector never has opened his heart for public display; odds are, he never will. He never has cooperated with a biographer; he sued the last one, in 1989, for $30 million. (They settled.) He has three ex-wives, four grown children – one of his sons died at age nine, of leukemia – a million jokes and anecdotes, vast wealth, singular talent, a permanent artistic legacy, and nobody to share any of this with. The people he sees now are on his payroll.

In late 1964, with both "Walking in the Rain" and "You've Lost That Lovin' Feelin'" zooming the charts, a not-yet-founding-father-of-New-Journalism Tom Wolfe profiled a twenty-three-year-old Phil Spector for the bygone *New York Herald Tribune*; that article, "The First Tycoon of Teen," published in '65, has been Spector's official media portrait for forty years. When a four-CD retrospective of Spector's music was released in 1991, Wolfe's piece ran in the companion booklet, right after Spector's own dedication – to Ben Spector, his father.

Forty years ago, Spector boasted to Wolfe that he was spending $600 a week to see a psychiatrist. In an interview with a writer for London's *Sunday Telegraph*, published just before Lana Clarkson's death – Phillip had been in London for much of last year, working with a band there called Starsailor – Spector rattled on at length about his medications and his mental illness. After February 3, a sampling of his quotes from that interview – "I have devils inside that fight me" was, hands down, the most popular – became embedded in the coverage of the incident and bounced around the planet.

Grant him his pain, but I don't think Phil Spector's devils are all that special, just better-fed. I don't think half a life spent disconnected behind a gilded wall of silence, without much work and mostly alone, is good for anyone.

After a long time staring into the mirror, he turns away and sits back down in the seat across from mine. His eyes are red and wet. His hands shake.

"It's 'Anatomy of a Frame-Up,'" he says, still softly, not much above a purr. "There is no case. They have no case. I didn't do *anything* wrong – I didn't do anything. I called the police myself. *I called the police.* This is *not* Bobby Blake. This is *not* the Menendez brothers. They have no case. If they had a case, I'd be sitting in jail right now.

"She kissed the gun. I have no idea why – I never knew her, never even saw her before that night. I have no idea who she was or what her agenda was. They have the gun – I don't know where or how she got the gun. She asked me for a ride home. Then she wanted to see the castle. She was loud – she was loud and drunk even before we left the House of Blues. She grabbed a bottle of tequila from the bar to take with her. I was *not* drunk. I wasn't drunk *at all. There is no* case. She killed herself."

Spector tells me that he was Tasered by the police, that they stripped his day-old Mercedes limo of anything that might contain a molecule of evidence, ransacked the castle, seized his guns and his computers, and ran gunshot-residue tests on him. He's angry at Marvin Mitchelson for speaking with reporters about the incident, furious with Robert Shapiro – his attorney for the case and also a close friend – for charging him a huge fee, and mad at Nancy Sinatra, to whom Phillip has referred in the past as his "fiancée," for failing to stand by him.

"You know what she told me?" he snarls. "She says, 'My mother told me, *Omigod – Nancy, it could've been you.*' "

Chapter Thirteen: Phil Spector

In early March, Michelle Blaine sent out an e-mail proclaiming that an L.A. radio station would report that the Sheriff's Department was going to announce that Lana Clarkson's death was the result of an "accidental suicide," and that Spector wouldn't be charged. The Sheriff's Department responded by saying that the matter was still being investigated as a homicide. Robert Shapiro issued a statement expressing confidence that a thorough investigation would show that his client had committed no crime. Lana Clarkson's family and agent insist that she would not have killed herself. She was shifting gears, her agent said, hoping to land a sitcom part, trying stand-up comedy, and took the hostess gig at the House of Blues VIP room to make her rent and hook up with some showbiz heavyweights.

And there it sits: Two people alone in the castle at five A.M., and one winds up dead of a gunshot wound. The cops say that they have the gun that fired it. They autopsied the body – Spector tells me that Shapiro hired two forensic pathologists to sit in – and ran their tests. And?

And?

Well, hoss, Lana Clarkson, God rest her soul, is gone, and whatever her agenda, and however sunny her memory, the chance that, after twenty years of swimming after stardom in Los Angeles, she didn't know exactly what she was up to – and who she was riding with, and why – when she left the House of Blues that night is exactly the same chance she had of becoming Marilyn Monroe: zero. And Phil Spector, who has realized that the presumption of innocence is nothing more than a pretty concept even among friends, is flying to New York City for a few days of what he hopes will be carefree fun. Robert Shapiro will not answer my request for his comments. And Los Angeles County Sheriff's detective Lieutenant Daniel Rosenberg, heading the investigation, assures me that this case is "not particularly unusual. We're completing our investigation – waiting for evidence to be analyzed at our lab.

"When we're done, we'll be presenting this thing to the district attorney's office. We're not rushing anything. This is just one more case. We handle them all the same. We'll see how it plays out. We don't wanna taint the jury pool; we're not gonna try the case in the media. The jury's gonna be the tryers of the case – *if* it gets to court. These are all ifs – and if he ends up goin' to jail, it'll be very hard on him. It's important for me that he gets a fair shake in this."

Lieutenant Rosenberg sounds like a decent man on the phone.

Patient. The man with the badge has all the resources your tax dollars can buy, and all the time in the world to bring a homicide charge.

Spector never listens to his hits. He listens to Tony Bennett and Billie Holiday and Frank Sinatra singing Gershwin and Irving Berlin.

"Real American music," he says, nibbling at his cheesecake.

Louis Armstrong?

Spector nods. "He never played a wrong note. He never sang a wrong note. Everything he did was perfect. You know what Dizzy Gillespie said when someone asked him about Louis? 'No Louis, no Diz.'"

He wants to work again. He wants to work with Radiohead. He wanted to do something with Bono, who wanted to do something with Phil and called to talk about writing a song together and made plans to hook up – and then came February 3: Spector never heard from him again. He says that he enjoyed working with Starsailor but ran out of patience.

"You can't spend three months of your life making an album with guys who play pinball and video games all day. These guys are very good, but they're dumb. They're idiots. There are no Rolling Stones anymore. There are no Beatles."

I fish *All Things Must Pass* out of my bag – the two-CD reissue from 2001 – and read aloud this sentence from George Harrison's notes: "I still like the songs on the album and believe they can continue to outlive the style in which they were recorded."

Spector laughs. "Jesus fucking Christ," he says. "I gave him a coproducer credit just to get the fuck out of there. The slide guitar on 'My Sweet Lord' – he did ninety fucking versions of it. Then he had to do ninety more with a bottleneck. Then he brought Eric Clapton in to do another ninety."

That was Phil's first comeback: After "River Deep – Mountain High" tanked in 1966 – it spent a week on the charts, at number 88 – he closed the shutters and hid away for nearly three years. Spector has cowritten and produced hundreds of great songs; "River Deep" is the best, mono dropped from God. Phillip was twenty-five years old; he had the Wrecking Crew, he had Tina Turner, he had a string of top-ten hits that had made him the first brand-name producer in rock history – and still the record died.

"River Deep" was a huge hit in England; in America, it didn't even get played. Payback is a motherfucker, and Spector had made enemies on all sides. Disc jockeys hated him because he never bribed them to get airplay or respected them as music brokers; his B-sides were studio doodles put there to prevent them from flipping his A-sides over. Record distributors, who had shortchanged and extorted record companies for years, found out that doing business with Spector's Philles label meant paying him every penny due for his last smash if they wanted to get delivery on the next one. He had fought off the musicians' unions, who felt his use of overdubbing took money out of their members' pockets; he had outhustled the hustlers, outmuscled the mobsters, outjewed the Jews, and out-produced the Brill Building mavens who'd mentored him; and he had crowed about all of it. Loudly.

Spector's self-exile ended in 1970, when the Beatles handed him the mess of tapes they hated nearly as much as they hated one another by then, and Spector shaped the tapes into *Let It Be*. Then George asked Phil to do *All Things*, and John and Yoko began working with him, too. Spector produced and played some piano on *Plastic Ono Band* – still the rawest, most searing and honest rock album ever made, and perhaps the most beautiful – followed by *Imagine.*

The Lennon-Spector collaboration ended badly, in early '74. John was in such awful shape that Yoko threw him out; he went to L.A. to make an album of oldies with Spector. Legend has it that both men were at their worst – Phil and Ronnie were fighting for custody of their kids – and drinking hard. At one session, Phil produced a gun and fired it into the ceiling of the studio. Not long after that, John returned to New York City.

"He was my brother," is all Spector says about those days. "He was my brother and she was his wife, and I was never going to win that war."

He pulls out a small DVD player and cues up *The Awful Truth,* the Cary Grant-Irene Dunne screwball comedy made in 1937. "This is a great movie," Phil says, and we watch it as dawn breaks across the horizon. It's cold and rainy when we land. Phillip, Helmut, Michelle, and Pavelic ride the waiting limo down Route 3 to the Lincoln Tunnel and into the city; I call another car to take me home. Young Captain Bayar, as peppy now as he was six hours and three thousand miles ago, spots me waiting by the door.

"Can I help you with your bags?" he asks.

"Nah, but thanks. And thanks for getting us here. That was some sweet ride."

"Thank *you,*" he grins, waving me off. "I love my job."

Rock 'n' roll was never built to last – not

brick by brick and song by song – until Phil Spector came along. Mono wasn't merely his method: It was as timeless as religion. Spector's commemorative four-CD package came with a little red-and-white button that said it all – BACK TO MONO. Even as he crafted his symphonies, he never tried to refine the roar. Start doing that – separating sounds, parceling the noise, moving notes around, balancing the mix, expanding the number of tracks, gettin' all *stereophonic* and shit – and you kiss off any prayer of rhapsody.

Yeah, with mono you get some distortion with the soundboard needles pegged at the red zone's far edge. It isn't perfect, you understand – but it is real, as close to perfection in this one sense as you can ever hope for. What hits the ear inside the studio bleeds into that kid's ear pressed upon the pillow the same way you heard the Wrecking Crew play it. And if it's cranked high enough to numb the skull and crack open the sternum for a little heart massage, well, then you've got something special. Something great.

Phil Spector should've come back to New York City a long time ago, should've come back for good. Here it's mono 24/7; we've got your frigging wall of sound, right here. Here, a man can't disintegrate into wispy silence under a blank sky. That's L.A. – no feelings at all, only impressions, the vapors, thin air. It's hell sealed up tight, with a doughnut shop on every corner.

Spector and crew are at the Plaza, heading to Elaine's tonight for dinner. What once was hip is now kitsch, but still – it's the Plaza and it's Elaine's. Spector's resplendent in a gray waistcoat, a black linen shirt with big, round gold buttons, black pants, black boots with big heels and platform soles, shades. His hair is...perfect. He's seated at the head of the long table with his daughter and a friend of hers to his immediate left – their anonymity is preserved here – and Paul Shaffer and Richard Belzer on his right. Not A-listers, no – more like the J-list: Jews of middle vintage whose showbiz lives let them hang out and on for eons without having to smile in the middle box on *Hollywood Squares.*

Belzer begs off after dinner; the rest of us pile into a big-ass Navigator stretch and head downtown to a basement club called Fez, where Sue Mingus, Charles's sad-eyed widow, presides from a far table over the ferocious, protean Mingus Big Band. Charles Mingus – as pure a genius as America ever mainly ignored – was reared in L.A., in Watts, but this is the only place on God's earth where you'll hear his works played by the best jazz musicians alive.

No more than three dozen people are in the club, but the band is *blazing*, trading trumpet solos like left hooks, and Paul Shaffer is shouting "*Yeah!*" as they swap punches, and Spector is trying to get a fortyish schoolmarm type – don't ask me where he found her – all liquored up. For the Big Band's last number, they slow to a bluesy lope and invite Paul to the piano. He's up there comping, trying to find his way in, and Spector leans over and says, "He's the world's greatest clone, but he's lost up there. He can't keep up – they'll have to find him some music."

Paul lands on his feet quickly enough, and Spector smells a rat. "He *rehearsed* it!" he shouts. "The bastard *rehearsed*! I'll blow his brains out!"

Pavelic, who hasn't said boo all night, looks thunderstruck. Michelle screams, "*Phillip! You can't say those things anymore!*" But Phil's having a ball, and after the set, we all go to the upstairs bar, where the crush of toned young flesh is throbbing long past midnight to machine noise. Pavelic clears our path to a banquette, where Phillip occupies the center pillow like a pasha. Schoolmarm has taken her pie-eyed leave; on either side of Spector hunches a wide-thighed tart – younger, but hardly young – one of whom is braying something about having a million dollars to purchase airtime. Perhaps she is a media buyer, or just drunk.

I'm not sure that the women know who he is, but he looks cute enough, and no doubt he emits a moneyed scent, what with the waistcoat and shoulder-length curl. His voice is not audible in the din, but he looks like he's having hisself some fun.

I can't see Pavelic, Michelle, Spector's daughter, her friend, or Paul Shaffer. Hours, days, weeks seem to drag by. It's too hot and crowded to draw much breath. When Pavelic looms out of the murk and says that the limo is waiting, it's a relief. But not to Phil. When we reach the lobby and push open the door and see that the Navigator *isn't* waiting, he ain't happy.

"What the *fuck*," he says. "It's *raining*. Where the *fuck* is the *fucking* car? I'm not standing here in the fucking rain." And he darts back into the lobby. He's still fuming when the limo comes. He thought he was gonna get laid – and maybe he was. Hell, hoss, maybe he still will. It's only three A.M. in the city that never sleeps.

As soon as we're back in the car heading uptown – Paul, it turns out, was the one who wanted to leave – Spector, sounding wobbly but determined, wants to know who'll go back to the club with him after we drive Paul home.

Not Phil's daughter and her friend, who get dropped off next. Not Pavelic, who's up front next to the driver, behind the glass partition. Not

Michelle, who keeps hiccuping and throwing her hand mouthward, as if she might hurl at any moment.

Me? Sorry, hoss, no. This cowboy's still whipped from the all-nighter on Bayar's Gulfstream fewer than forty-eight hours ago. Besides, Michelle's hissing, "Tell him – *hic!* – that girl is gone. Tell him the place – *hic!* – is closed. Tell him – *urp!* – anything. You can't – *omigod!* – let him go back there."

I'm asking myself, What would Tom Wolfe do? – because if I can figure that out, I'm doing the opposite – when Phillip announces that he has to take a leak. Unfortunately, it takes a little while to relay this information to the Navigator's cockpit.

"Can we go down a side street for a minute? No, no, no – just go straight ahead. Jesus *fucking* Christ. Just tell the guy to find a side street. What seems to be the problem? My goodness gracious. My goodness."

The driver pulls over at the curb in front of a diner, and Pavelic escorts Phillip inside. They're back in a couple of minutes – and now Phil is ready to head back to the club, alone if need be. But the next time we stop, we're somehow at the Plaza's side entrance.

"What are we here for?" Spector asks. "We're at the wrong place. Why are we home?"

Some skinny kid pulls open the back door of the limo and starts babbling in heavily accented English. He's French. Or Italian. Or a Turk. Who the fuck knows? "We take ze cah," he says. Phil shrinks back into his seat. Pavelic finally gets to the back door, clears the kid away with a sweep of his arm, and holds the door, waiting for Spector to dismount.

"Why are we here?" Phil asks, his voice rising in petulant command.

Pavelic mumbles something I can't hear.

"I don't care who said that," Phil tells him. "I make the decisions."

Pavelic says, "I was gonna – "

"I don't care what you were gonna do. I make the decisions."

"Michelle," Pavelic says. "Let's do it." Then, to Spector, "She needs to go to the bathroom."

"*That's not why we're at the Plaza,*" Phillip's yelling. "I went to the bathroom. She could've gone to the bathroom then. *Tell me* – not, 'We're at the hotel, get out' and some fucking prick comes and opens my door. What the hell was that all about?"

Michelle gets out of the limo. Pavelic closes the door. Spector turns to me. He isn't drunk. He isn't yelling. He's upset, angry, and embarrassed at being tricked and treated like a child.

"Jesus fucking Christ. What the hell is wrong with these fuckin' people? I have no control over my life."

All his life, Spector fought for control: of his image and his privacy, of his power to shape popular music, of the publishing rights to his songs, of the sounds and ideas raging inside his heart and head – fought and won. His fate dangles in other hands now – the law, his lawyer, the press, the jury – and nobody's got him covered. No one has Phil's back.

I say, Phillip, look, I think they're trying to help you. Maybe they're being overprotective, I say.

"No," he says. "This is not 'overprotective' – this is stupidity. What is wrong with me? I *am* in control. This is what Robert Shapiro charged me seven figures about. *Bullshit!* I was *never* involved in a murder – and he should've said to me, 'Mr. Spector, I am your friend, I am your confidant, but lemme tell you something: You didn't commit a homicide, and I'm outta here now. Get Gerry Spence to come in and kick ass – because I gotta go schmooze with the sheriffs, because Nick Nolte may kill his wife tomorrow, and I gotta make deals with them. I gotta say to them, 'Remember what I did with you on the Spector case.'

"I wasn't drunk – I remember exactly what happened. But when you're Tasered and beaten up and lied to and crapped on, you don't know what the fuck happened. When Robert came in, as a courtesy, as a favor, he shoulda gotten me outta jail. As a *courtesy* – not for seven figures. As a courtesy. I've taken him for *three hundred thousand dollars*' worth of gifts and rides and plane trips. I wasn't a referral – I was his best friend. Nancy Sinatra, Marvin Mitchelson – they all proved to be fucking wastes of time. Bill Pavelic, my chief investigator – look what he's doing tonight. He's tired, so my evening's over. And then you suddenly get angry – so you're drunk."

It's getting close to four A.M., and Phil Spector is wide awake. I say, Phillip, you know what? Maybe it's just hard to keep pace with an old rock 'n' roll soldier like you.

He smiles, calmed by memory. "It's 1989," he says, "and Jack Nicholson and myself go to the Rolling Stones concert at the Coliseum. First we go to the Four Seasons, and we're sitting in Keith Richards's suite. At the fucking time he had two little blond girls, three and four. And the three-year-old flushes down her teddy bear. Down the toilet. And it gets stuck. And the toilet won't flush, and the teddy bear won't come out.

"The mother's a beautiful blond model and the mother's panicking.

And the little girl is crying hysterically. And fucking Keith don't give a shit. And Jack's saying, 'Man, what are we gonna do?' I said, 'I don't know what the fuck to do – get her another teddy bear.'

"They can't get the teddy bear up and the toilet won't go down. The little girl won't stop crying. So they call the plumber – and he can't get the fucking teddy bear up. So he takes the toilet out.

"Water everywhere. Shit everywhere. Shit *everywhere*. Gets the teddy bear, but the bathroom looks like hell. The place is ruined – and the Rolling Stones have to go now. It's showtime. And Jack says, 'Well, I guess we'll see you over there.' Because they go in the van.

"So then the chief of security comes up, knocks on the door, says, 'Hello – I'm chief of security. Everything's under control. I'm gonna look around the place.' And he goes in there, and he looks at it, and he says, 'Goddamn Rolling Stones – fifty years old and they're still fuckin' up suites. Goddamn bullshit – damn! Damn!' He's talkin' to himself as he's goin' out of the goddamn place. And Jack looks at me and says, 'Wel-l-l-l, whaddaya gonna do?' "

The old rooster cackles with glee. Pavelic and Michelle are back in the limo, and we head back downtown. Phil's on the cell, chatting up the soused schoolmarm. Asking for an address. The night is young yet. Dawn may never come.

The Navigator pulls up to the parking garage where I've left my car. "How are you on cash?" he asks.

I'm fine, Phillip. Thank you.

"Good night, buddy," he says.

Chapter Fourteen

Ike Turner

Lover

Musician, at 70*

"I'm pure with myself, man. I don't bullshit Ike. I bite the bullet. I don't lie to me.

You can feel when people are yessin' you. You can feel the real.

I always showed them what to do. I can go and record any girl you bring in here right now and you would swear to God she's coppin' off Tina – because there is no Tina. You hear me through Tina. I do it all. I do every bit of it. Every note that's played. When you saw Ike and Tina, every step came from me. All that shit came dead out of me.

You got to stand for somethin' or you'll fall for anything.

I know that people are stuck in cocaine, and I know that you feel it start off as fun, and then you wake up lookin' for it, and then you want out, because you see your life and you feel there's no way out. I say it like this: It's like you have glasses on and you can really see clear. So once, man, you put the stuff on it and it's a little brighter, but what happens is, when the stuff dies, now it's dull. You can never get it back clear unless you put some stuff on it. So every day you wake up, you put some stuff on it to clear it up, and you never can get it back clear. So you gotta go all the way to zero, where you can't see shit, and then you can find a light down there. There is a light there, but you have to really want it to get it.

I had to hit bottom. And when I hit bottom, it was like jail was the best thing ever happened to me.

People meet me and say, "Man, you're nothin' like what I thought you were. You're nothin' like that movie." But, man, that movie is not me. They had to have a villain. They assassinated my career with that damn movie, man.

My mother's a woman. I mean, I loved my mother to death. I ain't gonna do nothin' no more to nobody else than somebody might do to my mother, man.

Where's the Ray Charleses, the Sam Cookes, the Jackie Wilsons, the Louis Jordans? Where? It's no more. Black radio died. Kids took to the street with rap and hip-hop. "Shoot him. Kill him. The bitch this. The bitch that." This is what they had to do to sell records. So they did it. But the rest of this life that I got in me, man, I'm gonna use it to get black music back on the radio. Because there's very few of us left. Motown sold out – that's dead.

It make me happy to make you happy, but I'm not gonna make you happy by makin' me sad – and if I got to marry you because you want a husband, uh-uh. That's dead. I'll never get married again. That was number thirteen I just got a divorce from. Took a long time for me to learn, didn't it? I'm through, man. You can bet your bottom dollar.

The first drink of whiskey you take, you feel like a peacock; you want to get up and stroll around. It's just like peacock blood. The next drink you take, you feel like you can whup the world – that's the lion blood in it. And then the last drink you take, you're so drunk you want to lay down and wallow – that's the hog blood.

What am I? I'm an organizer. Next, I'm a piano player.

I'm alive today and enjoying what the fuck I do.

To me, the onliest two people that ever had freedom in America is a white man and a black woman. They can do what the shit they wanna do. A black woman in Mississippi could slap the shit out of a white man – there ain't nothin' gonna happen to her. Rosa Parks, if she hadda been a black dude that done that, they woulda hung him on the highest tree. I'm just bein' real about it.

When you don't like whites, or you don't like blacks, well, you're just cheating your own self.

I call some people RadioShacks – if you got questions, we got answers. They got answers for every fuckin' thing.

One of the wrongs that I did in my life was that I fired this guy because he was too slow with them pedals, and come to find out ten or twelve years later it was Jimi Hendrix. You can't win 'em all.

If he have millions of dollars, I been there. If he's poor, eating out of the garbage can, I been there. If he have fifty women, I had that. If he lookin' for one, I been there, too. I've lived my life.

Don't do shit about me when I die. Let me rest.

Everything is a hole. When you're born, two holes – there's a hole at the head of your penis, and you come out of a hole. So you come out, and everything is about holes. When you eat? Hole. When you breathe, it's a hole. When you see, it's a hole. When you hear, it's a hole. And when you die, where you goin'? Right back in the hole. If you get too much money, you gonna be in a hole. If you don't get enough, you're definitely gonna be in a hole. So to me, the best thing to do is stop tryin' to stay outta the hole: Get in the hole and find out what's happenin' with the hole and try to control the hole. And then you can have the hole, because you understand the hole.

I know you heard what I said, but did you understand what I mean?"

– interviewed by the author, fall 2001, San Marcos, California, six years before Turner's death

Chapter Fifteen

Alex Rodriguez

Collector

Satan wears a sweater-vest. Scott
Boras – Scott Freakin' Boras, the Most Hated Man in Baseball, the heart-
less bastard hell-bent on destroying our National Pastime, the keen-eyed
pimp of ball-hogging, bat-whipping, splitter-hurling youth – he walks
among us, here in the lobby of the elephantine Wyndham Anatole Hotel
in Dallas, during the long December weekend of the game's annual winter meetings, in his blue sweater-vest, blue denim shirt, and jeans, his
cloven hooves hidden in soft brown shoes, toting a tan leather satchel as
battered as Yogi's old catcher's mitt.

Boras has a suite upstairs, but nowhere does he ride – not even the
elevator down to the hotel café – without the satchel. The satchel doesn't
touch the floor, either: It gets a chair all to itself.

"Every contract I've done has been carried in that." Boras nods at the
satchel. "Six different handles. People see a bag; when I see this, it's no different than a cow – I'm close to that leather."

Boras grew up milking the cows and riding the tractor on his parents' small dairy farm – they raised alfalfa, too – not far from Sacramento.
He is plain of face and speech, stocky and squint-eyed, piercing and
direct. He played minor league ball for the Cubs and Cardinals in the

1970s – rose as high as AA – but never even sipped a cup of coffee in the Show. Even in the minors, though, Boras kept up with his college courses; by the early '80s, he'd earned a Ph.D. in industrial pharmaceutics and a law degree and spent five years in a large Chicago firm defending drug companies against product-liability lawsuits before pledging his soul to the financial ruin of God's favorite pro sport.

It was either Vito Corleone or Vin Scully who first said that one lawyer with a briefcase could heist more cash than a hundred men with guns. Boras is proof: He represents only fifty-five major league players, but three of his pitchers have signed record-setting deals in the last four seasons; he also represents forty minor-leaguers, and with them he has thrown the game's amateur draft system into fiscal chaos, consistently plucking the ripest of young plums, forcing ball clubs to fork over fair market value for them before taking the first bite; and by the time this weekend is over, he will have bamboozled the Texas Rangers into making twenty-five-year-old shortstop Alex Rodriguez an offer he can't refuse: $252 million over ten years, plus bonus and escalator clauses, exactly twice the dollar amount of the previous highest-priced player contract in the history of American sport.

And Scott Boras, who takes 5 percent, will once more be vilified – along with Rodriguez – as the cancer killing the game.

"The greedy agent," says Boras. "When you bring a player to a team, they don't reward you for it – the team recruited him. But if you take a player, the team didn't lose him – the agent took him away. For money. Everything is about money; nothing is about anything you do to accentuate the performance of the player. None of *that* is ever talked about. It's money. It's contract. It's not talent assessment. It's not doing things that help the player – his career, his life, his family. It's money. I used to fight that battle early on. I stopped. I go into a city now and I say, 'Okay, where're my horns?' "

I wasn't expecting horns, really, but at least an Armani suit and a shiny pair of Pradas.

Satan gives up a dry chuckle and a grin that flashes like a dagger.

"I worry about what's in *here*," he says, reaching to pat the satchel. "We've got very dressed-up computers. Our data – it's very polished. That's the extent of our style."

He is picking at his salad, a Cobb salad, at a table on a terrace open to the lobby proper, and two separate clusters of reporters in the near distance stand watching him carefully.

"You see that bunch there?" Boras asks, jabbing his fork. "That's the L.A. group. They know their shit. I have great respect for them – the beat writers. Their problem is they love the game."

Everyone at the winter meetings loves the game, including Boras, but few know it so well or get so little sugar in return. Scouts hate Boras because his nose for the scent of nubile, unsigned talent is at least as sharp as theirs and because the financial demands of any draftee linked with Boras will scare off some clubs regardless of their scouts' recommendations. General managers fear him because he doesn't schmooze away trade secrets or play scratch-my-back. Owners dread him because he shapes his monster deals and arbitration battles with a database that includes every pitch thrown in every major league game since 1979 and because when an owner says, "Well, those are some impressive numbers, Scott, but the truth is I just can't afford to pay that much for this player," Boras will say, "Then let's take a peek at your balance sheet and see how we might make it work." And the commissioner despises him because Boras has no patience for Bud Selig's death-rattling about how payroll disparities and the lack of competitive balance can't be helped until the players make the owners stop paying them so much money.

"Hocus-pocus," says Boras. "Players have to meet standards or they're released. The same thing should apply to baseball ownership. You wanna talk about traditions and the betterment of the game? If you have not achieved a standard of performance as a team, you should be required to sell it. If for ten years you are outside the playoffs, if you're just sitting there riding the tide of inflation and you really don't care, then give it to somebody who *does* care."

Satan has no need of sugar now: He's got *leverage*. Never has any sport's finest player been dangled at so tender an age before the open market. Boras will get 150 phone messages before this day is done, and the media will stand sentry at the elevators to mark his every coming and going, and starry-eyed general managers will paw at the door of his suite like prom-bound schoolboys.

"You know the great thing?" Boras says. "We don't know where he's going, neither I nor Alex. We've got it narrowed down, but we don't know. As exact as this game is – are you gettin' three hits tonight? – that's exactly how you know where you're gonna go. You don't know."

He grins again.

"But you know what they say about Dallas – you never get out of this town with your gun."

The title of the book is *Alex Rodriguez: Historical Performance.* The Scott Boras Corporation published an edition of fifty, at a cost of $35,000. Light on character development, barely seventy pages long, with more blank white space than John Rocker's brain, it offers a vivid, nay, compelling plot: A-Rod, a bilingual Latino American heartthrob middle infielder, natural-born leader of manly men who take group showers, smashes all-time career records for home runs, runs scored, and runs batted in, becoming, by age forty, the greatest baseball player who has ever adjusted his cup.

Cutting Room Floor: Rodriguez

THE PITCH: Are superstar Alex Rodriguez and superagent Scott Boras ruining baseball, or saving it?

SCENE: The VIP lounge deep in the bowels of the American Airlines Arena in Miami, where Alex Rodriguez and his agent, Scott Boras, relax after watching a humdrum Heat win from their floor seats. The room is dark and crowded, filled by rich guys, hot women, and a parade of dressed-to-kill basketball players fresh from the showers.

A-Rod, fresh from signing a $250 million contract, is the quiet center of it all, the golden homeboy. Everyone, even the NBA vets, looks at him sideways, in silent appraisal. In a room full of stars, this 25-year-old is king.

BACKSTORY: The few lines in the story where Alex speaks somewhat disparagingly of Derek Jeter became huge news in the baseball world as soon as the issue came out. A few days later, A-Rod called and said that by quoting him thus I had ruined his friendship with Jeter. (To his credit, he never said he had been misquoted him or had his words taken out of context, maybe because I always use a tape recorder.) He seemed to be genuinely upset, so I said I'd send Jeter a fax attesting

---

And then, just before A-Rod's induction into a wing of the Hall of Fame built especially to house his plaque, bat, glove, cleats, and wristbands, his jealous evil twin, Nim-Rod, threatens to nuke the sleepy village of Cooperstown unless...okay, so I'm making this part up. But the rest of it is there, ten chapters of data comparing A-Rod at age twenty-four with everyone from Junior Griffey and Big Mac back to Willie Mays and the Georgia Peach, all spiced by paeans to A-Rod's unquantifiable but no less precious valor and virtue as sung by teammates, coaches, managers, executives, even journalists, including one long quote from a *Miami Herald* writer that ends as follows: *Yes, Alex Rodriguez can save baseball.*

The odd thing is, you meet Alex Rodriguez – born in New York City of Dominican heritage, six three and 210 pounds, with skin of gleaming

---

to all the nice things Alex had said to me about him that had not run in the story. So I did – but by all accounts, and even though they're now teammates, Jeter's still mad.

CONFLICT: Fast-forward to 2007: The quarter-billion dollar contract with the Rangers is history. The new deal's even bigger – the Yankees will still be paying A-Rod $30 million per year when he's 42. Word is, he did the deal himself – without Boras – rebuilding bridges Boras burned.

Baloney.

WISH I'D WRITTEN: Scott Boras wasn't shy about trashing his former clients and various other major-leaguers, and he never went off the record. In our first conversation, I asked him about another high-profile free agent that off-season – not his client – and Boras said, "Of course, everyone knows ____'s 'enhanced' " (meaning, he confirmed when I asked directly, whether ____ was using steroids).

It wasn't something I could use for the story I was writing – not without a whole lot of extra time and reporting – and it may have been no more than scurrilous gossip (the player in question has not been publicly accused of steroid use), but I realized then that a big part of the steroids-in-baseball story was how many folks knew about the breadth of the scandal-to-be long before Major League Baseball acknowledged it.

---

caramel and an easy, honeyed smile, well-spoken both *en Español y en Ingles*, sober and self-controlled – and even the claim of saviorhood comes to seem, ah, not modest, certainly, but not as far-fetched as it first sounds.

Boras wears sweater-vests; A-Rod is the spiff. Tonight, taking in a Heat-Lakers game in Miami with Boras a few days after the deal was done, he's all in black – wide-wale corduroys, cashmere crewneck, leather car coat, and a pair of black-and-white lace-ups that just may be the swiftest kicks humankind has ever seen.

On and off the diamond, Rodriguez glides and smolders at once. Model handsome, yes, but he also has the *presence* that some great athletes possess, a coiled charisma, a blend of size and mastery, muscle and confidence, the aura of self-knowledge and -belief forged and tempered by a life in competition.

Oh, and he admires Leonardo da Vinci. The kid collects art, for God's sake, real Art: Chagall and Miró and Picasso.

"Because I love art," he says shyly. "It brings happiness and life to my house."

Speaking of art, Alex, have you seen that A-Rod book?

He nods, straight-faced.

"I've got a lot of work to do," he says, "a lot of motivation. I'm chasing all those things – internally. It's not good to talk about it. It's hard to compete when you don't have a place in the game now as a shortstop, so you have to look years back to find someone to compete against. That's what I do. I'm playing against guys like Ernie Banks or Hank Aaron or Ozzie Smith."

If this assessment ignores the most gifted shortstops he actually plays against – Nomar Garciaparra of the Boston Red Sox and the Yankees' Derek Jeter – well, Alex is better than they are. He has far more power at the plate (41 home runs, 132 RBIs, and a slugging percentage of .606 last season), more range and arm in the field, more speed on the bases, and now more – lots more – money.

Alex Rodriguez now has so much money that when he hands the VIP-lounge waiter a hundred-dollar bill to cover four bottles of spring water, the waiter asks if he needs change.

"Yeah, I need change," Alex says, shaking his head in disgust.

So much money that the Heat's Tim Hardaway, no peon his own self, comes bopping through the lounge, spots Alex, and heads over for a handout.

"Alex! Man. *Da*-yam!"

"What's up, Timmy?"

"*Da*-yam! Congratulations, man."

"What's up, big boy? How you feelin', man?"

"*Da*-yam! I need a loan, man. *Da*-yam!"

So much goddamned money that he spends most of his public time pleading not guilty for taking it.

"When I signed out of high school, that was the biggest thrill of my life, because I could buy my Cherokee, my black Cherokee, for thirty grand. I thought, Man, I've never been happier. You go up to an $11 million contract for four years – that was really neat, too, because I could buy my first house.

"I was ridiculed for four years about my contract in Seattle, people telling me that I was grossly underpaid, that Scott's a bad agent. Now I'm grossly overpaid, and he's too greedy. Everything I've ever wanted, I already have. I'm already spoiled beyond anything. I feel like my life is a dream.

"My talent, what the man upstairs blessed me with, hiring Scott – the result was my contract. But my work and my love for the game come way before that." He shrugs. "People are going to make up their own minds. I only worry about the people I love and the people who love me."

You almost feel bad for the kid, for the edge of hurt pride, the high-pitched plaint, in his voice. His father deserted the family when Alex was a lad of ten. His mother worked two jobs to make sure her children wore decent clothes to decent schools. His nose is clean, his Website, arod.com, is simple to navigate, and his Range Rover is three years old. The Rolling Stones rake in $75 million on their latest Swollen Prostate Tour and no one sermonizes about cancer-research funding, but let Alex Rodriguez earn a deal that vaults his annual salary up there with such living saints as Celine Dion and Tom Cruise, and baseball has been stained beyond redemption.

He doesn't wear makeup or croon, but A-Rod is no less an entertainer. Fans pay to see him play – the Rangers' *advance* ticket sales for the 2001 season are expected to reach nearly two million – he plays on TV, and he does all his own stunts. Plus, he risks his livelihood each time he takes the field. No pre-free-agency baseball star ever got paid close to what he was worth, in dollars and cents, to his team or his sport. Thanks to Scott Boras, A-Rod will.

Not that the men who run baseball know or care what a jewel like

Alex Rodriguez might be worth in terms of attracting young and unwhite fans and all the future stars now shooting hoops and catching passes. In fact, you'd have thought from their reactions to his deal that A-Rod had been convicted of conspiring to shoot his pregnant girlfriend dead.

"The system has to be changed, and it will be changed," said commissioner Bud Selig from his burrow in Manhattan.

"Stupefying," said Sandy Alderson, Selig's right-hand man, in Dallas for the winter meetings. "Every club will be affected by this.... There will be people who say, 'Stop whining.' But clearly we have a crisis situation, and it's time for us to deal with it." Alderson, by the way, is the same guy who, in 1990, as general manager of the Oakland Athletics, inked gun-toting hulk Jose Canseco to a record-setting five-year, $23 million deal. (When we asked Sandy Alderson to speak with us for this story, his spokesman said that he would prefer not to.)

A-Rod, he gets it: Business is business, and in the baseball business, owners crying poverty is a century-old tradition. "When Babe Ruth first signed for a hundred thousand – there were the same issues then," Alex says. "This is a large business, and it's getting larger. This has been blown up, all these numbers. It's over. Now let's go play ball."

You wonder if the kid will find it harder to focus on the field now. He looks you right in the eye. "No. My responsibility increases. I'm under a bigger microscope. But I always go back to the beauty and the clarity of the game."

Big Tom Hicks, he ain't been stupefied. No way,

nohow. "For Sandy Alderson to come into my city and trash our signin' the best player in baseball...." Hicks weighs his verbal options while his left hand slowly curls into a meaty fist. Hicks is a bull of a man – six three and well north of the Mendoza line weightwise – with a dry husk of an east Texas drawl. There are 381 names above his on *Forbes* magazine's list of the 400 wealthiest Americans – but I'd bet green money that the fifty-five-year-old Hicks could kick their butts, one at a time or all at once.

"Well," he finishes, lips pursed in a sour smile, "I thought that was pretty inappropriate." Hicks collects companies – close to two hundred over the past ten years or so – as cofounder, CEO, and chairman of Hicks, Muse, Tate & Furst, a leveraged-buyout firm. In 1998, he bought the Texas Rangers from his buddy George W. Bush; in 1996, he bought the Dallas Stars. That ring on Big Tom's fist, crusted with big ol' diamonds – that came with the Stars winnin' the Stanley Cup 'bout, oh, two years back.

Somebody here digs art, too, although it's more along the lines of furniture and statuary than all that painty crap. The Hicks, Muse offices are one whole floor – you step off the elevator and turn right into a four-rod-square waiting room full of marble and dark wood and sculpted cherubs and tufted chairs with tiny curved feet and gilt-edged clocks that stopped running a couple of centuries back, and then a voice in your left ear says, "Can I help you," and it isn't the receptionist and it isn't a question: It's the brawny security guy whose name might be Earl or Raymond but whose suit is better than yours, and from the tinge of malice in his smile you can see that, Earl or Raymond, he knows it.

Big Tom's own office is more sedate, with kind of an attached executive maid's quarters where two assistants work, and a desk you could land a corporate jet on, and shelves full of actual books, leather bound, some of which he may have actually cracked.

"Our model is to keep payroll to 50 to 55 percent of revenue," Hicks says, "real payroll, real cash. We're gonna be a little over $80 million, and our revenue this year will exceed $160 million. Our payroll goin' into free agency was $49 million. Compare that to where the Yankees were, where the Dodgers were, the Mets or Atlanta or Boston. We knew there was a bumper crop of free agents, and we didn't like the team we had. We got cheaper, we got younger, and we put ourselves in a position to have the flexibility to do what we've done."

Hicks opened the A-Rod book and didn't see only the shortstop who'd shatter Henry Aaron's records and deliver another ring or three unto his hammy fist: He saw Tiger, too, and Michael, and ol' Roger Staubach himself, all rolled into one.

"I read in one of the New York papers that I fell in love with Alex. I didn't fall in love. Alex Rodriguez is a good asset, and he's gonna own this city. Traditionally, the marquee athlete here has been a Dallas Cowboy. Alex will wear that cape. At his age, with his success and potential, he deserves to be the highest-paid guy in baseball – no question. After the first time I met him, I knew he wasn't goin' back to Seattle. I only worried about Atlanta and the Mets."

So while A-Rod spent the weekend of the winter meetings playing golf in Las Vegas, Big Tom Hicks and Scott Boras got after it good up at the Anatole. Real good, with Boras ducking out of the room to phone updates to Alex as Hicks kept upping the ante.

"Scott's a good negotiator," Hicks grins. "He was tryin' to get a twelve-year contract that could be repriced after three years. If we were gonna invest in Alex, we wanted to give our team a chance to really benefit from what he brings. And if our fans are gonna fall in love with A-Rod, we want him to be here for a while. The most important thing was to lock him in for seven years, particularly in the early years, at reasonable numbers."

What Big Tom did – "Very smart of the guy," says Boras, "very smart" – was to jack up the salary, all the way up to $242 million for ten years, with $36 million of it deferred. Slowly they worked out the deferral schedule and interest rates, the option and escalator clauses, and a list of twelve award bonuses so minutely crafted by Boras as to guarantee Rodriguez an extra shiny nickel for each time he appears on camera in uniform without spitting or tugging at himself.

"The last thing he put on the table," says Hicks, "was this signing bonus. He said he talked to Alex and that it was important to Alex – he needed $10 million to get situated, he wanted to buy a home in Dallas. So we swallowed hard and said yes to the $10 million on the basis that it would be deferred over five years."

Hicks gulped it down, but something still sticks in his craw. "Two, three days later, I told Boras, I said, 'I've been thinking about this, and I never look back on a deal at all, but I *do* keep score. I could've stared you down on that $10 million. You bring another player in here someday and I'm gonna get that $10 million back.' "

Hicks didn't wait long: When he took Rodriguez to lunch a few days later, the subject of signing bonuses somehow came up. "Alex looked at me with that boyish grin and said, 'Mr. Hicks, when you renegotiate my contract in seven years, I'm gonna give you back the $10 million.' So we shook hands on it. And he'll do it."

As soon as Boras heard about the lunch, he called Hicks. "I get you around my client for fifteen minutes and what do you do? You get $10 million out of him? You're killing me." Maybe Hicks could've stared down Boras on that $10 million, but I doubt it: Boras is always the guy with the ace showing, and the next time he blinks at the poker table or turns over his hole card will be the very first.

But then again, the Braves had folded their hand by refusing to give A-Rod a no-trade clause, and the Mets had beshat themselves back in November by claiming publicly that Boras had tried to shake them down for all manner of perks, which Boras steadfastly denies. The Mariners' best and last offer was a halfhearted five years at $19 million per, with less than $60 million guaranteed. The Orioles and the White Sox made late, hapless plays. The Rockies spent their free-agent dollars on pitching, and the Dodgers, with all their Murdoch money, never made it to the table.

Which left Big Tom. Maybe he could've stared Boras down. But he didn't. "I assure you," Hicks says, "he had other ten-year offers, and he had other offers over $20 million per year. I assure you."

And right there is the tell – proof positive that this is one deal Big Tom is damned sure looking back on. Because I had not said one word about the chance that Hicks had indeed been bidding against himself. Which doesn't make Hicks anybody's patsy. He got what he paid for: brilliance unto genius.

Nobody ever misjudged Alex Rodriguez

– not Tom Hicks, not the scouts who saw him as a schoolboy, and surely not young A-Rod himself, who would look up from his geometry homework and see agents flitting across his lawn like geckos.

"They had to buy a new front door," Boras says. "I scratched off the first one. I came here nine times in two months. Alex was so busy with school and baseball that it was hard to get time."

Boras and Rodriguez are kicking back after the Heat-Lakers game, reminiscing. It's their first chance to toast the deal; Boras flew in today from Baltimore, where he completed a four-year, $28 million deal for another free agent, David Segui. He was here in Miami a few days before that, but he'd been busy hammering out a five-year, $35 million contract with the Florida Marlins for catcher Charles Johnson. The winter meetings ended a week ago (lost in all the A-Rod hoo-ha in Dallas was pitcher Darren Dreifort, yet another Boras guy, signing for five years and $55 million with the Dodgers, which brings his grand total for the past ten days to, um, what's 5 percent of $370 million?), and Scott Boras has spent nine hours at home since.

"You remember the guy," Boras says, starting to giggle, "that one guy who brought you – he brought a bag." Alex dissolves in laughter while Boras continues. "This was the last couple of months of high school – that's when all the agents come because they hear it from the scouts."

Boras, of course, had been scouting Alex for three years by then. The kid was hardly a secret: A three-time high school all-American, Alex was named U.S.A. Baseball's Junior Player of the Year and Gatorade's National Student

Athlete of the Year. As a senior, he hit .505 with thirty-five stolen bases.

"This guy comes and takes you to lunch at Denny's...."

"Not Denny's," Alex gasps. "It was Hooters!"

"What'd he whip out on the table? A batting helmet?"

"Batting gloves. Shoes. Bats."

"He brought the equipment bag with him."

Suddenly Alex isn't laughing.

"A lot of Latin kids have nothing," he says. "They love it. But to me it was insulting. The limos – they came into my living room trying to wow me with all these things. And Scott never once said anything like that. He was factual: 'Let me tell you why you and I make a great combination. Let me tell you why if you do your job, I can do mine.'

"Those other guys were just a bunch of baloney – they shot themselves in the foot. I don't want to hear stories. I want to hear facts. I don't need you as a friend. I need you as my attorney. The advantage I have with Scott – like I already told him, I can fire you now, because you've got your job done for the next ten years – but seriously, not only do I think that I have the best negotiator in the big leagues, but I have a good human being, a family man who sets a good example for me. The contract's over – now I'm paying for the advice he can give me on a daily, weekly, yearly basis as I go through my career."

Boras glows fondly. "The thing that made it easy was that Alex always loved baseball," he says. "That was our common love."

Alex gloves the lob and crosses the bag. "I have a love affair with the game of baseball that is so sincere and genuine – I don't know. I don't know where it comes from, to be honest with you."

Me: "'The clarity and beauty of the game' – like you said before. That says it all."

"*Hah*. Tell Mike Lupica that," Boras says.

"He's killin' me, man," says A-Rod.

"Eleven times he left his job to go for higher compensation," Boras says.

"He kills me on national TV," says Alex, his voice rising. "On *The Sports Reporters*. I would like to ask that guy, *What would you do if you had this guarantee?* He's barkin', 'You wanna win? Seattle gave you a winner.' So what? I made a business decision. An economic decision. It was simple."

"The thing that bothers me the most," Boras says, "is that this guy doesn't understand baseball. He doesn't understand why Seattle won last year. This year he's gonna find out why they won."

Alex is unsmiling, hard-faced. "The thing about Mike Lupica that pisses me off," he says, "is that he makes me look like the biggest dickhead in the world, and then he takes a guy like Jeter and just puts him way up there."

So much for the brotherhood of shortstops united under the fatherhood of Honus Wagner.

"There's a big difference," says Boras. "Jeter had seventy-one RBIs and fifteen home runs. Jeter and Nomar last year had fifteen and twenty-one home runs. You can have a golden bulldozer, but if there's no dirt to push..."

"Jeter's been blessed with great talent around him," Alex says. "He's never had to lead. He can just go and play and have fun. And he hits second – that's totally different than third and fourth in a lineup. You go into New York, you wanna stop Bernie and O'Neill. You never say, *Don't let Derek beat you.* He's never your concern."

"Remember," Boras says, "when the troops are marching, who's the first to die?"

"The leader of the pack," Alex answers.

"The leader. Being a leader, you're always gonna take the bullet. Whenever one of these contracts is done, it's the worst decision in baseball. This is part of the tradition of our game."

"But the 250 mark, Scott. How long do you think that will take to break?" Alex asks.

"Aw," Boras says, smiling wide, "gimme a week."

A-Rod collects art. Tom Hicks collects compa-
nies. Scott Boras collects talent.

"The privilege and respect in this game have always revolved around one thing," Boras says. "Talent. The only power that any of us have in this game – teams or agents or whatever – is players. The talents. *That's* the commodity."

Bleary-eyed and hoarse, Boras sits at his desk in a nondescript third-floor suite in an island of smoked-glass buildings in Irvine, California, two minutes from John Wayne Airport, itching for the next deal, the next flight out. He flew home from Cleveland on Christmas Eve at 10:00 P.M., then zipped off with his wife and their three children on a five-day ski trip to Colorado, where Boras and the satchel holed up in the lodge while his family hit the slopes. Last night, he and his team banged heads in the conference room until 1:30 a.m., pitching arguments for Jason Varitek's arbitration hearing, and in an hour he heads back to Cleveland to complete a one-year, $10 million deal with the Indians for Juan Gonzalez.

"We could've gotten thirty million, guaranteed," Boras says. "But we would've had to do it for two years in a place Juan didn't want to play. I always do what's best for the players. Money is one thing, but putting them in an environment where they can succeed? You have to."

There are two theories put forth to explain why Scott Boras is the devil. The dumber one cites his insatiable greed. Oh, the money counts, yeah: Sweater-vests don't grow on trees. But Boras is already famous for being the sharpest lawyer and negotiator in sports; if it was all about the money, he could go cherry-picking among the five or ten best players in the NFL, NBA, and NHL, too. Shaq's daddy, Oscar De La Hoya, Hollywood's A-listers: Boras gets plenty of feelers. Two years ago, he spurned a nine-figure offer – not just money: *A-Rod money* – to sell his agency outright.

The other theory posits an embittered ex-minor-leaguer – call him Bo-Rod – who couldn't make the majors and decided to avenge himself on the game by wreaking legal and financial mayhem upon it. This theory might hold water if Boras hadn't wrecked both knees. Hadn't gotten that doctorate in pharmacy. Hadn't practiced medical law. And hadn't known, all along, that he wasn't good enough to make the Show.

"I tried," he says. "I really gave it my all. And it was so much fun trying. In the end – my knees. I had to have 'em drained all the time. I had no lateral movement. When that went away, my opportunity to be a competent major league player went away."

Scott Boras stepped to the plate for the last time in 1977, at twenty-five years old. He had watched tough men break down in tears in the parking lot after getting released, hometown studs invincible to everything except truth and time. They'd hung on in the minors year after year, without training or skills beyond baseball, hoping for a shot that never would come.

"Everyone's goal is a long-term major league career," Boras says. "They use that term – *career*. I say, *That's not in our vocabulary.* This is an opportunity; it is *not* a career. The number that we crunch? A six-year major league career – .0025 percent. It ain't happenin'. It's a wonderful, wonderful game. And it's a wonderful opportunity. But it is not a career."

Boras left the field on his own terms, but he never forgot what he'd seen. When a couple of former teammates who'd made it to the bigs sought his help in negotiating their contracts in the '80s – Boras was practicing law in Chicago by then – he said yes. By '85, he was a full-time agent, focused mainly on the amateur draft. For four consecutive years, beginning in 1988, his picks got record-setting signing bonuses. Boras recognized even then that good pitching would forever be in short supply; today, more than two thirds of his clients are pitchers, including Greg Maddux and Kevin Brown, who signed contracts, in '97 and '98, that made each of them, for a while, the highest-paid player in baseball.

The first time Boras saw Alex Rodriguez play, A-Rod was a spindly-legged fourteen-year-old. Boras didn't see 5 percent of a quarter-billion-dollar contract. He didn't see a shovel he could use to bury Bud Selig 'neath the hard-packed dirt. He saw talent. Phenomenal talent.

"Alex was in the big leagues at age eighteen. I never told him this, but I was just scared for him. Here he is, in the big leagues, and I was just sitting there thinking, *I've got this guy who could be the greatest player in the game, and they're gonna damage him.* "But every time I'd go to the ballpark, I'd think, *What am I worried about? This guy – he's got it.*"

Managers and general managers – without talent, they're quickly out of work. Sometimes, they rush raw players, overpitch young arms, destroy confidence and careers. Owners will bargain hard and then present themselves as victims of greed. Commissioners will poor-mouth the product and scapegoat the talent. The players are the game, but sometimes the men who run the sport lose sight of that.

Never Boras. Yes, he is shrewd. Tireless. Calculating. Wickedly smart. That doesn't make him Satan; if you're a ballplayer, that makes Scott Boras the guy you want covering your back. He has a staff of fifteen; eight played big-league ball. Some coached and managed; some went to Harvard, Stanford, Duke. They wear T-shirts and jeans to work; they eat lunch at a sports bar, order chili, and make fart jokes; they spend eighteen-hour days at the office six, seven days a week; and they can't wait to tell you why Jason Varitek deserves to be paid more for his fourth season than Jorge Posada got. Boras has ten scouts planted in baseball hotbeds from Cape Cod to Venezuela, a full-time sports psychologist, and a computer engineer who used to work for NASA.

"Every working hour is the game," says Boras. "I wasn't playing baseball for the money – I knew that early on. I was playing to *compete*. It was a kick. It was really, really challenging. This is my life. That's what I do. It's a privilege. It's just great. It's just never anything but absolutely intriguing for me."

A-Rod said it: Before the money comes the love. Find the work you love: *voilà!* – you've found all the beauty and clarity one battered satchel of a heart can hold. You've found your game.

Framed on his desk is a small photo of Boras in his early twenties. It must be spring training: He's wearing a Cubs uniform. There's a bat resting on his shoulder. His hair is fat and blond under his cap, his smile is sunlit.

"I wasn't going back to that farm," Boras says. "I hated it. I was in jail. Out on that damned tractor all day long. I didn't mind the cows so much. But I wasn't going back." Boras laughs and walks over to the window. The bat's over there in the corner – the Louisville Slugger S361 he carried to home plate that last time up, in San Antonio, in 1977, with Bob Welch on the mound. Bob Welch, who went up to the Dodgers in '78 and spent seventeen years in the bigs.

"I always hear it – *Man, I'd do this for a million dollars.* I say, *Look, we all would.* This is about mystery. The real mystery of this is, Why would someone pay someone? 'Cause all these players would play this game for love."

Boras holds the bat in front of him, the handle resting in both palms, weighing it, bouncing it, feeling the heft of the barrel.

Welch goes into his stretch.

"Fastball," Boras says, open-eyed and dreaming. "Outside corner."

The fingers of both hands wrap above the knob. Gently, gently.

"Double," Boras says, nodding, grinning, rocking on his feet.

Double?

"Double. Left center-field gap."

Chapter Sixteen

Mickey Rourke

```
Thug
```

Lost inside a huge sweater and a baggy, low-slung pair of jeans, an oversized brown fedora slumped well down on his forehead, half walking, half leaning against a young woman with long brown hair, actor/boxer Mickey Rourke trudges down a hallway of the Plaza Hotel in New York City. It is two o'clock on a winter afternoon, early for him, and he has a meeting scheduled, although he can't quite remember with whom. At the door of the Oak Room, where we have arranged to meet, he shakes hands tentatively. Turning to the young woman, he asks, "Is he the stunt coordinator?" His smile is off-kilter, the fogged grin of a sot trying to remember where he parked the car. His sunglasses have upswept tortoiseshell rims and teardrop lenses.

The young woman he's with, Robbie – "my special assistant in charge of international affairs," he calls her – reminds him of who I am and what we are doing here. She carries his money, his smokes and his cellular phone. The trappings of his fame, even here at rock bottom, still require that he be coddled like an infant. He is not left alone, not even to go from the second floor of the Plaza to the first. When he wants or needs something, someone must hand it to him. Preferably a woman.

The assistants, the publicists, the friends/bodyguards/gofers – they all have the same job these days: holding Mickey together. They tell him what he wants to hear – above all, by their hovering concern, that he still matters very much – and they say nothing that might register in his ears as unpleasant, such as the name of his wife from whom he is at this moment estranged. Carré Otis, whose presence is palpable, and not only because her name and visage are variously tattooed all over his body. Back in Los Angeles, a spousal abuse filed by Otis is scheduled for trial in a few weeks. Rourke stands accused of slapping her, knocking her down and kicking her. In a few days Otis is due to arrive here in New York, attempting to resurrect her career as a model. She has a new boyfriend, a clothing designer. And here sits Mickey Rourke, his phantom acting comeback now at four years and counting, staring into the abyss through a pair of Edith Prickley shades.

At a table in the back of the room, Mickey takes off his hat; underneath it is a 'do-rag. He removes the glasses His face is wan, hard-used, his cheeks rutted with nicks and scars, his chin stubbled. Despite this scruffy machismo, his air is feminine: the delicate dark eyes, the moue of his Kewpie-doll mouth, every movement and expression styled and marked with the peculiar self-regard of a creature obsessed with its own appearance. Like a doll, he has different looks to reflect his various personae: Biker Mickey, Mickey the Fop and, today, Hip-Hop Mick. Like an old-time actress, he is coy about his age: He claims 38, but some reports have him as old as 43. He sports a fortyish blonde at a nearby table staring his way. She has finished her lunch and is getting into her coat. She smooths her leather pants with her hands, takes her purse from the table and pushes in her chair, never taking her eyes from him. "They still look at me," he says, smirking, after she is gone.

At this moment, Rourke is the snake man, the character he played in *9 1/2 Weeks* and *Wild Orchid*, who, armed only with a hoarse whisper and a bloated script, ignites the loins of any female, however reluctant. To most of us, this is simply a tired cinema fantasy: the tender thug, soft beneath the manly chest, and hard beneath the zipper, the male equivalent of the whore with a heart of gold, who beds and weds the ur-female mannequin, gorgeous but cold, half-human, half-puppet. He reveals her to herself, brings her to life; in return, she becomes the beautiful mirror who exists solely to reflect his own hard but sweet face and larger-than-life force. Fade, the end, roll credits.

"Women do what I tell them," Rourke says. He's serious.

And how, exactly, does the work?

"You've got to tell them what to do." Big smile.

Reality, which plays out in three dimensions according to a mostly hidden script, is usually more complex than this. But not for Mick, whose grip on a certain type of woman – models, exclusively, whose careers require the submission of body and will – is the last vestige of his potency. It began with Otis, Rourke's *Wild Orchid* costar. With his fame fading, he married Otis, demanded that she give up modeling and began photographing her himself, hobbling her in chains and smearing her with oil. Now, during their separation, Rourke works the fashion industry soil. At a party Mickey threw for himself, a modeling agent regaled me with the story of a friend whose recent liaison with Rourke had left her feeling unsatisfied with other, lesser men. "I've been bitten by the viper," the friend had said.

Mickey orders roast beef, cold, no bread. He says his trainer, an Argentinean woman, has had him on an 800-calorie diet for three months. Twice he lifts his sweater to demonstrate the flatness of his stomach. It's a nice stomach, a fine stomach, a proud stomach. He travels with a Gym In A Bag. His Cuban sparring partner shares his suite upstairs; together they work out. Still, he smokes many Marlboros and does not seem fit. His stomach is toned, yes, but he looks thin, battered. He weighs 163 pounds now; he boxed at 178. The boxing may be over. "I don't know yet," he says. "Last year, I fractured my cheekbone, I broke my fifth and fourth metacarpal, broke my knuckle twice, my big toe, and I've got an eight-inch scar underneath my tongue." Pause. "Well, it's about four inches. I had to go back to the boxing because I was self-destructing. I had no respect for myself being an actor. So I went back to a profession which really humbled me."

Mickey says that he fought nine times over two years, mainly in Europe. He does not say that the dawn of his boxing career coincided with the demise of his career in mainstream movies. One opponent, he says, had fought for the middleweight and light-heavyweight championship of Canada. He does not say why such a consummate pugilist would take a six-rounder with a fortyish actor. He claims a ring record of seven wins and two draws; six of them, he says, were knockouts. He does not say that his pro debut in fact came in 1991, that it was a four-round decision in Miami over a moonlighting auto mechanic.

He is ready, now, to forsake boxing, if only Hollywood will finally take him back. He's in New York shooting *Bullet*, a low-budget gangster flick out in Brooklyn, costarring the not-yet convicted, not-yet-gelded rapper Tupac Shakur. This is what it's come to: "I'm playing a Jewish guy who gets out of jail after eight years," he says. "There was an actress we wanted to play the mother – her agency called back and said, 'I'm not going to stick my talent in a movie with Mickey Rourke and Tupac Shakur.'"

I ask about Carré Otis: Would he like to patch things up? "Don't talk about that at all," he warns. "Not at all."

I venture that he sounds like he's hurting over her, like he hasn't let go. "I don't let go," he says, his voice nearly breaking. "Ever. Of nothin'."

"What do you want to know?" he asks after a moment. "Because I'd rather give it to you straight than have you paraphrase some quote that's not true. Her agent has been using my celebrity to try to get her career off the ground. So I don't want to give it any play at all."

Suddenly he puts his arm around my shoulder and pulls me to him until my head is against his. In a hoarse whisper, he says she has a big problem, that it was someone else who slapped and kicked her, or maybe she just fell down.

It's at this moment, tête-a-tête, that I realize that Mickey Rourke has no smell, no odor whatsoever. None, bad or good. Not even his breath.

A woman answers the door of his suite at the

Plaza the following afternoon and introduces herself as Karen. She is full-lipped, brown-haired, blue-eyed, tight-jeaned, sweet-assed, heart-stoppingly fine. She looks, in fact, a lot like a vest-pocket version of Carré Otis. She says she is a singer/model; she once was a model/singer, but she has chosen to put her music first. Mickey is on the phone to L.A., pitching a script he wrote. He describes it as "an ethereal Western."

His phone call finished, he escorts Karen to the door and stretches out on the couch, stripped to the waist. It is mid-afternoon, but the large room is darkened, lit by a single lamp; the floor-to-celing draperies look as if they haven't stirred in months. Despite the burnished wood and gilt-framed art, there is a whiff of decay. Sweat socks, perhaps, or a remnant of his twin Chihuahuas, who are in another room, asleep. The couch is silken gold, except for one large stain, a smudge on the fabric at the precise spot where, if he were sitting up, his head would rest. His stomach looks excellent today, and his face seems fuller, more robust, less sallow. His hair

Cutting Room Floor: Rourke

THE PITCH: If they handed out Oscars for career trainwrecks, he'd have eight. On the other hand, he loves little dogs, leggy models, and Tupac.

SCENE: A small restaurant on the Upper East Side of Manhattan. Fashion Week in New York City – as bizarre and degrading a non-surgical rite as ever devised by any tribe on the planet – is nearly over, and Mickey Rourke is co-hosting a dinner party for dozens of models.

Never do I get near enough to talk to Mickey, but that's fine, because never before have I found myself in a room filled by dozens of models – all young, lithe, and dressed to kill. For a half-hour, the effect is literally astonishing – so many flawless faces flawlessly made-up; so many long legs and heart-stopping asses – I'm dumbstruck, agape. Then, just like that, the effect wears off, and they all look sort of...silly. You can waste a lot of hot air debating the subjective nature of beauty. That night, I found living proof.

BACKSTORY: Poor Tupac, *alav hashalom*. He and his Thug Life posse were rolling in Mickey's wake the whole week, and while his vibe was anything but warm, he was willing to pass a joint to a strange magazine writer at Club Expo. His too-slim corpus of work on film is powerful; his weed, sad to say, was weak.

CONFLICT: Bad, bad mojo, what with Rourke shooting a movie he knew stunk (*Bullet* wound up going direct-to-video, but only after Tupac's death), and chasing his ex-wife all over town while I chased after him. I don't think we had one moment together that felt pleasant or easy, and I'm not sure I got one straight answer from him. To this day, when I see or hear his name, the first words to come to mind are 'full of shit.'.

WISH I'D WRITTEN: Well, I wish I hadn't written Rourke's acting future off so glibly. Not only did he keep plugging away, he also became a better – darker, deeper, more interesting – actor, scary fun to watch. To wit, the "new" Mick in 2005, in *Sin City*, and later the same year, in *Domino*, holding his own and then some with Keira Knightley.

seems to have a separate, darker existence, as if someone had dipped a sea anemone in motor oil and sewn it to his skull. His mood is improved, reflective but not somber. He's still talking about his acting comeback.

"I think people know that I'm making a genuine attempt to come back and ask for redemption," he says quietly. "It's up to them to say, 'Okay, Mickey, we'll give you that opportunity.'"

The phone rings and he rises to get it. He's in the process of having several of his tatoos removed by a laser surgeon in Miami, but above his left shoulder blade a large, fine-line portrait of Carré Otis is untouched. Her face, gentle and smiling, rises above dark clouds like a sun; her hair billows around it. When he answers the phone, no one is on the line. One of his two Chihuahuas, perhaps awakened by the ringing, trots into the room. "C'mere, baby," he coos and carries it back to the couch with him. The tiny dog is trembling, cradled in his arms. "They're not used to New York weather. They have sweaters somewhere. We bought them sweaters."

Marlon Brando's autobiography sits on the coffee table between us. "It's happened to Brando and a lot of people," he notes, "where they were put on a shelf." Last year Mickey made a Japanese cigarette commercial and a movie called *Fall Time*, which, after a tepid reception at the Sundance Film Festival, has yet to be released. He says that if he does not get another offer soon, he may call his boxing promoter again, try to find another fight.

His Cuban sparring partner enters the room. The phone rings again: another hang-up. Mickey and his sparring partner have a brief conversation in Spanish. They suspect it's Carré who keeps calling and hanging up.

Mickey grew up in Miami's notorious Liberty City; when I asked him how he came to live there, he snapped, "Because my mother married a pig." That would be his stepfather, a cop who regularly slapped Mickey and his brother around. Mickey missed his own father fiercely, with a grudge he held for decades. Before he came to New York to study acting, he was a penniless thug, beering and drugging with the boys, fighting in the streets.

"I am trying," he says now, "through a lot of therapy and a lot of growing, to get the chip off my shoulder. Anybody who's got demons inside him and, let's say, comes from a background, let's say, of being physically abused to a certain extent, you have an innate hatred that never goes away. Never goes away. Because of the hurt, because you can't defend yourself when you're little." Prizefighting, he says, helped him outgrow this. "I had to come to terms with the demons about not feeling like a piece of shit as a man," he explains, and stops talking for a long minute. "I think the boxing is coming to an end," he sighs. "I have no choice; it's time to take the acting, this year, as far as I can take it. I'm not going to get a lot of opportunities. I've gotta do it."

At moments like this, it's apparent that some part of Mickey Rourke knows he's finished. He has spent his entire adult life convincing audiences that he is someone else – speaking other people's lines, investing in the psychic landscapes of men who don't exist, wearing their clothes, fighting their battles and suffering their wounds. If Hollywood refuses to offer him identities to slip into, if the boxing is over, then he's left with only himself, a lost and beaten little boy whose father left him long ago. So he does what he can. He's the name in boldface in the gossip columns; he's the tough guy, the fashion plate, the stud the models dig. Self-parody, it seems, is better than no self at all.

The sad thing, the thing that makes Mickey Rourke in descent so fascinating, is that once upon a time this guy could act. His small, dark eyes, his twisted, closed-mouth smile, the weary husk of his voice: He was a kid in 1981 when he had his first standout role, a small part in *Body Heat*, but every word and gesture said he knew about rage and desire, about feeling caged and doing whatever has to be done to break out.

People noticed, particularly serious directors. Barry Levinson gave Rourke his first featured role, in *Diner*. Coppola made him a Motorcycle Boy in *Rumble Fish*. Then came *The Pope of Greenwich Village*, his breakthrough, the performance that his fans still recall with passion. He played Charlie Moran, an Irish tough with mob problems, a volatile relationship with his woman, and a self-immolating attachment to the macho, inane code of honor that, at least in the movies, rules the mean streets.

For Mickey Rourke, of course, the role was not exactly a stretch. And while that hard-guy persona he needed to survive growing up the way he did may have helped drive him to acting success, it translated poorly to actual stardom. Even in Liberty City, when you call your job bullshit and your boss a scumbag – as Mickey publicly described *9 1/2 Weeks* producer Samuel Goldwyn Jr. – and showed up at work with a posse of Hell's Angels and demand work for all of them, you are begging for the shitcan.

Yet he was still a star then, still had his choice of roles, could have cleaned up his own mess. Instead, as the bleak non-hit parade of neo-noir detectives and mumbling losers grew endless, he became too painful to watch and too difficult to bother working with. However deluded Rourke may be about his past and future in Hollywood, viewing his films in chronological order, watching a fine young actor re-create himself as a stumbling hack – without range, without craft, without even giving a damn – is both astounding and tragic, like seeing a wrecking ball slam a building into dust.

"I need character witnesses," he says, the Chihuahua next to him on the couch. "Publicists can't really do it – it's gotta be people within the industry. They gotta say, 'Hey, you know, Rourke's ready to start workin' again.'"

That night, on the movie set, the playground of a public school in Brooklyn, I'm waiting for Mickey to let me into his trailer, where, I've been promised, the soul-baring is to continue. "We'll have all night," Mick had assured me. "I'm a night man, anyway; I'm a very free spirit at night. There's no rules."

Every hour or so, the unit publicist knocks on the trailer door. The door opens slightly and the publicist cranes his head inside. There is a brief conversation and then he returns, shaking his head. "Not yet," he says each time, as if one of us believes that eventually I'll get inside. One who belongs in the trailer is in the trailer. One who is outside the trailer belongs outside the trailer. No way exists to get inside the trailer except to be inside the trailer.

The unit publicist was ever so much more cheerful on the ride out to Brooklyn. "Mickey's incredible," he had said then. "We heard that he was difficult, but he's been just incredibly cooperative. He brings everyone on the set into his life." This may explain why Tupac won't let anyone into his trailer, either.

When filming breaks for lunch around 11 P.M., Tupac and Mickey dine alone, in their respective trailers. I go into the school cafeteria, grab a plate of tepid catered chicken and sit across from Matty Powers, an actor who looks remarkably like a younger, fresher Mickey Rourke. He admires Mickey, feels grateful to be working with him, but he's worried about the mood swings.

"I can't get the guy to take his hands out of his pockets," Matty says. "I said, 'Mick, how are you?' He says, 'Ah, fifty-fifty.' I say, 'Mick, you're not even twenty-eighty.'" Matty says that Mick has agreed to get tested for depression after the shoot is over.

Mickey has a brief scene after midnight. He comes out of the trailer and walks past me without even a nod. At 2:30 A.M., Robbie emerges to confirm that I have no chance of being inside the trailer tonight. Tomorrow is possible, she says, and provides the cellular number. When I phone the next morning to check if it still is possible, MIckey answers. "How the fuck did you get this number?" he says. It sounds like another bad day, so I hang up.

I catch up with Mickey a few days later, early on the Saturday evening that marks the end of Fashion Week in New York. His people have spent the week planting breathless stories in the tabloids about Mickey's romp through the spring collections.

First, the [New York] *Daily News* ran a front-page photo of the begowned Carré Otis and an inset of her hubby; "DON'T LET HIM NEAR ME," screamed the headline. On Friday it was reported that Rourke had trashed his suite at the Plaza to the tune of twenty grand and that owner Donald Trump had banned him from its hallowed grounds for life. The same day, the *Post* ran a four-column picture of Rourke smooching with some 16-year-old supermodel.

Now he's in his favorite little café on Madison Avenue, dressed in his hip-hop best, sans hat, with a fresh scrape underneath one eye and his hair waving in lank little tendrils, looking as if it has spent the week at the bottom of a service bay at Jiffy Lube. the entire Rourke troupe is present: Pink, Mickey's longtime companion/bodyguard; Matty Powers; Robbie, his publicist, who has flown in from the coast to assume wet-nurse duty; and both Chihuahuas. The evening is warm and the dogs are sweaterless.

"Whaddaya got?" as soon as I sit down.

"Huh?"

"Whaddaya wanna know?" He's pissed off.

"What's with the hair?" I ask.

"The what?"

"The hair."

"It's growing back. Next question." The table gets quiet; someone asks Mickey for a smoke. One of the dogs, apparently sensing Daddy's nasty vibe, leaps from Pink's lap onto the floor. "Loki, baby," Mick calls, "it's okay. What are you looking at, my little angel? I love you." Mickey gives the dog an air kiss and I ask him about the 16-year-old supermodel.

"I would not go near a 16-year-old girl. I don't even fuck. I've gotta be in love to fuck a woman. I'll get a blow job, but I won't fuck. I cannot fuck unless I'm in love."

"Me neither," I say. "How about a blow job?"

"Open it up," Mickey says, laughing, pointing at my crotch. "I'll suck your dick. Got twenty dollars?"

My zipper stays closed, but the exchange relaxes the conversation somewhat. I ask him how the last couple nights of filming *Bullet* went.

"You missed the fight scene, schmuck," he answers. "What a schmuck. You missed it. You missed the most difficult night." He turns to the publicist. "He misses the fight scene. What a schmuck."

Oh, yeah? "How was Fashion Week? They let you into any of Carré's shows?"

"I did go. We're not gonna mention her name in the article, though. You understand what I'm saying? They're just trying to get her movie career off, and it's not gonna happen. You understand? They're using my good name to make me look like a piece of shit. I don't want you to put that in – I just want you to call other people and put in that she can't act. That's all. All right?"

Talk turns to finding a place to watch the George Foreman and Michael Moorer fight for the heavyweight championship in a couple of hours. Robbie brings out the cellular, but the midtown sports bar Mickey instructs her to phone is already fully booked. There's an alternative, a topless club, but first, Mickey says, he has to call someone himself to obtain clearance. Both clubs are mobbed-up, but not with the same family. I ask him why he has to make the call.

"Because there was life before acting, okay?" he says mysteriously.

When I press him on this, he tells me that his real father was a shooter, a Mob hit man known as "Two-Gun Philly." Narrowing his eyes and dropping his voice, he adds, "That's a piece of information that'll put you in the ground if you use it."

Yeah, Mick's been friendly with guys, used to hang out at the Ravenite Social Club and so forth. He was caught on-camera outside the courthouse during one of Gotti's trials, yapping to the local news about how tight he was with the capo. Ever since, Mickey Rourke has been considered a loudmouth and a punk, and he knows it. That's why he makes those phone calls.

At the topless club, Tupac Shakur and a couple members of his Thug Life crew join us. No problem: The entire center section of the front row has been reserved for Mickey and his group. Tupac and Mickey grew tight while filming *Bullet*; they sit side by side in the middle of the row. The fight has not begun, so the mirrored stage is held by a series of women thrusting about to the most irritating crap-rock imaginable. The overall effect is as exciting as toast, and Mickey and Tupac, huddled in discussion, never look up. They may be comparing legal notes: Tupac's sodomy trial begins in two days.

When the lights go down and the fight begins, all conversation halts. A series of young men appear at my side – I'm at the end of the row – and ask me if it's all right to approach Mr. Rourke for an autograph. Since I am large and tattooed, I assume that they have mistaken me for one of his bodyguards, and I turn each of them away: Mr. Rourke can't be bothered now. Mr. Rourke takes boxing very seriously.

Mickey's rooting loudly for the 45-year-old Foreman, along with everyone else in the room, but there is little to cheer through the first nine rounds. Moorer, in fact, is pounding Foreman's pumpkin face into mush. Suddenly, in the tenth round, Foreman clubs the younger man with a sledgehammer right and knocks him out. "See? See?" Mickey screams, leaping from his chair. "Age don't mean shit!" As the group is escorted to a table for dinner, Mickey tells me that he won $30,000 betting on Foreman. After the meal, the waitress shyly asks Mickey if she can perform a couch dance for him in a private room at the back of the club. "I would love to so much," she says. "Please." Mickey graciously ascents.

Mickey's back at the table in fifteen minutes; given his normal state of dishevelment, I can't tell if anything fellationic has transpired.

It's after midnight, time to head to Club Expo, the trendy dance hall where Mickey hangs regularly. Mickey's arrival at Expo is precisely chore-ographed. He has removed his sweater to reveal a white sleeveless under-shirt and an enormous wooden cross hanging from a cable-thick rosary around his neck. His jeans droop stylishly below the waistband of his chalk-striped boxers. At his side, Tupac is an encrusted version of gold subtly accented by a blue New York Rangers jersey and a no-label 'do-rag. We're met by club personnel, ushered quickly into a side entrance and escorted up to the roped-off velvet-cushioned VIP section, where, on most Saturday nights, Mickey leans against the railing and scans the throng below. Occasionally, he'll spot a young vixen and have her brought to him. It's a nice setup.

Tonight, however, Carré Otis herself is planted on the burgundy cushions in Mickey's section. She's wearing a tight black dress that plunges midway down her creamy bosom. Her hair is pulled back tightly; her immobile face is a still life of pink, untouchable lust.

"She looks ravishing," I say to Mickey's publicist. "Don't tell Mickey that," he squeaks, working hard to appear stricken. "I just can't believe this is happening." That's when it becomes clear that this is only another staged event, a show. Carré Otis knows exactly where she's sitting, as did the Expo people who met Rourke at the door. As does every tabloid photographer in New York City. When your career is down the crapper, even bad publicity is good publicity, and each moment of this charade reunion is captured on film. Carré moves out of Mick's section shortly, and the Rourke party spreads out. A tray of drinks arrives, sent by Otis. Mickey orders a bottle of Cristal for Carré; Tupac delivers it.

In his VIP section, Mickey swigs from a bottle

of red wine; Tupac rolls and smokes joint after joint. As if the scuzz-celebrity quotient here tonight isn't quite high enough, Shannon Doherty appears on the cushions. She and Tupac talk; Mickey is busy scanning the floor below, where someone has hoisted Carré atop a huge speaker on the floor. She is dancing, stiffly, alone, above the crowd. I notice two girls who have been allowed beyond the rope; they are standing at my side, staring at Mickey's back, whispering and giggling. The one with raven pigtails, her midriff bare, approaches Mickey. The other, blonde and bubbly cute, asks me who I am. She and her friend are models, she tells me and begins to laugh. "Look," she says, pointing to her friend, whose hand is now down the back of Mickey's jeans. "He's so gross. I can't believe it."

She wants to know what Tupac is like. I tell her all I know is that he's smoked a lot of weed tonight. "He'll probably want to do that anal thing," she says, laughing, and moves to him. In a little while it's time to go home. The blonde leaves with Tupac, and Mickey and her friend take the next cab. Before he gets in, Mickey comes over to give me a hug. His lips brush my cheek. "Take care of yourself," he says warmly. I still can't smell a thing, not even the wine.

Tempus fugit, they say, and lives change, but not all

that much. Shortly after I felt Mick's farewell kiss, a Los Angeles court dismissed the single count of misdemeanor spousal abuse against him. The city prosecutor's office was ready to go ahead – Mickey faced a maximum one-year sentence – but Carré Otis simply didn't show up to testify.

"Apparently," said Rourke's attorney, "these two wonderful people have been able to work things out between them without it becoming a public spectacle."

On Valentine's Day, 1995, with newspaper photographers in tow, Mick and Carré announced their reengagement. They had not actually been divorced, of course, but this way they were able to buy new rings.

Poor Tupac was not nearly so fortunate. He was convicted of sexual abuse and sentenced to four and a half years in prison, which turned out to be the good news. The bad news arrived on the night before his conviction, when he was shot five times in a mysterious ambush in the lobby of a Manhattan recording studio. One bullet hit a testicle. "Thug Life to me is dead," he told *Vibe* magazine from his jail cell. Eligible for parole in eighteen months, he plans to team up with Mike Tyson to help save young blacks from violence.

As of this writing, according to Mickey's publicist, Rourke and Otis are very happy. "Mickey looks incredible, better than ever," he told me, "and Carré is modeling full-time." Yes, he confirms, Mickey definitely has retired from boxing.

Any current movie projects?

"He's not really working on anything right now," says the publicist.

Chapter Seventeen

Christy Turlington

Scholar

And then I saw her face. That face. I

had seen it before, of course, somewhere. Ten thousand times. I hadn't known its name, or, rather, I knew its name but didn't know that this name, half stuffy, half silly, went with that face. She wore nothing special – a plain black pants suit, a high-necked jersey of dark green, black wedge-heeled shoes. Nudity would've been welcome relief. That face makes demands beyond the imagination. Each plane of it – even the philtrum, the rectangular cleft above her upper lip – perfectly formed and entirely symmetrical, each a separate, swelling voice in a choir of pure praise.

Christy Turlington, returning the favor, believes in God.

Christy's search for meaning began here, with faith, after she was named godmother to her niece. "My understanding," she says, "is that the godparent really is supposed to be a spiritual influence, and so I thought, Okay, well, I've got certain issues, and I want to start, like, looking at them."

I know, I know. She doesn't sound like Hannah Arendt. Cut Christy a break. At 28, she has been a supermodel nearly half her life. Now, in addition, she is a student. "I'm constantly being told, 'Ha, ha – she's going to school. Maybe she'll learn how to spell.' It's just the kind of thing that comes along with this job that I didn't actually choose, that I fell into. There are negative associations, and amongst them are that you are just completely worthless."

Some blessings, says that face, are worse than a curse.

Christy Turlington goes to church – she is Catholic – and to school. She is a junior at New York University, torn between majoring in art histo-

Cutting Room Floor: Turlington

THE PITCH: If you're going to carry a girl's books to school, she may as well be a supermodel.

SCENE: Walking to class at New York University with Christy was the nearest I've ever come to invisibility. For ten minutes, as we made our way through the first-week-of-class throngs on the downtown Manhattan streets, her face cleared our path like a hurricane. Seeing her, people froze. Looking back over my shoulder, I saw them behind us wearing goofy, astonished smiles – and nobody would have noticed me had I been prancing naked beside her.

In the course of my professional duties, I have spent a fair amount of time in the presence of four semi-officially designated supermodels – Christy, Carré Otis, Rebecca Romijn, and Naomi Campbell. Each of them was stunning to behold. Ms. T, however, was the most beautiful. Yeah, I know there's no disputing taste, but trust me – Christy, by far, hands down, end of story.

BACKSTORY: The original conceit was for me to carry Christy's books to class for her, but because it was the first week of the semester, she had no books to carry – which was just as well, because Christy's not the kind of girl who wants some dope carrying her books.

I found this out at the NYU bookstore, where we went to buy her textbooks after classes ended. Christy did let me carry the two bags from the shelves to the cashier, then up the stairs and out into the street, where she asked me – in a sweet, firm voice – to hand 'em over.

ry, literature or religion. Of her three courses this semester, the toughest is Theism, Atheism, and Existentialism, with Professor Leahy. "I heard it was really hard," Christy says on the first day of classes – classes to which I accompany her -- "but it sounds fascinating. And because it's scary to me, some of those ideas, and because I don't know anything about them, it's like, that's the class. The thing that's hardest and most difficult – that's the

---

CONFLICT: Supermodel or Elephant Man, the curse of knowing that everyone is looking at you everywhere you go requires a certain mindset.

"I can't be completely oblivious to it," Christy explained. "I can see if someone's looking at me a little bit too long. I can hear it out of the corner of my ear when someone mentions my name as I walk by. I just choose to ignore it. It's the only way that I can be comfortable. You have to pretend you're deaf and stupid. I'd rather have them kind of confused, and then, while they're thinking about it, I'm gone."

And it's even worse, she said, on the job. "Whatever they say is distracting. I don't get off by somebody saying, 'You look great,' or, 'You look really sexy.' That, if anything, would make me freeze and be a lot more self-conscious. I don't take any of those kinds of physical compliments seriously. I couldn't absorb those words the amount of times that I do and be a person living on this planet today."

WISH I'D WRITTEN: After the bookstore, Christy did let me buy us banana-strawberry smoothies, and we walked to Washington Square Park and sat on a bench and talked.

The way I wrote the piece, there was no way to make a scene out of it, but that was really nice, to sit in the park on a sweet, sunny autumn day in New York City and talk.

With Christy Turlington.

---

one I aim for."

The search for meaning is fraught with fear and, therefore, fearless.

Professor Leahy's syllabus vows a month of Sartre alone. Kierkegaard. Nietzsche. "I'm serious," Leahy warns at the first class meeting. "I'm dead serious. This is my life." I believe him. In his forties, thin, balding, bearded and ponytailed, he's clad in a short-sleeved mango-colored shirt, wrinkled white slacks and black Kmart sneakers.

Christy takes notes in a neat, rounded script.

The fingers curled around the pen are like good legs: creamy, tapered, supple. Each ends in a squared, shortish nail, buffed with pale pink. That face betrays nothing, a qualm least of all.

"Plato" – Leahy caresses the name as if he and the Greek were old lovers – "said that the ideal of the good transcends reality and knowledge."

Perhaps. It is a large lecture hall, but Christy likes to sit down front. So the time will come this semester when the vortex of that face yanks the scales of received truth from Leahy's vision and he is forced to confront an ideal carved of flesh. Watch him retreat behind the master's toga then.

"In the beginning," Christy says of academic life, "it's easy to have all your reading done. I always do this, every semester. You want to be really on top of things. I'll definitely do my reading tonight, tomorrow night, over the weekend."

I ask her her grade-point average.

"Three-point something," she says. "It doesn't really matter, because I'm just kind of growing."

That is Christy's quest: to grow. And, perhaps, someday, something more: to share that growth with others. "I grew up wanting to be a writer. I thought it was, like, the most noble profession. I loved to read so much. I thought, Oh, my God, if I could make somebody feel like this, if I could do that, that's gonna be the most incredible thing. So I do hope to write."

This strikes me as both greedy and unfair – isn't it enough to see your face on every magazine rack without ever dealing with an editor? – until I recall that as a lonely teenager I yearned to be a gorgeous woman whose sole quest would be to play with herself all day. Writing, of course, is not so different. I mention none of this to Christy. She will find her own meaning. She will find that everything she reads and writes and sees is a mirror.

After Leahy's lecture comes the class about dreams. A small, fun class, although no less replete with meanings. This professor is also a practicing Jungian therapist and so was far too busy deciphering mandalas to prepare a syllabus. Next week, he promises, and asks for questions.

"Is it, um, like, possible, you know," squeaks the hip-hop halfwit next to Christy, wearing an auburn goatee and jeans whose waistline seems to occupy the same longitude as his balls, "for, like, you know, other people to, like, you know, control your dreams? Like, um, voodoo?"

Christy asks nothing. At the next class meeting, says the professor, the students will introduce themselves briefly. Christy has done this in other classes. "I keep it really brief," she says. "I'll just say, 'I'm Christy, and I'm a junior, and I heard this class was really good, and I was curious. If you can find some message in your subconscious that could help you in your day-to-day life, I would like to know that. I would like to know how to be in touch with that.'"

Most of her dreams now are of her late father. "His last words, that he actually never said, but ones that I kind of created for him." In another recent dream, she has killed someone. "Nobody knew, and then there was something in the *New York Times*, and someone came up to me and said, 'Don't you know that it's come out that you've done this?' I don't know what that means. It's all very complicated."

It is. Very complicated. "An uninterpreted dream," said the Jungian professor, quoting the Talmud, "is like an unopened letter." So Christy will read her Jung and Freud, her Nietzsche and Sartre; she will open the letters she is writing to herself, and she will read them. One will be particularly difficult to make out, the writing too faint to discern, the language foreign to her, or the paper blank. Finally, she will press it to the lamp at her desk, looking for an impression, a watermark, anything that might yield a clue from the realm beyond reality and knowledge. And she will see in its blankness, in its seeming absence of meaning, a face.

That face.

Chapter Eighteen

Dennis Rodman

Champion

Dennis Rodman addresses the last of his sushi with the feathered delicacy of a geisha. His long, leathery fingers lever the chopsticks deftly, cradling the yellowfin. He does not neglect the wasabi, but he's gentle with it, painterly. You would not suppose that he'd spent his evening banging elbows and buttocks with the Miami Heat. With his tattoos mostly buried beneath nondescript grunge and his nappy pink do under a cap, he looks like a goofball savant; large, liquid eyes; a nose like an upturned rutabaga; a scruffy goatee framing a steam-shovel mouth whose teeth are too small for its gums.

Finished, Rodman sets down the sticks and pours more sake for his companions. "Have some, cuz," he urges, tilting the flagon to my empty thimble. A latecomer, I'm on the cushions next to Tommy, a self-employed music producer with short, chipping deep-purple fingernails. Across from me sit Larry, a leather merchant, and his wife. Rodman has one side of the table to himself; in the far corner, grunting into the cell phone welded to his hammy fist is George, a fortyish cop whose work arrangements with the city of Chicago somehow permit him to serve as Rodman's bodyguard, driver, and major domo. At the oak-and-rice paper sliding door stands my escort, Kelly, another policeman who moonlights on the Rodman detail.

I hooked up with George and Kelly after the Bulls-Heat game at the United Center, where they triple-dip as gray-blazered security men. "You don't understand," George snarled when I asked if the taxpayers foot the bill for Rodman's protection. "We don't get overtime, OK? We get *comp* time. This is *comp* time."

I've never met any of these people before, except for Rodman, and that was back in 1994, when interviewing him required no more than showing up at a tattoo parlor in Dallas shitfaced and sleeveless. [Back then, I was all-but-obligated to ask: 'What's Madonna like in bed?' To

Cutting Room Floor: Rodman

THE PITCH: What's the difference between Alice in Wonderland and Dennis in Chicago? Not a whole lot.

SCENE: The near-empty transgender bar in Chicago in 1996. Dennis Rodman isn't here to slum or show off or knock back a drink or two. He's a regular, a friend of sorts to one of the queens, and he's trying to get as drunk as he can as fast as he can.

BACKSTORY: The following few sentences further describing the bar scene in were edited out of the story as it ran in *GQ*: Larry the leather merchant sidles up. "You ever get sucked off by one of these guys?" he asks me.

"Not that I'm aware of," I say, whereupon he reaches into his pocket and yanks out a wad of cash. "No, thanks, really," I tell him, "I promised my honey I wouldn't act out on this trip."

He waves me off. "Come on," he says, "She doesn't have to know. My treat. Come on." The problem turned out to be something more complicated than a simple matter of editing for taste: some car company had just signed on for a big ad package with the magazine, and the powers-that-be felt that this passage went just a bit too far for a brand-new, very conservative client.

which Rodman replied, 'Fuckin' great. Nothin' like it, bro. It's like takin' the ultimate challenge...fucking at its highest peak. Then fallin' off the son of a bitch and wakin' up thinkin' it was a dream.' But we're past that sort of talk now. I'm no longer a Rodman interview virgin.] So I listen politely as they sip their sake and chat about Ferraris.

After dinner we head over to the Baton Show Lounge. I ride with Kelly, and by the time we get there, Rodman, George and company are standing at the bar, bolting their drinks. Huddling with Rodman is a female impersonator in a blond wig, a low-necked silver-sequined gown and high heels. I shake hands and introduce myself. Her name is Mimi,

CONFLICT: During the two years between my Rodman profiles, I had quit drinking; Rodman, meanwhile, had become an outright lush.

Because he's impossible to dislike – an innocent, trusting, vulnerable child of a man – it was impossible also not to worry about him, not to soften things in the story, not to take him aside man-to-man and tell him to dump the sycophants and get some help. His life after the NBA – he's still trying, ludicrously, to get back – has been a tale of lonely, drunken woe.

WISH I'D WRITTEN: He was bitter, and prescient, about the state of the league, especially with regard to rookies coming into the NBA making stupid money before they'd ever suited up:

"These coaches, these fuckin' dumbass owners, these fuckin' stupid-ass people that's fuckin' payin' these guys don't understand – you can get young players, but you gotta understand what you're getting in these young players. They have no concept of what the NBA is all about.

All they want to do is make the NBA, and say, 'I finally made it, I got millions of dollars.' Don't get your fuckin' occupation confused with your paycheck."

It was a couple of years later that the NBA finally restructured its salary system to make sure that players who'd proved themselves weren't being paid a fraction of a first-year player's paycheck.

and she is flawless. Her mouth is a sassy bow of lipstick red perfection. Her breasts are full, milky globes. Her legs are... George motions me over.

"You wouldn't know, would you?" George sneers, looking Mimi up and down.

"I would know," I tell George. "In fact, just so happens that I'm wearing a black camisole under this sweatshirt." Mimi excuses herself: The show is about to begin. The rows of folding chairs in front of the small stage at the back of the room remain utterly empty. Rodman hangs barside, hunched on a stool, downing kamikazes. After each round is poured – I count six in an hour – he clinks glasses with one and all and gulps his down clean.

A Divine look-alike, mammoth in a black sheath, opens the revue, lip-synching and stomping in place to some campy show tune while her bosom struggles vainly to pout over the thin fabric. Mimi's next, vamping, hands on hips, but too fettered by her corset to strut her ersatz stuff. Rodman sits gaping at the stage, heavy lidded, expressionless. When Mimi's number ends, he boos lustily. Mimi, squinting into the spotlight, shakes a fist in mock anger.

Mimi returns for a farewell hug from Rodman, who promises her he'll phone when he gets back to town – the Bulls are flying to Charlotte the next afternoon. I kiss Mimi good-bye when she offers me her bone-white cheek, which smells faintly of vanilla. "Dennis and I are such good friends," Mimi whispers. "He's a very special man."

I may not know Dennis Rodman as Mimi does, but I, too, have plucked the dulcimer of his specialness. Back in Texas during the summer of '94, his appeal consisted mainly of his not being special, just another big doofus with tattoos and a nose ring who hated his job, his boss and, beneath it all, himself. Above the din of all the shrapnel rattling in his head, the loudest sound was the howl of a deep-voiced kid done wrong.

"I'm the fuckin' bad boy of the NBA," he said. "They look at me as, like evil. And I'm not really evil; I'm just mad. I just wanna lash out at all the shit that doesn't make sense.   "

Coming from a fellow in his early thirties, a man without much education or training, a former airport janitor and petty thief who was at that point raking in a couple of million a year, gunning a Ferrari, straddling a Harley, shtupping Madonna, hitting Vegas whenever the fever struck – well, his protests all sounded a trifle silly. What, exactly, was he lashing out at?

"People try to embed this certain image in me and make me believe in it," he said. "It pisses me off and makes me more of an enraged person than I am. I want to think the way Dennis Rodman thinks. That's why God put you on this earth, to be an individual person – not to be the same as some other person."

Here was the voice of every pustular butt-head sulking in the detention room. Which might explain why, two years later, Dennis Rodman has a show of his own on MTV.

Where are we going?

"Crobar," George mumbles, as what's left of the crew walks to Rodman's truck. Kelly has departed, as have leather larry and his wife. Rodman, George, Tommy and I are about to climb into Rodman's pickup – a big-tired, high-riding, chrome-flanged, fat-bodies virgin white Ford F-350 – when I notice, bolted down onto the truck's bed, two large steel-mesh dog cages, locked and empty. Above the door of each cage is a strip of lettered masking tape, one marked KELLY, the other GEORGE.

What's that about? "What's what about?" snaps George. Um, your names on the cages. "That's *his* idea of a joke," George mutters, getting into the driver's seat.

What happens next is, like astral projection and my grandmother's potato kugel, easier described than explained. Rodman's riding shotgun; I'm in the rear of the extended cab, next to Tommy. George, apparently certain that everyone else on the road will apprehend immediately that our vehicle is being driven by a drunken off-duty cop hired to insure that no harm befalls the $9 million-per-year athlete-cum-civic treasure who sits beside him, races insanely through a series of solid-red lights, gunning full-bore across four-lane, two-way downtown intersections, barely glancing through the tinted side windows to check for cross traffic.

There is plenty of cross-traffic – yes, it's nearly 3 A.M., but we're not in Peoria – yet no one inside the truck says a word. Actually, no one inside the truck seems to be breathing, except for George, who every now and then emits a yawp of deranged pleasure. Silently, I recite the Sh'ma like any good Hebrew about to meet his Maker. Whatever comes to pass, I remind myself, I'm only a professional witness, strictly and totally detached. If we get broad-sided, it's great for the story. But how in heaven's name does Dennis Rodman just sit there while this porcine yobbo endangers his life?

We come very close, very close. On our left, a dark limo cruising toward its green light nears an intersection as George bolts through the red. Rodman sees the limo coming toward us and reflexively raises his knees and jerks up both arms to steel himself for the impact, which makes an impression upon George's numbed retina sufficient to cause him to stiffen, look left, tap briefly on the brake – long enough to see that the limo is not slowing – and tromp on the gas.

"Bro," Rodman gasps, long after we are safely past.

"No problem," says George, turning to him with a jackal's smile. "We're almost there."

Dennis Rodman has a death wish,

and says so right on page 213 of *Bad As I Wanna Be*, in chapter 11: "Death Wish," in which he discusses crashing his Ferrari or his Harley, or putting a bullet in his brain. He's unafraid of death, he boasts, except for the pain, and says he's already old, considering that he came from the projects. Yet for such a balls-out, spit-in-the-Reaper's-face motherfucker, somehow Rodman still walks the earth. Which raises the question: Is Rodman just lucky, or is he full of shit"?

Well, people with a genuine death wish rarely brag about it to their ghostwriters or schmooze about it with Barbara Walters. They die.

What Rodman does have is a stunted teenager's bottomless capacity for loud, self-inflicted suffering: the piercings, tattoos and bleach jobs; the way he baits referees to eject him and the league to suspend and fine him to that he can claim a ludicrous martyrdom; how he bitterly recalls the day when he discovered that the NBA was – gasp! – "just a business," as if any other sort of endeavor would pay seven figures a year to an ill-tempered yutz in Nikes.

Of course, now he's an icon of popular culture, which means that if Michael Jordan appeals to the happy, hopeful strivers who eat Wheaties and drink Gatorade because they want to be like Mike, Dennis Rodman is a magnet for the sullen masses who think they already are like him because their navels are pierced, work sucks, and the world just can't see how exceptional they are.

Or maybe *Bad as I Wanna Be* has sold nearly a million copies because Rodman is a great rebounder.

The Crobar is a warehouse of choreographed hip.

The body-piercing booth sits empty, awaiting Bondage Night. The gum-chewing, jackbooted babe in the black vinyl bikini on the swing above the dance floor looks hydraulic: Back and forth she arcs, over and over, oblivious to the loop of pneumatic, ceaseless, deafening sound. It's all so techno-craphaus-industrial, so, so...lame.

Rodman's designated spot is at the far side of a large central bar, a five-by-fifteen-foot rectangle of low-lit space between the rear of the bar and a wall framed by massive steel girders. Led by George, Rodman reaches his space. He leans forward against the bar, orders kamikazes, lights a big cigar. He bobs his outslung chin to the beat. If he sees the legion ringing the bar, milling to the very edge of his turf, if he senses their eyes, he shows no sign of it. He simply towers above them, drunk, impassive, smoking.

As if on some unseen, unheard cue, they begin to step into Dennis Rodman's box of a shadow, these beggars of his fame. The men just stand and gawk. The women move close, needing to touch and smell him. One snakes an arm around his waist and slips her fingers inside the back of his pants to stroke his ass. He shimmies and grins and leans down to place an ear against her whispering lips. Then he tosses back his head, laughs and buys another round. And another woman comes. And another. An endless stream.

I have seen Troy Aikman in a Dallas country-and-western bar. I have seen Mickey Rourke in a room full of fashion models. I have never seen a vulva magnet like Dennis Rodman.

When the area behind the bar fills until there is no separation between Rodman and the throng, the winnowing begins. George inches toward Rodman, tapping shoulders as he goes. The men follow the jerk of this head and leave quickly; a few women are allowed to stay. Leather-jacketed bouncers appear, hauling sawhorses to close the rectangle.

Latecomers gather at the barricade, hoping. One persistent young man, failing to sway a bouncer, buttonholes George. He jaws until, without warning, George explodes: "YOU AIN'T SHIT!" George rages at him, his face flushed, spittle flying, his hands curled into fists. "FUCK YOU! FUCK YOU! FUCK YOU!" The young man cringes at each shouted repetition. Finally, he turns his back and looks up to see the babe on the swing. She is blowing bubbles now.

In the shadows, Rodman tosses back another kamikaze and exchanges half-spent cigars with George. At 4 A.M., we leave. Rodman has practice at ten and a 4 P.M. team flight. On our way out, one burly patron grabs my shoulder. "Keep him well," he says, obviously mistaking me for a bodyguard. His voice is trembling, thick with love.

In the summer of 1995, when the San

Antonio Spurs traded Rodman to the Bulls even-up for seven pale feet of
hoops ineptitude named Will Perdue, I went back to check the transcripts
of my talks with Rodman from the year before.

"Oh, I'm gonna have one," he had vowed then, when I asked him
about winning another NBA title. "I guarantee you: I'll have another one."

With the Spurs? "No, It could be any-fuckin' body. I don't give a fuck.
Any team I play on, I'm gon' kick ass. Simple as that."

On the court, it *was* simple. The Bulls, eliminated the year before in
the conference semifinals, added Rodman to their frontcourt and stam-
peded the league. As for the rest of it – the business, the bodyguards, the
crush of fame – the core tenet of Rodman's off-court Weltanschauung has
remained a model of Confucian depth-in-simplicity: I Don't Give a Fuck.

He is managed now by the Rodman Group, i.e., a 31-year-old former
coin dealer named Dwight Manley, who met Rodman at a craps table in
Las Vegas and offered to become his agent. Rodman agreed, becoming
Manley's first and only client. Numbered among Manleys' accomplish-
ments are the Worm Pop, a peach-sized, multihued sucker shaped like
Rodman's face; Dennis "the Worm" Rodman Temporary Tattoos; and a
one-year contract with the Bulls that penalizes Rodman hundreds of thousands of dollars for missed games and defers a full third of his salary until
the year 2024, when Rodman will be 63 years old, if his bodyguard does-
n't kill him first. At the age of 35, with three league championship rings
and five rebounding titles, Rodman will most likely pull down fewer on-
court dollars this year than, say, NBA perma-stiff Derrick Coleman.

As with many pro athletes, Rodman's savvy and strength end with
the buzzer; faced with an adult challenge – a wannabe agent with a soft
suit and a shiny watch, a cop with a brain cloud – he merely goes along
for the ride, limply, a victim who's destined to stay that way. It's much
harder to imagine Dennis Rodman dead five or ten years from now than
it is to see him as Hulk Hogan's tag-team partner, or at the Mirage, working as a greeter. The big drawback to I Don't Give a Fuck is that it's too
passive, especially when you deal with people who don't give a fuck about
you, who see you as the means to their ends.

On the day after Crobar, I meet

George and a woman named Erika at the Berto Center, Bulls Central, to catch Rodman after practice. Erika has flown in from Los Angeles to spend some time with him. She is not as ravishing as Mimi, but she is awfully good-looking; plus, if I'm not mistaken, she is an actual woman. Rodman seems groggy and looks red-eyed. (This morning's *Tribune* says Rodman's recovering from a "nasty encounter with some bad sushi," which is apparently code for "massive hangover.") He wants lunch. Taco Bell. At a nearby mall food court.

George drives much slower today on account of the heavy midday suburban traffic, for which I'm particularly grateful because I'm up front. Rodman and Erika cuddle in back. The phone in the truck rings. It's Stacy, Rodman's longtime squeeze. Rodman's end of the conversation consists wholly of monosyllables. I turn around and see Erika scowling at him. Rodman has his sunglasses on. The cap on his head is from L.A.'s Viper Room, the site of River Phoenix's final collapse.

As we walk into the mall, Rodman turns to me. "You gonna write about last night?"

Sure. Why not?

He shrugs.

What part of last night don't you want me to write about?

Rodman shakes his head. "Whatever," he says.

This shades-and-cap disguise fools no one: The entire population of the food court is gaping even as George cogitates over which plastiform picnic bench provides the worst sight lines for any prospective snipers.

As soon as we're seated, the parade begins. Erika goes for the tacos. Rodman wants a baked potato, too, from the baked potato hut, and George disappears. Fucking vanishes. Leaving me to fend off dozens of desperate and well-meaning folks who just want a moment with Rodman.

"Please read this," one middle-aged man says, sliding a handwritten letter onto our table. "My son – you're his biggest hero." He stands there, waiting; Rodman just looks up at the ceiling.

The poor guy scurries away with his mash note. I suggest to Rodman that maybe a drive-through would have been a better choice, tacowise. "You can't go anywhere," he snorts. "You're trying to do normal things – sit in this fucking mall without fucking people coming up who want your fucking autograph. They don't think, 'Well, fuck, he's eating; he's relaxing.' They say, 'Fuck that; he owes us this.' They can kiss my ass. We don't owe dick."

What about at Crobar? "I have a great time at Crobar. A wonderful time. It's free, it's energetic, it's vibrant, it's alive. I can just be myself."

They keep coming – young and old, men and women, shoppers and mall employees – all so goddamned delighted at being in the same food court as Dennis Rodman that it breaks my heart each time I send them packing.

How long do you think this kind of worship is going to last?

"I know people are getting sick and tired of Dennis Rodman. You have your time, and then you move on. I want people to look at me not just as an athlete; I want them to think of me as a universal person. Dennis Rodman's a multitalented, individual person. I think my next forte will be doing movies."

Rodman acted for the first time during the off-season, playing the sidekick in a film with Jean-Claude Van Damme and Mickey Rourke. I ask him about working with the always-prickly-when-not-comatose Rourke. "He was real cool. He said that I have a lot of ability."

I find this strangely touching. Mickey Rourke praising your acting is not unlike Ronald Reagan admiring your alertness.

Erika returns. Most of the tables around us have emptied. Rodman wolfs his food and says something I can't hear. He repeats it, a little louder. "I think I have a stalker" is what he says, darting his eyes to the left. Two tables over, a man no older than 30 is sitting alone. Lank black hair, black glasses, sallow features compressed into a pinched frown, a beige down jacket, brown polyester slacks. There is nothing on the man's table except for his tiny hands, so tightly clasped that the tips of his fingers are beet red. Every minute or so, he unlocks his hands, places them under his armpits and hugs himself tightly. Rocking almost imperceptibly, he is alternately staring sideways at Rodman and turning away.

"I've seen him in my yard," Rodman says. "He follows me."

You're serious.

"Um-hmm. When I walk out, he'll follow me."

Rodman doesn't sound the least bit alarmed, but the guy I'm looking at definitely fits the Chapman-Hinkley profile. I see George at the far end of the food court, near the stairs, walking toward us, waving. As we get up, the stalker gets up, too. He doesn't trail us, exactly; he's charting a parallel course along the other wall. When we get close to George, I ask him if he knows that Rodman has a stalker. "Yep," he says.

We're on the stairs now. I look over my shoulder.

"Let him come," George says, patting his coat pocket.

The guy isn't there.

"That's OK. Just let him come."

Jesus.

Rodman lives within sight of the

mall, in a nondescript rancher on a tree-lined street. The most striking interior features of the place are the sixty-inch television and the huge mattress on the floor in front of it, a Lava lamp and the velvet Elvis on the wall behind the TV. I want to ask him about the Elvis – I've got the same one in my house – but Rodman's in a back room, packing for the two-day trip to Charlotte. Or maybe poking Erika – I haven't seen either one of them in twenty minutes, and the low noises I'm hearing don't sound like packing. George is in the front yard, pouring food for the two police-trained German shepherds, Katy and Aran, fenced in between the garage and the front door. "Not *I*-ran," George says when I step out for a smoke. "*A*-ran."

Back inside, Jerry Springer is on, bigger than life, talking to an armless, legless woman. At the next commercial, I walk into the kitchen. Cereal boxes atop the refrigerator: no Wheaties. Frosted Flakes. Mimi's number is scrawled on a cabinet door. The counter is lined with children's drawings of Rodman.

Not long after my visit, the Bulls ground Rodman for two games without pay, ostensibly for saying the "f" word into a live microphone during a cable-station locker-room interview after a loss to the Toronto Raptors. Rodman had been thrown out of the game for a hand-to-the-groin gesture interpreted by a referee fifty feet downcourt as obscene. Rodman claimed that he was merely pulling up his shorts.

Chicago is, as everyone knows, a prudish sports town, where the fans will not abide profanity from anyone. So it was only coincidence that the suspension came after the Bulls' second straight defeat, ending a week in which Rodman played so badly that the SpaceJamming Colognemeister himself suggested publicly that Rodman was distracted by his off-court pursuits. Pundits nationwide, writing in their ususal Rodman-as-a-sign-of-the-apocalypse orgy, penned their huzzahs.

Dwight Manley told the press that his sole client was "weighing his options." Rodman filed a grievance with the players' union and announced that "it feels like there's a conspiracy out there for Dennis Rodman this year."

With Dennis Rodman, of course, the conspiracy dwells mainly within. When a player head-butts a referee, as Rodman did last March, he can expect no breaks from the zebras. When a 35-year-old pro athlete stays out boozing until four in the morning, what's left of his ability will dissipate quickly. When Michael Jordan makes plain that he can play without you, it's time to call the movers. And when Mickey Rourke is your Tinseltown rabbi, you're already living in direct-to-video hell.

But just now Dennis is merely running late. He finally emerges, toting an athletic bag large enough to hide a Volvo. Outside, he tosses the bag into the truck bed next to Erika's luggage and offers me his hand.

"Let's go," George shouts.

"See you down the road, bro," Dennis Rodman says, folding himself into the passenger seat. George is driving.

Chapter Nineteen

Ray Romano

Dweeb

The maestros make it seem easy. It's the mojo, the chi, the flow. They don't work the job; they work *wonder*. They be what they do. Plumber, barber, shoedog, chef – you know a maestro when you find one. You brag him up to all your friends: He's the best. The *best* – trust me. He'll take care of you.

A comedy maestro? That's solid gold, brother. A guy who makes me laugh, I owe him somehow. I love him like sunshine and tell my friends to look for him. *Everybody Loves Raymond*, yo – check it out.

They didn't like it. Twenty million people watch the show every Monday night, millions more dig it in syndication, and I don't know any of 'em. *Seinfeld*? Sure – best sitcom ever. *The Simpsons*? Genius. *Everybody Loves Raymond*? Eh.

Maybe it's the Edge Factor, that thing HBO milks so well: *It's Not TV Because Someone Just Said "Cocksucker."* Hell, maybe you don't love Raymond, either. Maybe you think his show, despite its Chekhovian probing of the delicious miseries of marriage and family, is a bit too Bea Arthur for a hipster like yourself. Maybe if you're gonna watch any show about an East Coast Italian clan stuck in the sludge of love and hostility, it'll be the stiff, gassy corpse of *The Sopranos*, where the mope-opera Grand Guignol bushwa is so untrue to life, it makes *ELR* play like a newsreel.

Well, you can have the depressive brute with the cash-stuffed duffel bag and the endless string of yielding, wet-lipped women. Me, I'll take Everyman. I'll take the nebbish who can't get laid, won't grow up, and does-n't want anybody mad at him. I'll take the mama's boy who – in real life – was still living in his parents' house at age twenty-nine. In their basement. I'll take Ray Romano, the leading man of weenie, the maestro of morose.

His show's funny, but it ain't pretty; it isn't edgy, but it cuts deep. The most painfully poignant TV moment I've seen in years – not counting Jason Alexander's first ad for KFC – came during an episode in which Ray's wife is trying to get him to at least consider marriage counseling because she just can't seem to nag his sorry ass off the sofa.

"Can't I sometimes watch TV?" Ray whines, pouting. And Ray's TV mom, hovering nearby, tells his wife, "Raymond is a very hard worker and sometimes needs to relax."

"Of course," his wife says to Ray, ignoring her mother-in-law, "but why is it such a battle to get you to do anything?"

"I dunno."

"That's why I want to go to counseling. I don't think it's that you're just lazy – I think there's a deeper reason behind it. If we could just figure it out, you and I could be happier."

"You know me," Ray says. "There's not much deepness. I just – I like to be taken care of."

"But you gotta understand, Ray, that that's not a wife – that's a mother."

"Well," squeaks Romano in a ten-year-old's voice, "maybe that's what I *want*."

Everything stops dead right there. No big deal – a Psych 101 insight. But who ever admits it even to himself, much less confesses it out loud?

The actors hold the take. The studio audience laughs, but their laughter is soon buried in a long "*Oooooh* . . ." They actually sound fright-ened. And Raymond, agape at what he's just heard himself say, shouts, "Holy crap!" in a dead-on impression of his TV dad's voice.

He knows he's stuck. And you know he's stuck, too, one foot in his parents' marriage, one in his own, half boy and half man and too half-assed to move. And it's a pain in the butt to be stuck there, but it's even more of a pain to do much about it, which never happens on *ELR*, and rarely in real life, because getting stuck right there is what we all do: Homer and Marge, Ralph and Alice, me and my wife, you and yours. Every one of us.

That's why, sooner or later, everybody loves Raymond – except, of course, Ray Romano. It's one thing to get the boy out of the basement, another to get the basement out of the boy.

He's bigger than you think, six

two and solid, slope-shouldered and long-muscled. He's wearing the blue shirt, of course, his comedy shirt, with a twenty-dollar Casio strapped to his wrist. His shiny black hair is cowlicked. He's got an oversized, old-country nose – hell, his whole noggin is huge, a big boy's cantaloupe, except for the eyes. They're close-set, dark, and hooded, tired after the flight from L.A., wary from forty-five years of fretting, asking the stand-up comic's eternal hangdog question: "How'm I doin'?"

Ray's doin' all right. He's back home in New York City for Thanksgiving, the boy next door made good – the People's Choice, the only stand-up ever to win the Best Actor Emmy, a top-ten show, a near-million bucks per episode (plus a slice of the $300 million syndication pie), a new ten-thousand-square-foot SoCal homestead with a putting green out back, four healthy children, a good marriage. The evidence is everywhere: Even the Lord loves Raymond.

Which means, as far as Ray's concerned, he's going nowhere but down. He's worried. His hands natter like a pair of peasant women at their baking, kneading and twisting, patting and squeezing, fluttering to and fro while the rest of him slouches in a cheap motel chair upstairs at *The Late Show*. Ray's worried about Dave's mood – never mind that tonight marks his sixteenth appearance on Letterman's show, that it was Dave himself who, back in 1995, saw in Ray the possibility of sitcom glory, which led to *Everybody Loves Raymond*, which has showered gold upon CBS and Dave's production company, Worldwide Pants. Ray's worried that it's cheesy to go out there and plug the DVD release of *Ice Age*, a smash kiddie flick starring Ray's humpty, dweeb-outta-Queens stammer. And he's worried that a bit about helping his four-year-old son wipe his tuchus is too poopycentric for Letterman, whose goyish distaste for toilet humor is legendary.

But mainly, right now, Ray's worried about the Turtle Guy, about wounding the Turtle Guy's feelings with a new bit. Ray tries it out in the dressing room on Anna, his wife, and Rory Rosegarten, his longtime manager, and me and my tape recorder, which Ray eyes with fear.

"I don't know if this is gonna be off the record or not," he says.

"Leave it on for now – because if I do the bit, then it's obviously on the record. So we have this new house – it's big, blah-blah-blah – and we have a guy to take care of the pool, and a gardener, and, my wife told me the other day, we have a *turtle guy*."

Anna, small and blond and perfectly sweet – they met twenty years ago at a bank in Queens where they worked as tellers – says, "We have turtles."

"*Lemme do it!*" Ray hollers, and then remembers my tape recorder. "I

Cutting Room Floor: Romano

THE PITCH: A humble-sad comic from Queens endures the living hell of having everybody love him, even David Letterman.

SCENE: Backstage, Broadway and 53rd, after Letterman's show. Everyone's ready to go, but Letterman's taping a second show tonight – it's the week of Thanksgiving – with Liza Minelli as a guest, and Phil Rosenthal, one of *Everybody Loves Raymond*'s creators, can't leave because his wife adores Liza Minelli and this may be her only chance ever to bask in her actual presence. So everyone stays and waits. "I can't believe that she's here," says Phil. "And I can't believe that I'm married to someone who's this obsessed with her."

Liza finally appears, a sad-eyed doll whose "Hello" sounds faintly British. Phil's wife swoons, hand to heart. "We love you," Phil says, steppng up.

"Thank you so much," says Liza, turning. "And this is my husband, Phillip." Only at that moment did Phillip achieve actual visibility, although he had been standing there, a little behind Liza, indistinct, waxen. His small nod and bleak smile seemed to require all the energy he could muster.

BACKSTORY: One of the pleasures of writing about comics is their genuine humility. All right, it's not humility: It's self-loathing, but it is genuine. Romano felt his sitcom's title was so repugnant that he spent countless hours conjuring alternatives. A scrap of paper framed

---

wasn't yellin' there," he groans.

The voice was definitely raised, I say.

"Yeah, yeah, because I had to cut her off quick, before she gives it up."

Rory, pacing across from Ray, points down to Ray's unzipped zipper. Ray zips.

"Full service," Rory beams.

"So we have this fountain," says Ray, resuming, "with a little concrete

and hung on his dressing room wall is full of them – That Raymond Guy, Raymond's Show, Ray, Ummm, Raymond, on and on and on. CBS President Les Moonves liked the name but got so tired of Romano's kvetching that he promised Ray he'd change it if the show ever made it into the Top Ten. When it did, Ray called Les and said he wanted to change it. "You can't change the name of the show," Moonves said. "We're Top Ten."

CONFLICT: Money is always a touchy subject, and when I ask Ray about recent reports of an *ELR* syndication deal for $300 million, he gets cranky. "I don't like to talk about it – the syndication sale, that has nothing to do with me. Yeah, I have a piece of the back end, but when you throw figures out like $300 million, that means nothing to me. That's their money."

But you get a hefty chunk, right? "I don't have a hefty chunk, no. I'm the low man on that – I have the lowest piece of the back end of everybody involved. I get a piece of the back end in a year from now."

WISH I'D WRITTEN: How does a guy who still hangs out with old pals at the Jersey Shore every summer make new friends out in Hollywood? He doesn't. "That's the sad part. I'm startin' to realize – ya gotta get into that little bubble. You've got your friends who are your lifelong friends, and your family. Look, there are people who wanna be friendly with me who are genuinely the nicest people in the world. Still, even though they're the nicest people in the world, the truth is they're not talkin' to me if I'm not on a TV show. That's nothing against them – that's just the nature of it."

pool around it that has turtles, and once a week they have to be serviced. They have to be fed, whatever, so we have a turtle guy. So I tell my wife, 'Look, do me a favor: Just don't have an affair with this guy, okay? Because I don't wanna have to tell my friends that my wife left me for the *turtle* guy.'"

Rory laughs. I'm laughing. Anna's not even smiling.

"My thing is," says Ray, "is it insulting to the Turtle Guy?"

"Come on," Rory tells him, "it's in fun."

"Yeah, yeah – but am I demeaning his thing, you know?"

"No, it's funny. What, he's gonna poison your turtles? It's funny. I think it's great, and I'll tell you something – he'll love the bit, and he's gonna know it's him, and he'll tell all his friends."

"Maybe I can say afterward, 'By the way, I know the guy, he's a good guy, he's a decent man.'"

"Just listen to what you're doing," Rory pleads, throwing up his hands. "Just listen to what you're doing here."

Maybe Ray's worried that the Turtle Guy might take offense and quit. A Turtle Guy has to be tough to replace – how many could there be, even in L.A.? – and Anna will be pissed at Ray if he goes. Or maybe Ray's a really sensitive guy himself. Or neurotic. Or all of the above.

Ray looks over at me. "I have negative grandiosity," he says. "That's what my therapist said."

"I think it's absolutely fine," sighs Rory, "and it's gonna get a huge laugh."

"Yeah," Ray splutters, "but, but, but, but, but . . ."

"I don't think it's slamming the Turtle Guy," says Rory. "It's fine."

"All right," says Ray. He pulls out two sheets of paper, notes for what to cover out there with Dave. He looks up at the monitor in the corner of the room when Letterman starts talking about him after the monologue. "Great guy," Letterman's saying. "What a nice guy, what a nice man, couldn't be more successful, and it's all well deserved."

Ray winces. "He don't mean a word of it," he says.

Out in the hall, the ganja fumes wafting from the dressing room of tonight's musical guests, Jurassic 5, smell like trouble to Ray.

"Jesus. I gotta get outta that – I don't like that. I'll be more paranoid. Believe it or not, I can get more paranoid. Dave will become the Turtle Guy."

Ray does fifteen minutes with Dave, his hands and his uh-uh-uh nasal drone working the whole while. He plugs *Ice Age*, leans over to the desk after the Turtle Guy bit to add, "By the way, he's a great guy," and tells the poopy story without curling Letterman's lip. Afterward, back in the dressing room, a producer assures Ray that Dave seemed to be enjoying himself.

"Yeah, yeah, yeah," Ray moans. "But was he *forcin'* it, though?"

Nebbish. Dweeb. Mama's boy.

I say these things with utmost respect. With love. With awe, even. Because it takes a certain greatness of soul to be Any Guy, to work a clean act, to connect with our collective Inner Weenie, the archetype of every man addled by his mom, busted by his wife, commanded by his toddler to the john to help wipe ass. He must let their songs sing him. He must keep close his doubts and fears. He must be fucking nuts.

Here, too, the evidence is everywhere. Just check out the metal storage cabinet across from his desk in his office out in Burbank and you'll see a dozen or more uncracked economy-size bottles of Scope filling three shelves – mouthwash enough to float a yacht *and* freshen Andy Rooney's bung.

"I'm very nervous about my oral hygiene," he confesses. "We eat a lotta sushi. We come back from lunch, I don't wanna smell like halibut all afternoon. I got tongue scrapers in there, too. One year, I gave everybody tongue scrapers. I got Letterman a tongue scraper."

He's wearing the blue shirt. Not the exact same blue shirt anymore – that was in the old days, twelve years of stand-up to make the mortgage and feed his first three kids; he'd go from club to club polishing his act, come home in the wee hours, and Anna would wash and dry and iron the blue shirt. Now he's got blue shirts for Letterman, blue shirts for the six-figure weekend stand-up gigs in Vegas, blue button-downs, blue plaids, and blue T-shirts for *Everybody Loves Raymond*.

"That's my color," he says. "Richard Lewis has black. And Johnny Cash. Rip Taylor has everything else. My wife – if she had her way, she'd have me in Armani shirts. What she doesn't realize is that it has to be conducive to comedy – and by that I don't mean it has to be a funny-looking shirt. If I wore a red shirt and I had a bad set, I'm not gonna blame the shirt, but I'm not gonna thank it, either. It's not superstition – it's just a matter of, *I can't be funny in this shirt.* I'll fight anyone who tries to disprove that. Blue just works for me."

Down the hall from his office is the writers' room, where Ray and a chorus of wits warble his song. It is empty now – after five on Friday evening – but you can feel their joyful agony as they punch up and stamp out episodes, twenty-four weeks per season, year after year. Well, you can't feel it, not really, but you can read it on the walls, up on the big marker boards they use for inspiration, one jammed with Raymondese – rows of words Ray has misused or mispronounced (*Kimono* dragon, *premeate* for permeate; the classics, like *Inesteen* for Einstein, are in red)--and a less crowded board listing the difficult or obscure words (*epiphany, hypnagogic*) he has used or pronounced correctly, shocking his more literary teammates.

"Yeah," says Ray, who flunked out of two high schools, dropped out of two colleges, pumped gas until he was robbed, twice, at gunpoint, and left the bank job to deliver futons by day while he found his feet as an open-mike stand-up, "these Ivy League fucks like throwin' their educations around."

There is a third board, a weirder board. "I have to have sex with my wife," reads one of the phrases written there. "That's the only way I can come." And, "The point is, poorly drawn Ray likes to suck even more poorly drawn penis."

"You shouldn't see that board," says Ray. "Those are things that've been said that people find quotable. You gotta remember, you're in a writers' room. You have to encourage all these things. Nothing is sacred."

Nothing sacred, no holds barred, nobody's hurt feelings truly matter – not the wife's, not the weenie's, and surely not the Turtle Guy's. The sole sacrament is the laugh. Ray Romano is a sweetheart, but you don't become a comedy maestro without leaving a spoor of blood. Twelve years of trudging the stand-up trail takes no less a battler than those bulvans with their scrota stuffed into spandex tights, crushing skulls to win the Ultimate Fighting Championship. Without the laugh, you don't kill: You die.

"I was never goin' for a treasure chest," Ray says. "I just dreamed of being a stand-up comedian – *that* was the treasure. I used to go into the city and do seven shows on a Saturday night; each club would give me $50, and I'd come home with $350 cash in my pocket. I was doin' what I loved to do, and I had the money to buy the kids sneakers. I'm nostalgic for that. I want that feeling again."

A stand-up warrior, impervious to pain, a *Star Search* also-ran – in 1990, he lost to some yutz named Geechy Guy – he soldiered on, bellied his way up to the middle, or maybe a notch above. In '91, a spot on Carson, then Leno, an HBO special, and, yeah, he was a name, a headliner, but there he stuck; at a time when every stand-up with a pulse had a TV pilot, Raymond was still gigging weekends in Atlantic City.

"This guy was getting a *development deal*, that guy was getting a *development deal*"– even now, he can't mouth the phrase without sneering. "Someone would see 'em at the Montreal festival and sign 'em. 'Here's a hundred thousand – we're gonna come up with sump'n.' Left and right, comics that . . . *ehhhhhhh*"– this ritardando, too, is part of Raymond's song – "I've been around twelve years, and these comics that'd been around three, four, five – all right, so what? They're entitled to get what they can get. But I had done all you could do – all the things you do to get seen. Nobody was knockin' on my door."

He had a wife and three kids and a small house in Queens. He was making, in a good year, $90K. Doin' okay. But when the sitcom suits would hit the clubs to roust stand-ups for the next casting call – lemme see him, him, and him – Romano would blow the audition.

"We would go in and read, and I would be horrible, and that would be the end of it. The auditioning thing – I was really bad at it. I would be really good in my bedroom, and then I would clam up with five people sittin' on a couch."

His big break appeared to come in 1994, when he was cast for *NewsRadio*. Eight thousand dollars an episode, national exposure every week.

"I couldn't believe it," he says. "I was gonna be on a TV show, and I knew the show was gonna make it, knew it was gonna get picked up."

The show made it. Raymond got the old heave-ho before the pilot was shot.

"It's gonna sound like bullshit, but I was a little relieved when I got fired – because I knew I wasn't cuttin' it. It's like if you were plopped into the PGA tournament, and you *know*, 'I'm gonna get exposed soon, it won't be long till I shank one.' I felt it during the rehearsals. It wasn't as devastating as it sounds. I lose that job and I'm still doin' what I love to do and makin' a living.

"Plus, failure – it centers me. Too much success has me thinking, *All right, what's goin' on?* The only thing that saves me now is it's so hard, the creative side of it. One show is over, the next one's gotta be written, and that is so fuckin' hard that you can't even sit back. Ya gotta be funny, ya gotta write it, ya gotta create funny stuff. You're consumed by that."

Ray's not complaining – he yells this into the tape recorder: "*I'm not complaining!*"– about the reality that actual failure is many years and tens of millions of dollars behind him. Any schmuck can fail without succeeding: That's easy to do and to explain. Failure after success – that's scary. Success gives you lots of things to worry about losing and plenty of time to stoke your fear into an aria of sniveling terror.

That's the tune he carries from the writers' cage back to an editing room, where he's at work on a tape he's putting together for a friend's fiftieth birthday party back in New York.

"I really wish I could be there, Harry," Raymond says on the tape, staring at the camera, "so we could swap antidepressant stories, share rashes, and exchange talcum-powder recipes."

Suddenly, watching himself on the monitor, he shrieks, "Turn that off for a second! One of my eyes is bigger than the other. Just look at that – look at the left eye and right eye. That's probably the beginning of that drooping disease – what's it called? Look at my left eye! Look at my right eye! Lisa Lopes – Left-Eye Lopes! *Christ!*"

As happy as a man alive in misery can be, miserable as any happy man alive: Sing, maestro, sing.

Next season will be *ELR*'s eighth and, odds
are, its last. Worried he has overstayed his TV welcome and grown fat on a diet of studio laughs, Ray will take a shot at fresh failure as a movie actor. Already, he has read many scripts and taken meetings with names even more freighted with intrigue and stardust than "Raymond," names like "Milos" and "Winona" and "Dustin." Romano has become a very good actor, an actor of range and nuance, but he has brought along his dread.

"It's very scary. There's a lot goin' against you when you come from a sitcom and you're doin' a movie. People are watching – 'All right, well, who are you to think you can play with the big boys?' You gotta be careful, man. You do that first one and – God, I don't know. I don't know what the right choice is, but if you make the wrong one? There are so many sitcom actors who did that – one movie and that's it."

This, too . . .

"You can look at it from a box-office point of view, and if you choose a project which you know is gonna make good money, then you will have an opportunity again to maybe choose what you wanna do after that. Or do you go for something that isn't gonna be a box-office success? There may be critical acclaim, but if you fall on your face, it's hard to recover from."

. . . is . . .

"This movie thing is new to me. When you wanna play a character, you need to explore the back story – you have to go in knowin' where this guy grew up and how he lived and what makes him what he is. I remember Dustin askin' me, 'Why's this guy livin' in this town? Why d'ya think he isn't married?'– and I hadn't even explored that. I thought, Dustin's dealin' with an amateur. It's not negative grandiosity – it's just negativity. He seemed like he liked me, but so do you."

. . . Raymond's song. . . .

"Next I heard, a week later, Dustin's out. In this business, you never know what the reasons are: He pulled out cuzza money, cuzza his schedule. You don't know. He's not doin' the movie. I swear to God, I think it was me. I'm sure they didn't offer him what he wanted, but he would've fought a *little* harder had he thought this has a chance of working with Ray Romano."

Misery ages; we die a little more each day, and yet our songs remain the same. Still, we can't leave Raymond – not yet, not out in Burbank, where the storm clouds spritz tinsel and even failure drives a Hummer.

No, let's leave him in Queens instead, where Raymond's song began, down in his folks' basement. His mom and dad, Lucille and Albert Romano, live in the same small Cape Cod – "That house I grew up in," Ray had told me, "is as big as my bedroom and my wife's closet" – where they raised Raymond and his brothers.

"We're just content here, you know?" Lucie says in a voice inflected just like Ray's. "It's more comfortable now than it was with three boys running around, so why should we move?"

Lucie, a Juilliard grad who still teaches piano, is the lively, outgoing one; Albert, a retired civil engineer who now works, when he feels like it, as a real estate broker, has the wry and stoic crust. Her eyes dance; his roll.

Sunlight pours through the kitchen window. A fresh dozen from Dunkin' sits on the table – Albert had a coupon – and the coffee is just ready to pour. Nice people, good people, proud of Raymond – it's always "Raymond" to Mom, although you get the feeling that when they're together, she calls him "Ray" once in a while – and proud of Richard and Robert, their other boys, too. "We're very lucky with our sons," Lucie says. "The three of them are dolls, yeah. They are."

On Monday nights, they sit in the den that doubles as a dining room for holidays and watch their son, and Lucie catches him six nights a week in syndication at 11:30. Other than that, and the trips to Los Angeles for the Emmys, life hasn't much changed.

"It's like it's the most normal thing in the world," says Lucie, "but I think about it once in a while. My friend said to me, 'You just don't realize the enormity of it.' Maybe not, I dunno. It still hasn't all dawned on us.

Raymond is Raymond still – he hasn't changed. He hasn't changed at all."

"He bought us a car the first year," Albert says.

"The one outside," says Lucie. "It's a Malibu, Chevy Malibu, brand-new."

"I'm upstairs," Albert remembers, "and I'm lookin' out the bedroom window, and I see a car, and it's got a big red ribbon on the top of it."

"I was crying," Lucie says. "It's a consolation to know I'm not gonna have to worry about my old age, ya know?"

"Ya know," says Albert, "he makes in one episode what it took me twenty years to make in salary."

"We never expected it," Lucie says. "When people used to ask me, What does your son do? I would burst out laughing. It was unbelievable to me that my son is this stand-up comedian."

"He had a variety of jobs," says Albert. "He used to wash trucks, then he was at a gas station."

"This was when he had quit college."

"He got held up a couple of times at a gas station."

"Well, the second time, we said, 'Out!' "

The basement has changed. Nobody's living down there anymore, of course, and when I ask to check it out, it turns out to be a battleground.

"He's a pack rat," says Lucie. "We cannot sell this house. You know why?"

"Oh, boy," Albert says, grinning like an angel.

"Because when we went down once to clean out the basement, he can't part with a rubber band. He's taken over the garage, the basement, and the front bedroom. Every box from every office he worked at, he's got."

Lucie's smiling, too. They've sung this song a few million times.

The door to the basement stairway is off the kitchen, just behind my chair at the table. Albert walks me down; Lucie stays put.

"It was fixed like a studio apartment, you know," Lucie shouts down at us, "with a little couch."

"That's some of their trophies yet, over there," says Albert.

The old softball trophies, the rusting Exercycle, the autographed photo of William Shatner still hung on one wood-paneled wall – I'm sniffin' weenie. And there it is, over by the washer-dryer: the water heater. This was one of Raymond's early bits, about living with his parents and bringing his date back to this basement lair: "Yeah," he'd brag, "that's the hot-water heater – right there. Anyone wants to take a shower in *this* house gotta go through me."

Upstairs, Lucie instructs Albert to give me a lift to the subway and tells me to catch the E train back to Manhattan.

"I tell a lotta my pupils' parents," she says before I go, "not all children go home and do their homework and get beautiful grades. I tell 'em, Don't give up. Some have to be worked with, ya know?"

Chapter Twenty

Robert Downey Jr.

Genius

Start in tight, Downey's puss full frame, like so: his creased Valentine of a face has some puff and scarification on it, some overtorqued, Dakar Rally, desert-of-the-soul mileage, but he's still hustling, still shape-shifting, still a man's man and a ladies' man, still a wanking matinee idol, liquid-brown boyish-shy eyes a-wobble, warm voice twanging from hoarse Jew's-harp burble to wheezing, pennywhistle laugh in a fingersnap. Words – thousands upon thousands of words – burst yawping from him, seemingly unfiltered and unbidden, overflowing an instrumental self whose sole means of control is a steady-Eddie self-surrender, hugging shores of work, Wing Chun kung fu, and love. Grinning prisoner in a loose-fit jailhouse of kinetic bliss, forty-one years ancient, Robert Downey's ripe and ready for his close-up.

Or maybe open in Playa Vista, inside the 315,000-square-foot wood hangar-turned-soundstage where Howard Hughes built the *Spruce Goose* and Jon Favreau is getting ready to direct the first of what everyone hopes will be an *Iron Man* trilogy. Swoop down from the laminate rafters to a human figure prone in a burren of painted Styrofoam caves. Stippled with muscle, roped with veins, gravely wounded, his pulsing diopter of a heart is a prop master's bauble, faint with ebbing life. He's Tony Stark – a lone warrior facing an ancient evil, blahblahblah, as the Invincible Iron Man...starring – pan up-body to the pain-twisted visage – R. D. Jr.

Or just let Downey himself rip this joint:

"Lemme tell ya what's happenin'," says Downey, " 'cuz I just figured it the fuck out. We're goin' to the Chateau – we'll go in the lobby there. We gotta be up the street in a couple hours. This gives us *time* – time that we *require*."

What's happening is that Downey's behind the wheel of this butter-fresh Mercedes – a newfangled silver E-Class sedan, a "lawyer's mistress's car," he calls it – inching east along Sunset Boulevard. "Complemented by a 6.3-liter engine. Thus, the E63. I like it 'cuz it reminds me of my dear sister, Allyson, born in 1963. It was her birthday a couple days ago. Who'da fuckin' thought – me and my sister, these wayward souls, wind up with –"

He's looking at me as a car cuts us off, and I reflexively reach for the wheel as he hits the brakes and the spring-loaded Buddha on the dashboard starts bobbling madly. He waves off my apology – Downey, not Buddha. Buddha can go fuck himself.

"I want you to feel completely free to let all your codependent neuroses out," he tells me. "You can grab the wheel, you can ask me if my tummy hurts, you can give me a foot rub later, anything. Enmeshment is really okay in small doses."

Small doses? A dab of Downey – trust me – would fill this magazine cover to cover. Which makes a couple of hours sitting and talking at the Chateau Marmont perfect; we have only met, and I've brought – just in case conversation lags – my carefully researched notes.

"Me too," he says.

You have notes? "I do, yeah. I actually already printed out the article if you'd like to read it. It really went great."

But I'm worried about the lead. I need to redo the lead.

"You don't need a lead," Downey purrs. "*Dude*, the lead's about to *happen*."

We'll get to the Chateau, but, please,

glance back up at that lead paragraph – I won't ask you to do this again, I swear – and note the phrase "prisoner in a loose-fit jailhouse of kinetic bliss." This is an allusion, of course, to the fact that out of all the big-name shitbags in the history of Hollywood – not just dime-a-dozen addicts, either, fucking *murderers* – Robert Downey Jr. may hold the record for doing hard-time time, a solid year in state prison plus some shorter stretches here and there. That's part of what it took for him to get where he is now – sober, working, remarried, present and accounted for as a daddy – but he's sick and tired of being sick and tired of being defined by it.

The first time I spoke with Downey was on the phone a couple of days before I flew to L.A. "This is little Bobby Downey," he said by way of introduction, and when I told him then that I couldn't avoid touching on his tabloid history, he sighed. "'It's all you talk about in the press junkets,'" he said, mocking Earnest Journalist. "'But you've never talked to *us* about *it*'– and they go back and flash the jailhouse pictures. Okay, I get it – it's still there – and then something just broke, like, three months ago, where people stopped asking. It became about more interesting things.

"*Iron Man* is kind of a definitive – something so possibly two-dimensional and vapid and pointless in the bigger scope of life – but it points to a dividing line between me being identified as one thing which I'll always be and me being identified as another thing which I'll always be – *someone who came out here to fuckin' make movies and I didn't wanna be a busboy anymore.*"

Maybe he's right, although *Iron Man* won't be out before May 2008, and there is no story in any language about li'l Bobby that doesn't devote significant space to the more sordid aspects of his past. But the more salient point – the here-and-now truth of the matter – is that, fancy allusions aside, the guy sitting out on the Chateau veranda with my tape recorder resting on his chest and the Camel straight dangling from his pillowy lips is more than the sum of his rap and call sheets.

For one thing, he just yanked the butts out of a zippered gray manpurse, where they nestle with a kaleidoscope of herbal supplements, oils, lotions, potions, and vitamins.

Camel *straights*?

"Yeah. There's a million fuckin' ways I can go with that. First thing is, I was told by the cosmos night before last, 'We got ya from here – you don't have to do any of the shit yer doin' that's yer story.' You know, 'I was fuckin' hard-timin' and here's my straights' – that whole thing?"

But you're that guy, no?

"I am that guy, but I'm also not the fuckin' story. I'm not the story just 'cuz the story really happened. But when it really comes down to it, I just want a *lot* of *fucking* nicotine. I want it *butch*" – and he smacks a fist into a palm. "The other thing is, they stand out from all the other packs. They're all *this* size, and this one's like, *boom*! This is the short dog. This to me is the .25 caliber in yer boot that yer gonna *use*."

Downey's story comes in every flavor

but linear. Daddy – "Senior," Downey calls him – was an underground six-

---

Cutting Room Floor: Downey

THE PITCH: Betting on any junkie to whip his jones is crazy, but not nearly as nuts as this guy.

SCENE: Saturday morning in Beverly Hills. Downey and I are heading to Nate 'n' Al's Deli to grab a nosh with Josh Richman, character actor/club owner/musician/raconteur and also one of Downey's oldest friends. I've never met Josh, but as Downey points him out on the sidewalk out front of the restaurant as we walk, I could swear I know who those two younger guys with Josh are.

Holy cow! It's Barry Zito, the Oakland A's ace lefty, at that moment a free agent and a month or so away from signing a $156 million deal with the San Francisco Giants. And Huston Street, the Oakland's baby-faced assassin of a closer. Yowza! Movie stars are cool, but this is cooler – a Mr. Cy Young and a Mr. Rookie-of-the-Year.

Downey has no clue who these guys are even after the introductions are made, but I think he can sense my own disappointment when it turns out that Zito and Street are not there to eat with us, but to meet a psychoguru coach Josh knows, a guy who'll supposedly help Zito figure out where he truly wants to play next year.

BACKSTORY: Downey's set for *Esquire*'s cover just before the release of *Zodiac*, so the good folks at Paramount go to heroic lengths to get me a screening of the film, which is still being fine-tuned post-production. And it's...okay. I expected much better, frankly. And though Downey did a nice job in it, his character more or less disappears about halfway through the movie.

---

ties filmmaker whose limited renown peaked in 1969 with *Putney Swope*, Mama was an actress, Junior was born in Greenwich Village in 1965 and began acting and drugging while he was still in short pants. As for further explication, Buddha can go fuck himself.

"You wanna know the timeline, dude?"

I do. Because I don't know the timeline.

So you've got Downey on the cover, and a six-thousand-word profile along with a big fashion photo spread of him inside, and not one word about *Zodiac*.

CONFLICT: When Downey ducks into a fancy soap shop on Beverly Boulevard to pick up some Yule gifts, and drops $700 in a manic blur, I can't resist the urge to scold him. I'm not your accountant, I say, but slow down for a second.

"These are all just quick hits," he snaps.

For Christmas?

"Whaddaya think – I'm gonna go hand 'em out in the parking lot?"

Fine. I only wanted –

"This is just management, dude. I gotta get down from the $500-and-above gift."

WISH I'D WRITTEN: Our colloquy on cunnilingus, which took place at the Chateau Marmont soon after we met. "I feel sometimes like I don't know how to eat pussy," Downey whispers. "Is that wrong?"

Yeah.

"Because I've had moments of fucking perfection – y'know, sometimes it's just like I am a vagina – I know exactly what I'm doin'.

Don't let 'em come.

"Really?"

Get 'em right there and then stop.

"Yeah?"

Yeah.

"Yeah."

"Neither. Do. Fucking. I."

So. No formal training as an actor, then?

"No, I had it better. I had my dad hangin' out with the coolest, smartest, maverick fuckin' weirdos of the twentieth century in New York. I useta fall asleep listenin' to my dad's poker games, and they were only playin' poker so that they could riff on lines and put-downs. So I heard this rhythm – it'd be quiet and then someone would hit it and they'd all fuckin' lose it, and it was like winnin' the pot wasn't about the chips. That, to me, used to be the most comforting feeling goin' to sleep at night, just hearing that. This is what men are supposed to do – this two-layered thing – and it's about wit and repartee and a lot of sarcasm.

"That's the hustle. I didn't come out here to figure out if I could be in some Lorimar pilot. I didn't even know what a fuckin' pilot season was. I just knew that I'd been raised in this, but it didn't feel like movies were something that you went away to do or this organized thing. It's a hustle. I got some fuckin' juice, man, I got some tools, I got some hustle. I learned some shit. I learned shit on the streets. It was providence, dude, and proximity to where I could get my grift on. Ya come out here, and all of a sudden some hot dark-haired chick named Amber is drivin' a green Fiat 128-4 – drivin' *stick*. Dude, seeing a seventeen-year-old girl driving stick shift, and she's driving you down Sunset Boulevard to go make out by the *water?* I'm like, I'm *never* going back *anywhere.* Why the *fuck* would I go back to New York? This is fuckin' gypsy *heaven*, dude – there's a million suckers out here.

"Why did it serve me to become a really good actor? 'Cuz if there were times that maybe you didn't really wanna go home, then how do you extend yer stay after the midnight show of *Rocky Horror*'s over? You better be the guy who they think would be fun to bring to the next fuckin' spot. And it's really only a coupla things, but it's how do ya harmonize those and do ya know when to pull back and how do ya really hit it, how do ya not be too inundating, how do ya play status to the person who's really the point guy–"

The waitress places his double nonfat cappuccino on the wrought-iron table between us.

"Do you like it?" she asks.

"I like it," he says.

"Would you lahk to have it in your hand?" she drawls. "I foamed it myself."

Downey picks up the drawl. "Do you *lahk* it?" he says, returning serve, and he laughs. Gently.

"I was trying out my best vocals for you," she smiles, and sashays back inside the hotel.

"That's the other thing," Downey says. "Now, like goin' into my fuckin' *fifth* decade – "

Robert, you're forty-one. Don't be such a drama queen.

"Oh, believe me," he scowls, "I'm continually put on point about that."

Sorry.

"I tend to bring out the codependent element in anyone I'm in close proximity to. I can have the yoga teacher come to the door, and if I don't answer it, and he's waiting outside for me, he goes, 'I thought you were fucking *dead*.' "

Team Downey?

"It is, dude. It's Team Downey. But it's Team Esoterica – kung fu, therapy. It's like I am surrounded like an MIT prodigy with teams and squads of experts and supporters. Some of it's some real grassroots shit, but it's that thing of, How much support do you need? What kind and for how long?

"Susan"– that'd be Mrs. Junior, a film exec who met Downey in 2003 and married him in August 2005 – "and I copped to it last night. How much support do I need? Uh, *tons*? Unless I finally get to that place where all the cylinders are firing and she's in London for the weekend and I'm wearin' a pair of *fuckin'* boxer shorts and finger paintin' mandalas and, like, singin' three-part harmonies to some kind of Paul Buckmaster arrangement weirdo-classical thing, and I look up and I go, 'Who the *fuck* am I? This is what I *really* like to *do*.'

"I'm *not* an actor. It's my day job, and I learned how to hustle it really good, and I have a love for it, and I *get* it, but I don't *know* what I'm doing. This is what I *really* like to do: I like to tweak around and make a fuckin' matte. I like to walk around like I'm in some sort of arts-and-crafts netherworld workshop. It's not mysterious, 'cuz it's usually the same three or four things, but it's this hands-on meditation on – I don't even wanna say *creation* – but on, like, *feedback*. That's what it is – instant fuckin' visual, auditory feedback."

Downey has to pee now, which gives me the chance to put a couple of things on the record. First, a fact: A hundred monkeys with a hundred tape recorders can spend a hundred years doing celebrity profiles and never catch a wave like this. Codependent, schmodependent – I put the plug in the jug and tossed the stash in the trash in 1994, so I know that every drunk and junkie has exactly the same time in sobriety: today. And Downey knows it, too. But today – out on this pillared veranda, with water trickling in some fountain hidden back in the shade and birds twittering in the bushes and Robert Downey Jr. alive and well and riffing – today's nothing short of an everyday kind of miracle, fleshy, low-hung, and slobbering delicious.

Beyond this – beyond the taste of today – forget about it.

"I'm not here to promote fuckin' anything," Downey nods, speaking of miracles. "I don't really understand what happened, but I'm okay with it. I know things changed, but I don't fuckin' – I can't hit my ass with both hands tryin' to figure this mystery. I just know that it winds up comin' back to all that old-time religion stuff, except ya add science and physics and all of a sudden *faith*. *Faith* moves mountains, and I go, '*Fuck*, yeah.'

"That's what I was talkin' about with Susan last night, and we just wound up having one of those talks where we talked about what we're scared of, about how we're really feeling, about every little fuckin' thing where we felt we weren't listening to each other – and we're just fuckin' weeping together outta left field because we hadn't had enough *contact*. Contact isn't 'I fuckin' see you in the morning and at night and we talk during the day.' That's just *fucking proximity*. What's the Cosa Nostra element? What do we share that you can't get from anyone else but me? And to be that vulnerable, for her to say, 'Nobody sees me like this,' and for me to admit, not 'I wouldn't be okay without you,' but 'I wouldn't be where I am if we hadn't met, and I'm *okay* now' – that's *huge*.

"And the funny thing was – seconds and inches, dude – I swear to God, we woke up this morning, and again she was the hottest fuckin' chick I ever saw. It was just like the first time I took her hand in the cigar bar in Montreal, 'cuz she had a headache, and I had to get my hands on her anyway, and I was like squeezing her between the thumb and the forefinger, goin' like, Man, she's got really long hands for a girl who's not very tall – it reminds me of an Egyptian cartouche. Guys say, 'Did she really like me?' but I'm thinkin' about the fuckin' hand-to-arm ratio – *wow*."

By this time, Downey's laughing so hard, he can barely catch his breath.

"Dude, I don't mean to be too basal, but I always think about, maybe it'll make my dick seem bigger if they have little hands and they're wrappin' 'em around, but I might also feel like I'm gettin' a hand job from a fuckin' mouse, which, worse things could happen, but I'd rather get a hand job from a squid than a mouse. Which is the essence of what I'm trying to say today." Just then, a little bird lands on the edge of our table, close to a big bowl of fruit Downey summoned on his way back from peeing.

"*Really?*" Downey asks the bird. "You like fruity berries? Lemme give you a choice. Here's the whole palate." And he takes a slice of strawberry and lays it on the table near the bird, who eyes him and the slice and decides not just yet. Or maybe he'd rather have an unfiltered Camel.

"How cool is that? In New York that would be a pigeon – a fucking rabid pigeon, with one leg, coming and falling over on its side and fucking yakking up everything it was trying to bring back to its kids."

You know he's crazy. I know he's crazy. *He* knows he's crazy.

Onscreen, over the course of twenty years and dozens of movies, Downey, whatever his character, is a bolt of human lightning, the most labile and accessible unacting actor alive. His physical gifts are stunning. His work in 1992's *Chaplin* was uncanny, and even in his fifth decade, he's lithe, fluid, panther-quick. But it's his rogue tongue and seemingly unmediated heartspring that make it almost impossible not to like him. Everything boils over; nothing is repressed. Intense, exhilarating – all artifice, yet done so well it feels like life.

Off-duty…well, what is acting anyway if not trying to be alive in the moment? And what do you do when you're trying to get back your acting career, your reputation, and your bankroll – Downey has done ten films since 2005 – and some dude sidles up to do a cover story about you?

"Essentially," says Downey, back in the car to visit a small clothing designer's showroom up Sunset, "I decided to welcome you into the arms of Morpheus without manufacturing some sort of fuckin' White House-y thing of how I'd like it to seem."

Great. But nobody, I add, is ever crazy enough to do that.

"If you have this false sense, this thing where you've compartmentalized who you really are, as opposed to how you allow yourself – like you can fuckin' control it – to be perceived by the public to begin with, *then* there's something to fear. Because then you're imagining you're going to control the flow of a fucking *river.*"

Buddha – bald-headed, squinch-eyed, red-lipped – nods. The right side of his saffron robe is sort of slipping off the shoulder, I see now, and his bulging earlobes quiver. I'm starting to like him. Buddha, not Downey. Downey I love.

"*Your move, Outlander!*" he shouts into traffic, and cackles.

The clothes place is where the nice ladies put

rose petals – *crystallized* rose petals – in your sparkling water and refer to Robert as "Linda's muse," Linda being the designer and inventor of a line of clothing she calls "luxury eco," spun of bamboo and seaweed and wood pulp and sasawashi leaf.

Sasawashi?

"It's L.A., bro," Downey says. "Get into it. I'm not fazed if I hear *sasawashi.*"

Sasawashi turns out to be the leaf that sushi's rolled with, and the clothes turn out to be lacy and frilly and sheer and gossamer gorgeous – and that's just the men's line.

"This is *so* fabulous," Downey coos, copping a pinkish-gold shirt patterned in a shiny, froggy green. It's diaphanous, with sleeves nearly down to his knuckles. "If you guys don't mind, I'm gonna shower with this on – a little bird-bathing – to see how it feels."

Instead, he tries on a plaid organic-poplin jacket and comes out of the dressing room looking positively feral – with maybe just a smidge of minced Mizrahi – as the costume designer for *Iron Man* arrives with her assistant and her dog, Hunter.

"Isn't that the oldest dog in Hollywood?" Downey asks.

"She kept her girlish figure," says one of the clothes ladies.

"I'm very careful about that," the costume designer says. "She was on a raw diet for most of her life, and then when she started getting older and couldn't handle that much protein, now she gets the juice pulp from the juicer every morning mixed in her food – living enzymes."

"I need ta take a bunch of herbs," Downey says, heading for where he left his purse on a table out back with the rose-petal water. "I'm gonna smoke a Camel non-filter in my sustainable T-shirt."

He looks good – Downey, not Hunter. He's lifting five days a week, taking pharmaceutical creatine to plumpen the muscle, and his upper body, front and back, is ten years younger than his face – smooth, hairless, blue veined, and rippling – and by Jove, I think maybe I've lingered too long in this witches' den of nancy-hip couture.

You look buff, I tell Downey, fairly certain that I have never before used the word *buff* in any form or setting in my entire life.

"Yeah," he says. "It's goin' up, too. I'm on swoll status."

You're Iron Man.

"I *am* Iron Man. Now, what *kind* of Iron Man do I wanna be? The Daniel Craig, someone-just-packed-clay-on-my-shoulders-and-chest thing is played out. So I'd rather go a little more *Enter the Dragon* style."

Either way, there's a whole cult of comic-book dorks who aren't gonna let you off easy.

"No, the geek closet has swung wide open. Dude, I'm running into guys – some Fortune 500 guy at some thing, and all of a sudden he unloosens his fuckin' Prada and goes, 'Dude, when fuckin' Tony Stark came back in the second incarnation and the Mandarin and *dadadada*' – and I'm goin', Wow, this is no joke.

"Here's how insane life gets – *I'm doing a fucking biopic?* It's the same pressure as *Chaplin*, except there's no reference. You're creating the reference. So again the hustle is, How do I write a line between doing something that *wasn't* expected and how do I trust my *brother,* Jon Favreau, and how do we have this fuckin' thing happen where we are *both* the guy – because to me, *that's* a movie, when the director and the lead guy create this third thing that is the character.

"Between where he's at and where I'm at, and the fact that he pushed for me and that panned out – because I was *not* on anyone's A-list for this part; why *would* I be? I came in and aced a screen test and was throwin' heat all day long. I prepped myself into such a tizzy. I whipped myself into a fucking fury, to where the entire house, everybody backed off, like, Oh, okay, fuckin' Shaman Boy's back, it's rain-dance central. I refused to lose this part to anything or anyone. I hadn't felt that way since *Chaplin.* The only time I've screen-tested since *Chaplin* was for *Iron Man*.

"Why am I the guy for this job? Because the story is the most duplicitous and conflicted of all the Marvel characters, because he's really just a guy who gets put in an extraordinary set of circumstances – partially due to his own character defects and partially due to his lineage – and you can pick a fucking million Joseph Campbell myths and look 'em up, but none of them apply more to me, and there's nothing I could bring more to than this job and this story."

Back inside, the costume designer's explaining why she can't explain why she may or may not be able to use some luxury eco clothes for *Iron Man.* "We have a whole massive part of our movie where he becomes sort of a POW, and the people who capture him give him clothes, so perhaps we could create something perfect. I'm not supposed to say much. I can't give you any more information. Truly, he" – she means Shaman Boy – "and I will be assassinated."

Which, it turns out, is not so far from the truth.

"I have an Airsoft assault rifle in the trunk,"

Downey tells me as we roll on to *Iron Man* HQ, "so I don't want you to be surprised if I descend on the production office like a sniper – 'cuz we're goin' from Earth Mother into Butchathon."

Planet Butch is unfazed by Downey's attack – nobody bats a fucking eye, frankly – but the atmosphere is quickly engulfed by a gaseous cloud reeking of corporate tension when the alien life-form with him hauls out a tape recorder and a digital camera.

"Is this supposed to be a natural conversation?" Jon Favreau asks. "Because with cameras and tape recorders and reporters, it's hard to be natural."

Favreau, bless him, does not seem pleased to be saying this.

He is but a simple director/actor/writer, a flannel-shirted honeybear in nominal charge of a Marvel Comics–financed film project with a some-what star-crossed history – *Iron Man* has ricocheted around Hollywood for years – and a dweeb brigade locked in vicious online debate over possible casting, villain selection, story line, and hero-suit design. Now, with shooting starting in mere weeks, his office walls are flush with hush-hush body-armor sketches, and only his wife and God know what nerdgasmic revelations lay in the black-and-white-marbled composition book on his desk.

No photos, little chat, and all the inchoate dread and paranoia a couple hundred million can buy. But *this* much – without fear of finding my spicy tuna roll dosed with polonium-210 – I can tell you: Unless Favreau's prop master can gin up a CGI catheter, Iron Man will piss into a bent-glass carafe, so that Downey won't need to be extracted from his armor every time he has to whiz on the job.

Also this: When we – Downey, me, and Downey's sidekick, Jimmy, a gruff young roughneck who hails from the capital of Butch, Pittsburgh, and has a Steelers logo tattooed on the skin above his heart, "my broth-er," Downey says, "my Secret Service, the guy who'd fuckin' take the bul-let" – duck into Downey's wee on-set office to wolf a take-out lunch and I decline the ginger ale on the grounds that soda makes me fart, Iron Man takes it as a personal challenge.

"Go for it, dude," he roars. "Dude, I'll fuckin' match you thunderclap for thunderclap. I'm chambering one up myself." On the way home, as the Mercedes' windows glide up and down, Buddha weeps.

Downey House sits at the end of a cul-de-sac in a staid, plush, peaceable west Los Angeles neighborhood called Brentwood. It's strange in the same wealthy way that nearby Bel Air and Beverly Hills are strange – no human being who is not a maid, gardener, nanny, or garbage collector is ever manifest – but Brentwood is almost completely devoid of hip, chic, fizz, or glitz.

"I swear to God," Downey says, sitting in his kitchen, "I've been quoted as saying if I ever wind up as a forty-somethin', remarried, marketable, big-action-movie dad of a teenager in a cul-de-sac in Brentwood, *please* run up behind me and pop two in my head – do me a favor." There's a hand-lettered sign taped high above the sink – THE RULES ARE THE TOOLS – and, close by, a photo of Mr. and Mrs. Junior with Laura and George W. Bush at the White House. A countertop holds an espresso maker the size of Mount Vesuvius. The missus is still at work, and Downey's thirteen-year-old son, Indio, is at his mom's – that's Downey's ex-wife, actress-singer-model Deborah Falconer. Jimmy Butch is here, and Christine, the "titular head of this whole fuckin' Team Clown we got goin' here."

"Should we have one of our business-therapy sessions so Scott can see how fuckin' sick we all are?" Downey asks. "I just wanna break the ice here."

And he farts once, short and sharp.

"That's fuckin' nothin'," he says. "I can clear out this whole floor."

Not bad for an overture, I say, unrolling a bassoon note of my own. "Dude, that was literally like an orchestral blip. That wasn't even the warm-up. That was like the fuckin' oboist's double reed hit the floor."

But truth is elsewhere. Downey's colon is ready to conduct.

"For reference," he shouts as he bolts the kitchen, "you may photograph whatever you like, except this three-coil steamer I'm about to fuckin' drop in Christine's office."

"Don't!" she screams. "There's a whole house – go in the *yoga* room."

Too late.

"Ohhhh," Christine moans. Then she gathers herself and yells, "Leave the fan on."

Back from toileting, Downey fires up the espresso maker and hands me two chapters of his memoir-in-progress. Good stuff – wiseass, trippy, dwelling mainly on the misadventures of Jailhouse Jim – and he's reading a second copy along with me on the marble kitchen island, orally annotating as the pages unfold.

"There was this one guy in county jail, all he did was abuse everyone who came by – male, female, CO, doctor. 'Goddamn mind-midget,' 'Hey, *Cunt*-suela.' I'm next door to this guy and I'm hearin' him. It got to where they did a cell extraction – they pop him in the cell, they come out, and this fucker, I love him to this day, he was an amputee. He had one leg. He was so hell-bent, he was standin' on one foot sixteen hours a day just to tell everyone what a piece of shit they were. *That* fucking guy had *moxie*."

This all fits perfectly in tone with the Wall of Shame, which is Downeyspeak for a family bulletin board hung on another kitchen wall, thumbtacked with layers of self-mocking photos, mainly of Downey – kung-fu Downey with a shiner, sad sack in stir, dewy Brat Pack bouffant-coiffed Bob with old-old flame Sarah Jessica Parker – but Downey's writing, to be blunt, feels *unfelt.*

If you're gonna write a book, dude, you maybe oughta get more real with it.

"I don't know if I can," he says. "And that's probably part of the reason I stopped and got a little scared."

Exactamundo. Gimme some scorch, Little Bobby. Less soft-shoe, more fear. Some grim, tortured-spirit-behind-the-light-'n'-lively veneer –

"Could I also have a chapter where I talk about the seventh ray of the ninth configuration and start using, like, 'magnificent' – kind of an Eckhart thing – that, too? I'd love to have the cover actually be me in a long, flowing robe – a jeweled robe – where I'm writing as an ascended master."

How can you *not* love this silly, laughing, wheezing, buzzing, tap-dancing motherfuck?

"You know what'd be the *best*, dude? I'm *standing* there, and there's literally sunlight comin' out of my ass."

You're on no meds?

"No meds. Look, Ma – no meds. Dude, that's a great chapter. That's *genius*. I gotta hit this whole thing about the bipolar. They called me up and said, 'Hi, we're from the Bipolar Association and you –' 'But I'm *not*.' 'Well, you've said –' '*No!* I haven't said shit. Dr. Malibusian said,' and they go, 'Well, it's been written, so we're going to quote it.'

"Is it all right if I weigh in here? Because although I can say sometimes I wanna shop a lot and sometimes I just wanna watch ESPN and jerk off and eat ice cream, I'm not fuckin' depressed or manic. I've been told I was an axis 2.94 *disorder*, but the guy I was seeing didn't know I was smokin' crack in his bathroom. You can't make a diagnosis until somebody's fuckin' sober."

Never used needles?

"No."

Black-tar heroin? *And* crack?

"Well, first of all, it was eleven years ago, right around this time of year, and someone said, 'We're smokin' some, ah, some, ah – whaddya call it? – opium.' And I was like, 'Oh, that sounds really fuckin' *boheme*.' But, of course, that first time it was opium. The second time, it *looked* like opium. Looked the same, smelled the same, a little dirtier, not quite as pristine a buzz, and by the time three weeks later, when I woke up, thought I had a flu, and took one hit on it, I looked up and said, 'Great. So now we're junkies. This is fuckin' great.' Six months later, I catch my first case ever of getting pulled over – and that was after una*bashedly* partying to my fuckin' heart's content for the first ten-plus years I was out here.

"I was always the guy who was like, No heroin, no crack. But it doesn't matter if ya go ten years without doin' it. Because on that 3,651st day, it's yer fuckin' turn, joker. First time someone took the powder outta the house and accidentally left a rock there – that's the problem. Hang around the barbershop, yer gonna get a haircut.

"At that point it was like, *Uhhhh*, will someone just tie my shoelaces together, 'cuz I'm fucked now, and I knew it and proved it rapidly. Because once yer doin' those things together, it's time to get arrested."

Then, if you're an honest-to-Buddha addict, it's time to get clean, fuck up, and get arrested again. And again. And again. And again. And again. And again. And again. Time to tell everybody who ever believed in you, loved you, and gave you another chance – including the judge – to get fucked. Time to lose the wife, lose the kid, lose the gig. Time to go from personage to punch line.

"I'm Retread Fred, serial relapser. That's the story."

Yep, that's the story. But that story isn't him; hell, it's not even *this* story.

In *this* story, the most flatulent actor of his generation swings by the next noon, and it's off to the races again. We hit a deli in Beverly Hills for a long nosh with an old pal of his, and on the way back to the car, Downey ducks into a soap shop to drop a quick $700 on gifts. He's hobbling like a man with a large pole up his butt, stiff from this morning's kung-fu sparring, stuck in a phase his *sifu* calls "tasting the cup of bitters."

"In essence," he explains, "every single thing you do is wrong, even though you're doing everything right – because you're not really *there* with the other person. It's just amazing. It's so hard to show up for a process that's so simple in its complexity – and this goes for gettin' clean, this goes for showin' up for a relationship, this goes for chasing your dreams –"

Oy. Me, I'm sore from *listening*. Exhausted. Shitfaced, whirling drunk on a bottomless cup of Downey.

Look, I say, you've given me three cover stories already.

"We need ten," he says. No. What I need is an ending.

This story ends late that night in Brentwood. Quietly.

This story ends with Mrs. Junior – her long-fingered hands are lovely indeed, and so's the rest of her – and dark-eyed Indio and Little Bobby wolfing some Thai, a little Saturday-night-in-the-cul-de-sac curry, delivered piping hot.

This story ends with two fat albums of wedding photos of the beaming summer day that Jailhouse Jim, Retread Fred, Tiptoe Terry, Half-Measures Hal, Steady Eddie, and Susie Q, a savvy Jewish girl from Chicagoland by way of the USC film program and obviously in no need of any hand-lettered reminder about rules and tools, all tied the knot.

This story ends with Iron Man, still sore from his cup of bitters, curling up on the couch under some kind of new-age Zen healing wrap to watch Helen Mirren in *The Queen* with the missus.

This story ends with Shaman Boy and the Young Master – with Robert Downey Jr. and Indio, with a forty-one-year-old man and his thirteen-year-old boy – facing each other in silhouette down a shadowed hallway.

They stand clasped, each one's head on the other's shoulder, without words or distance between them. Only their hands move, trading rhythm in turn, drumming love in call and answer upon each other's back. The beat flows and ebbs, crackling in the dark, numinous. I don't know how long it goes, don't know what it may mean, don't know if Downey is wet-eyed or grinning. I know that he is finally silent, finally beyond words.

Acknowledgments

I owe plenty of thanks to far more folks than I can name here – for guidance, inspiration, and friendship. The short list includes Curt Pesmen, Mark Warren, Andy Ward, David Black, Bill Shapiro, Helene Rubinstein, John Kenney, Bob Scheffler, Kevin McDonnell, Victor Ozols, Fran Kessler, Lisa Hintelmann, Flip Brophy, Jay Woodruff, Bob Ivry, Arnie Jensky, Eliot Kaplan, Larry Platt, Bob Shacochis, and the late, great Art Cooper.

Special thanks go to my long-time comrades, the incomparable Tom Junod and the poet Charles P. Pierce.

David Granger is in his own category. The best editor in America, he is an even better man. His faith, trust, loyalty, and love have been the pillars of my career, and I owe him more than I could possibly repay.

Likewise Lisa Brennan and Thomas Judah Brennan Raab – my wife and my son, the loves of my life, my heart and my soul – to whom I dedicate this book.

About the Author

Cleveland native Scott Raab (www.scottraab.com), an *Esquire* Writer-at-Large since 1997, is an Iowa Writers' Workshop grad. His work has appeared in *Best American Sports Writing* and *Best American Food Writing*, as well as in *GQ* and *The New York Times*, and his cultural commentary has been featured on NPR, NBC's *Today*, Court TV and A&E's *Biography*. He lives with his wife and son in a northern New Jersey borough 2,788 miles from Hollywood.